MATHEMATICAL MODELS IN THE SOCIAL, MANAGEMENT AND LIFE SCIENCES

Thi

20.

ELLIS HORWOOD SERIES IN
MATHEMATICS AND ITS APPLICATIONS

Series Editor: Professor G. M. BELL, Chelsea College, University of London

Statistics and Operational Research
Editor: B. W. CONOLLY, Chelsea College, University of London

MATHEMATICAL MODELS IN THE SOCIAL, MANAGEMENT AND LIFE SCIENCES

D.N. BURGHES, B.Sc., Ph.D., F.R.A.S., F.I.M.A.
and
A.D. WOOD, B.Sc., Ph.D.
Department of Mathematics
Cranfield Institute of Technology

ELLIS HORWOOD LIMITED
Publishers · Chichester

Halsted Press: a division of
JOHN WILEY & SONS
New York · Chichester · Brisbane · Toronto

First published in 1980
Reprinted with corrections in 1984 by

ELLIS HORWOOD LIMITED
Market Cross House, Cooper Street, Chichester, West Sussex, PO19 1EB, England

*The publisher's colophon is reproduced from James Gillison's drawing of the
ancient Market Cross, Chichester.*

Distributors:

Australia, New Zealand, South-east Asia:
Jacaranda-Wiley Ltd., Jacaranda Press,
JOHN WILEY & SONS INC.,
G.P.O. Box 859, Brisbane, Queensland 40001, Australia.

Canada:
JOHN WILEY & SONS CANADA LIMITED
22 Worcester Road, Rexdale, Ontario, Canada.

Europe, Africa:
JOHN WILEY & SONS LIMITED
Baffins Lane, Chichester, West Sussex, England.

North and South America and the rest of the world:
Halsted Press, a division of
JOHN WILEY & SONS
605 Third Avenue, New York, N.Y. 10016, U.S.A.

British Library Cataloguing in Publication Data
Burghes, David Noel
    Mathematical models in the social, management and life sciences. —
    (Mathematics and its applications).
    1. Mathematical models 2. Management — Mathematical models
    3. Social Sciences — Mathematical models 4. Biology — Mathematical models
    I. Title II. Wood, Alistair D III. Series
    001.4'24   QA401   79–40989
ISBN 0–85312–097–8 (Ellis Horwood Ltd., Publishers, Library Edition)
ISBN 0–85312–101–X (Ellis Horwood Ltd., Publishers, Student Edition)
ISBN 0–470–26862–X (Halsted Press)

Typeset in Press Roman by Ellis Horwood Ltd.
Printed in Great Britain by Unwin Brothers Ltd. of Woking

Table of Contents

Preface

In this book we aim to give the reader an appreciation of how mathematical models are formulated, solved and applied, and a concise description of basic mathematical techniques. Each mathematical topic is motivated with a case study; the mathematical technique is presented; the case study solved; and further case studies described. Problems have been set to test the reader's comprehension; and hints and solutions are provided.

The case studies have been taken mainly from management, biology, economics, planning, and sociology: hence our description of the book as 'an account of models in the non-physical sciences' may be seen to be fully justified and earned by its content.

It is written for students in the above disciplines who need a practical course in applying mathematics, and for mathematics students and teachers who want to see the importance of mathematical concepts in a variety of realistic situations.

We have tried to avoid burdening the reader with too many mathematical proofs, at the same time not attempting to conceal any mathematical difficulties, which are fully explained in the text. Our feeling is that over-emphasis of mathematical rigour would detract from our aim of providing an appreciation of the role of mathematics in society today.

In making corrections we wish to thank Mr R. Morrisson of Coldingham, Berwickshire, and various students at N.I.H.E. Dublin for drawing our attention to misprints and errors.

David Burghes
Alastair Wood

CHAPTER 1

Mathematical Modelling: Aims and Philosophy

1.1. MATHEMATICS AND SOCIETY

Few people will deny that the most spectacular successes of mathematics have been in the physical sciences. We have, for instance, the mathematical prediction of the existence of heavenly bodies, subsequently verified by observation, or, in earlier centuries, the formulation of the laws of motion of various bodies. On a more practical level, it could even be claimed that the spread of modern industrial civilisation, for better or for worse, is partly a result of man's ability to solve the differential equations which govern so many of our industrial processes, be they chemical or engineering.

But over the last few decades mathematics has broken out into a whole new range of applications in the social sciences, biology and medicine, management and, it seems, almost every field of human endeavour, providing qualitative, if not quantitative models where none had existed or even been contemplated before. Mathematical techniques now play an important role in planning, managerial decision-making, and economics, which has probably been the longest quantified of the social sciences.

Do we all understand the same thing by 'mathematics'? The man in the street will tend to equate mathematics with arithmetic. But what will children recently exposed to 'modern mathematics' syllabuses in some primary schools equate mathematics with? The engineer will tend to think of the techniques of calculus used to compute solutions to problems. The businessman may think simply of book-keeping. The medical or experimental worker will come up with computers or statistics.

All of these are in part correct, such is the diversity of mathematics, although its unity becomes more obvious with deeper study. Even mathematicians cannot agree. Some, who are usually called applied mathematicians, see mathematics entirely as a model for the physical world. In their view the motivation towards innovation in mathematics arises from the needs of physics. For instance, physicists required a function, with the property that

$$\int_{-\infty}^{\infty} \delta(x)f(x)\,\mathrm{d}x \; = \; f(0)$$

for a wide class of functions. It was found that δ could not exist as an ordinary function, and this led to the development of the theory of generalised functions or distributions.

At the other extreme is the type of pure mathematician who sees mathematics as a formal language constructed from distinct symbols which can be strung together according to well-defined rules to make formulae which have a unique interpretation. Certain formulae are labelled axioms, and others are constructed from them by applying rules of inference. A sequence of such formulae forms a proof. The whole structure of pure mathematics can be set up in this way from a very few axioms, such as 'if X is contained in Y and Y is contained in X, then X equals Y'. By and large the mathematics constructed in this way fits the physical requirements, and occasionally precedes its physical application, for example Kepler's work on the ellipse anticipated an understanding of planetary motion.

Whatever viewpoint we adopt, we must agree on the necessity of having a clear, concise language for transferring thoughts about relatively subtle ideas which may previously have been vague or non-existent. New mathematics is not discovered, but invented: it does not exist until it has been communicated between people. The language must be versatile enough to allow a school-teacher to clarify a point for a pupil while at the same time allowing researchers to be sure that a new result is proved without mistakes.

The contemporary language of mathematics manipulates such basic notions as sets, functions and relations and describes constructions using them. Mathematics is usually laid out according to the following convention.

(i)   Definition: this describes a new entity in terms of those that have been defined previously.

(ii) Theorem: this is a statement giving an answer (unfortunately not always complete) to questions raised about these entities. A theorem is sometimes called a Proposition, Corollary, or Lemma.

(iii) Proof: This gives a record of the manipulations necessary to convince the reader that a theorem is a true statement.

Many people regard only these manipulations as mathematics, but the task of formulating the questions and describing the entities is just as important, particularly where modelling is concerned. Ordinary language, for example elementary English, is too imprecise. Suppose that you have never seen a dog and try to find out exactly what it is by using a dictionary. The definition rapidly becomes circular, as we see below:

A 'dog' is an 'animal'
An 'animal' is a 'being'
A 'being' is 'something which exists'
To 'exist' is to 'occur'
To 'occur' is to 'exist'.

There are many paradoxes in the English language. For instance, can you decide whether the statement 'I am lying' is true or false? The advantages of using mathematical language in any situation, but particularly in the new areas mentioned in our introductory paragraphs, may be listed as follows:

(i) The mathematical language is more efficient and less bulky than the written word; it reveals the assumptions being made in their naked simplicity in a way which words do not do efficiently.

(ii) It is more difficult to cheat conclusion with a mathematical argument. The results of a mathematical debate are precise and depend only on the initial assumptions. For a given set of assumptions the mathematical conclusions are accurately expressed, and their results cannot be argued with. It is the assumptions that can and should be criticised.

(iii) With a mathematical description it is possible to arrive at optimal solutions, which would not be obvious without the analysis.

It probably has some disadvantages too. Much time and effort can be spent trying to find solutions for rather irrelevant problems, problems which are so far removed from reality that their solutions have little meaning. In many cases a manager's practical experience and intuition will enable him to make better and quicker decisions than those available to him through a mathematical analysis of the problem. Nevertheless mathematical analysis has had some important successes. For example the technique of linear programming has been extensivly used in transportation problems leading to significant savings in costs; differential equation theory has been used to make precise decisions in glucose tolerance testing for diabetics; and matrix methods are employed in the estimation of future population trends.

Thus we conclude that mathematics has an important role to play in a wide range of applications, so long as we are realistic about what it cannot do, as well as what it can do.

1.2. MATHEMATICAL MODELLING – ITS ROLE AND LIMITATIONS

The underlying theme in all applications of mathematics to real situations is the process of mathematical modelling. By this we mean the problem of translating a real problem from its initial context into a mathematical description, that is, the mathematical model. This mathematical problem is then solved, and the resulting mathematical solutions must be translated back into the original context. The main stages in the modelling process are summarized in Fig. 1.1.

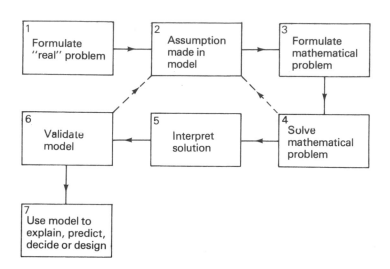

Fig. 1.1.

The left-hand column represents the real world, the right-hand column the mathematical world, and the middle column the connection between these two worlds where firstly the problem is simplified and formalised and secondly the mathematical solution is translated back into the real world situation.

In a straightforward modelling process we move from box 1 to box 7 in sequence, but most modelling is *not* straightforward. We often need to concentrate and spend significantly more time on particular stages. The model is sometimes not adequate for its purpose, and we must move from box 6 back to box 2 and repeat the process, using a more sophisticated model. In many cases, particularly in the social sciences, it is difficult to apply box 6 at all, and we move straight from box 5 to box 7. In other cases it might not be possible to solve the mathematical problem, the mathematics being too complicated to deal with. In this case we return to box 2 and weaken the assumptions. This of course takes us further from the real situation, but leads to an easier mathematical analysis. Whether or not the model is useful will become apparent when we reach box 6 and attempt to validate it.

We can summarise the main stages of modelling into *formulation, solution,* and *application*. The formulation stage is covered by boxes 1, 2 and 3, the solution stage by box 4, and the application stage by boxes 5, 6 and 7. All these stages are important in modelling. We must, though, emphasise that not all modelling will follow this exact pattern. This is just a guide to what modelling is about.

1.3 CASE STUDY

As a simple example to illustrate the modelling process we will consider the problem of a London-based managing director whose company has a factory near the centre of Manchester. Early one morning he is woken by a telephone call from the Manchester factory, where there has been a major industrial dispute during the night shift, and in order to prevent a total walkout of the day staff and a consequent shutdown of the production process (which would be very costly) he is required at the factory in Manchester as soon as possible. What is his problem? To get from his home in the suburbs of London to the factory in Manchester in minimum time. What are his possibilities? To travel by car, train, or plane. So his problem is to choose the form of transport that will get him to his destination as quickly as possible.

We now move from box 1 to box 2 in terms of the modelling diagram in Sec. 1.2 and formulate the model. Each type of journey can be divided into three parts, the time from his home to the starting point of the transport, including the waiting time for the transport, the time on the particular form of transport and the time required from the transport's stopping place to the final destination. To put this into mathematical terms let T_i denote the time required for the ith mode of transport where

$$i = 1 \text{ refers to car,}$$
$$i = 2 \text{ refers to train,}$$
$$i = 3 \text{ refers to plane.}$$

Then

$$\boxed{T_i = a_i + b_i + c_i}$$

where

a_i = time to get from initial point to start of transport i and waiting time;

b_i = time on transport i;

c_i = time from stopping point of transport i to final destination.

In terms of our original modelling diagram we are now moving into box 3. Before we do so it is important to note that we are setting up a general framework which will solve not only this particular managing director's problem but any problems of a similar nature.

On to box 3. Here we state the problem in mathematical terms. We require to find the value of i (1, 2 or 3) which minimises the function T_i, and we can immediately move on to box 4 and write the solution as

$$\boxed{i, \text{ where } T_i = \min(T_1, T_2, T_3)}$$

where the notation

$$\min (x_1, x_2, x_3, \ldots x_n)$$

means choosing the number x_i which is less than all other x values. So our mathematical world is soon dealt with and requires little sophistication. We just need to compare the values T_1, T_2, T_3, and choose the minimum one. The next box is straightforward as well. The interpretation of solution i is that the transport labelled i should be used. There is little we can do to validate the model, and so we move straight on to box 7 and apply the model to the managing director's problem.

The map below illustrates the geographical problem. The managing director lives just outside London at Romford in Essex, and the factory is close to the centre of Manchester. We now estimate each function T_i.

i = 1: CAR

Clearly for this form of transport $a_i = c_i = 0$, and we just need to evaluate b_i, the actual journey time in the car.

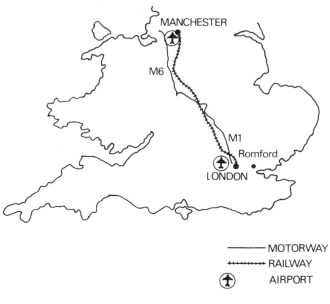

MOTORWAY
RAILWAY
AIRPORT

Fig. 1.2

There is first a journey on minor roads across to the M1 which he estimates to take 70 minutes. This is followed by 170 miles of driving at 70 m.p.h. which will take

$$\frac{170}{70} \text{ hours} = 146 \text{ mins.}$$

Allowing for a 20 minute journey from the motorway into Manchester and a 20 minute driving break (for breakfast!) we obtain

$$b_i = 70 + 146 + 20 = 256$$

$$T_i = 256 \text{ mins.}$$

$i = 2$: *TRAIN*

The first part of this journey is by car to Euston Station, and he estimates this as 70 mins, allowing for a possible 20 min wait at the station for the train to Manchester; that is, $a_2 = 70$. The journey time is 155 mins, that is, $b_2 = 155$; and the taxi journey from Manchester Piccadilly Station to the factory takes 10 mins, that is, $c_2 = 10$. Thus

$$T_2 = 70 + 155 + 10 = 235 \text{ mins.}$$

$i = 3$: *PLANE*

The journey across London to Heathrow by car is estimated to take 90 mins, and allowing 60 mins to wait and board the plane we have $a_3 = 150$. The plane time to Manchester Ringway Airport is 40 mins, that is, $b_3 = 40$ mins; and the final journey into the factory is estimated to take 30 mins; i.e., $c_3 = 30$. Thus

$$T_3 = 150 + 40 + 30 = 220 \text{ mins.}$$

The solution given by

$$\min (T_1, T_2, T_3) = \min (256, 235, 220) = 220 = T_3.$$

Using the above values, the answer is choose $i = 3$; that is, travel by plane. So we have completed our box 7 with the decision 'travel by plane'. Let us hope it is not a foggy morning at Heathrow!

The above example illustrates the modelling process. We are not advising that it is particularly helpful to use this formal process to solve this particular problem, but it does show clearly the various stages of modelling. We now fill in the relevant boxes corresponding to the modelling diagrams in Sec. 1.2 for this particular problem.

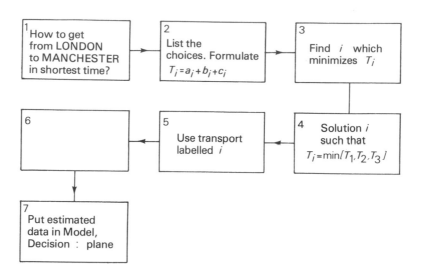

Fig. 1.3

1.4 FUTURE TRENDS

The trend towards more quantitive methods in the social sciences, management, planning, medicine, etc. seems likely to continue. As people become more confident in using mathematics they will find more and more applications. Models used will become more complex as the people using them become more expert in handling mathematical problems. In this way the models will have a far wider use than at present, and this itself will encourage further mathematical analysis.

The search will continue for underlying laws which govern, for instance, human actions, the behaviour of an economy, or changes in the stock market. In applying mathematics to the physical world, we already have available the governing laws, namely Newton's laws of motion, which give a very accurate mathematical model for nearly all physical phenomena. As yet in the social, managerial, and life sciences we do not have underlying laws, but the use of mathematical analysis in such subjects is still in its infancy. We have been applying mathematics to physical problems for 300 years, but to non-physical problems for only at most a few decades. Despite this, some laws have already been postulated and used. An inverse square law has made notable applications in the field of planning; there are now a number of laws relating to consumer purchase and laws governing social behaviour. In the future it seems probable that many more such laws will be postulated, verified, and then applied.

The use of the computer both to store and present data, and to take over automatic processes will also certainly expand rapidly in the future. As the technology improves, these improvements lead to wider and more successful applications of computer technology which have far reaching consequences for all society. Improved access to computers also means it is possible to solve mathematical problems efficiently and quickly, problems which could not be tackled at all a few decades ago. This means that the mathematical models used can become more and more complex, and therefore nearer to reality, and the resulting mathematical problems, although not soluble analytically, can be solved numerically by a computer. As computers become more efficient, so we can make our models more sophisticated and still manage to achieve a solution. The art of the applied mathematician is to get the best balance between the complexity of the assumptions in the model and the manageability of the resulting mathematical analysis. If the assumptions become too complex, not even the most efficient computer will find a solution, whereas if the assumptions are too far removed from reality, a solution will be found but it will have little use in practical implementation. The future will see, no doubt, both an improvement in computer technology and an improvement in the use of the available resources. More people will be trained in the use of such equipment, and in mathematical modelling it will lead to use of more sophisticated models; models which are more related to reality and so have more practical application.

We cannot emphasise enough that it is the role of the applied mathematician or mathematical modeller, through his choice of assumptions, to strike the correct balance between the demands of the real world situation and the complexity of the mathematics obtained through these assumptions. Too often in British schools and colleges applied mathematics has come to mean classical theoretical mechanics. This has not satisfied many of the better students, who have gone off into the more rapidly advancing abstract pure mathematics. But the frontiers for pure mathematics are now considered by many to be at least a generation beyond potential applications, if they are applicable at all, apart from a few exceptions, such as catastrophe theory (presented in Ch. 11 of this book), where the mathematicians themselves have gone in search of applications. As the gap widens between the level of modern pure mathematics and the level of the mathematics currently being applied by practitioners, this trend can only continue. The need now is for fewer pure mathematicians, to push back the frontiers of the subject, but more 'interpreters' of mathematics who can understand both the recent advances in mathematics and the problems and needs of workers in other fields, not just classical mechanics. We require mathematicians who can pick out the 'plum' of a real world problem 'ripe' for quantitive or qualitative analysis.

1.5 INTRODUCTION TO THE BOOK

This book aims at giving its reader

(i) an appreciation of how mathematical models are formulated, solved, and applied,

(ii) a concise description of basic mathematical techniques.

For those reading this text who are not trained in mathematics, we hope that you will see that mathematics is not a subject to be feared; rather one that has a fascination in its own right but also has a usefulness and applicability in almost all subjects. For those who already have some mathematical training, we hope that you will begin to appreciate the vast range of applications of mathematical concepts. Many of the mathematical topics you have met before probably seemed very abstract and of little importance. We hope that after reading this text you will realise that most, if not all, mathematical concepts, have important applications in some disciplines.

To illustrate the importance of each mathematical topic presented in this book, we have initially motivated the study of the topic by a practical example. So most chapters follow a pattern of the form

Sec. 1 – Practical example or case study.

Sec. 2 – Concise presentation of relevant mathematical techniques.

Sec. 3 – Solution of problem in Sec. 1.

Sec. 4 – Further case studies, using similar techniques.

Sec. 5 – Problems, both on the mathematical technique and its application.

For those familiar with the particular technique of a chapter, a brief glance at the material in Sec. 2 will probably suffice. For those who have not met the technique before, some time must be spent in Sec. 2 and the relevant exercises in Sec. 5. In fact for a complete understanding of the topic you might like to refer to a basic mathematical text since we normally only give an outline proof of theorems or refer to another text. So for those who have not met the technique before, to gain complete confidence in its application you will have to work hard on Sec. 2, referring to other texts if you feel that you need more elementary examples. We are not aiming to give a complete mathematical education, but more an appreciation of the role of mathematics in society today.

It is our hope that this book will help both in widening the range of mathematical topics which can be applied, and in extending potential applications from the physical sciences to the social, management, and life sciences.

A large number of references are provided at the end of the book. Some are basic mathematical texts, whilst others are aimed at students in particular disciplines and others at a broader audience. We gratefully acknowledge the debt we owe to the authors of these texts, who have provided the basis for much of the material in this book.

We also acknowledge the assistance of various secretaries at Cranfield who were responsible for transforming our rough drafts into typescript.

CHAPTER 2

Sequences and Series

2.1 THE GNOME CORPORATION REDEMPTION ISSUE

When an organisation requires money for an extended period, the amount needed may be too large for a single bank or lender to provide. One way of meeting this situation is to issue *bonds* which can be purchased by individual investors or insurance companies. Notice that *bonds* differ from *stock* in that the stockholder is a part owner or shareholder in the company, whereas the buyer of a bond is simply lending money to the issuing organisation. Bonds may be issued by governments, local authorities, national concerns such as electricity boards, or by private industry. The face value of a bond is usually some round number such as £1000, and it may be redeemed for this figure after some fixed period, usually 5 to 25 years, interest being paid annually (sometimes biannually) at a fixed rate.

Many bonds allow the issuing body the option of *calling the bond in* for repayment before it matures. Sometimes there is a penalty provision which the issuer must pay for calling the bond before maturity, but we shall assume in this case that the bonds are callable without penalty on any anniversary of their date of issue. This call provision is often exercised in a period of declining interest rates, the old bonds being replaced by a new issue paying a lower rate of interest. Conversely, if an organisation intends to make a new issue at maturity of the existing bonds, but expects interest rates to rise in the interim, it may be worthwhile calling the existing bonds a few years before maturity in order to make the new issue, or *redemption issue*, at a lower rate than might apply at maturity.

This is the situation facing the Gnome Corporation in the summer of 1976. They have one million pounds of 6% bonds outstanding. Interest is payable annually, and the bonds may be called without penalty on the 1st of October of any year before the maturity date of 1 October 1980. The board intend to issue an equal amount of new 20-year bonds at maturity of the present issue, but the general feeling is that interest rates on this type of bond will be running at 12% in 1980. The current rate of interest on such bonds is around 10%, and the board feels that it would be more profitable to recall the bonds on 1 October 1976 and issue redemption bonds at 10%, maturing after 20 years. Assuming negligible administrative costs in recalling and re-issuing bonds, is their conclusion correct?

To find out we begin with some simple results.

Additional interest costs from 1 Oct 1976 to 1 Oct 80
of 10% redemption bonds over existing 6% bonds

$$= £1\,000\,000 \times \frac{(10-6)}{100} \text{ for 4 years}$$

$= £40\,000$ per annum for 4 years

$= £160\,000$ in total.   (2.1)

Saving of interest costs from 1 Oct 80 to 1 Oct 96
of 10% redemption bonds over estimated 12% rate

$$= £1\,000\,000 \times \frac{(12-10)}{100} \text{ for 16 years}$$

$= £20\,000$ per annum for 16 years   (2.2)

$= £320\,000$ in total.   (2.3)

Subtracting (2.1) from (2.3) we obtain

Net savings from 1 Oct 76 to 1 Oct 96 $= £160\,000$.   (2.4)

On the face of it, the board seems to have made the correct decision, but no account has been taken of the fall in the value of money. With inflation at its present rate, the additional interest cost over the first four years must obviously be more heavily weighted than the saving over the subsequent sixteen. We must introduce the idea of *present value of money* and ask 'How much money must be invested today at a given rate of return (the *discount rate* – assumed to be 7%) in order to yield a given amount in a specified number of time periods?' In particular, taking expression (2.2), we ask how much must be invested on 1 Oct 76 in order to yield an annuity of £20 000 from 1981 to 1996 inclusive? On the other hand, considering expression (2.1), how much interest is lost by the corporation from 1976 to 1980 because £40 000 is paid out annually, rather than being retained for investment at 7%? Thus the question for Gnome is:

Is the total value of the money paid out in additional interest costs in the first four years less than the present value of the savings over the subsequent sixteen?

To answer this question we require some simple algebraic tools.

2.2 SEQUENCES; ARITHMETIC AND GEOMETRIC PROGRESSIONS

We begin by introducing the idea of a sequence.

Definition

A **sequence** is a correspondence between the positive integers $\{1, 2, 3, \ldots\}$ and the real numbers which associates with each integer n a real number a_n, which is called the nth **term** of the sequence.

For example,

$$1, -\tfrac{1}{2}, \tfrac{1}{3}, -\tfrac{1}{4}, \tfrac{1}{5}, \ldots$$

is a sequence whose nth term is given by $a_n = \dfrac{(-1)^{n+1}}{n}$.

Since there are infinitely many positive integers, it is possible for a sequence to have infinitely many terms, and we are often interested in what happens to the nth term a_n as n tends to infinity. If there is a real number L such that for any positive real number ϵ we can find an integer m such that whenever $n > m$ we have $|a_n - L| < \epsilon$ we say that the **sequence** $\{a_n\}$ converges to L or that the **limit** of a_n is L and write $\lim\limits_{n \to \infty} a_n = L$. Otherwise we say that the sequence is **divergent**.

The sequence in the example above, for instance, converges to 0 since

$$| a_n - 0 | = \left| \frac{(-1)^{n+1}}{n} \right| = \frac{1}{n}$$

which can be made smaller than any $\epsilon > 0$ simply by choosing n sufficiently large.

Let S_n denote the sum of the first n terms of a sequence $\{a_1, a_2, \ldots, a_n, \ldots\}$, so that

$$S_n = a_1 + a_2 + \ldots + a_n = \sum_{r=1}^{n} a_r.$$

We call S_n the **sum to n terms** or nth **partial sum**. For example, for the sequence

$$\{1, -1, 1, -1, \ldots\}$$

it is clear that

$$S_n = \begin{cases} 0 & \text{if } n \text{ even} \\ 1 & \text{if } n \text{ odd.} \end{cases}$$

An **arithmetic progression** (A.P.) is a sequence $\{a_1, a_2, a_3, \ldots\}$ such that each term is obtained from its predecessor by adding a constant quantity d, known as the **common difference**.

Thus an arithmetic progression always takes the form

$$\{a_1, a_2 = a_1 + d, a_3 = a_2 + d = a_1 + 2d, \ldots, a_n = a_1 + (n-1)d, \ldots\}$$

Examples of arithmetic progressions are

$$\{2, 4, 6, 8, \ldots\}$$

$$\{2, 1, 0, -1, \ldots\}$$

$$\{\tfrac{1}{2}, 2\tfrac{1}{2}, 4\tfrac{1}{2}, 6\tfrac{1}{2}, \ldots\}.$$

The common differences are 2, -1, 2 respectively. Note that the common difference, d, may be positive or negative.

It is straightforward to find a formula for the sum of the first n terms, S_n. For

$$S_n = a_1 + a_2 + \ldots + a_n$$

$$= a_1 + (a_1 + d) + \ldots + (a_1 + (n-1)d).$$

Rewriting the terms in the reverse order gives

$$S_n = (a_1 + (n-1)d) + (a_1 + (n-2)d) + \ldots + a_1,$$

and then adding the two expressions for S_n term by term gives

$$2S_n = (2a_1 + (n-1)d) + (2a_1 + (n-1)d) + \ldots + (2a_1 + (n-1)d)$$

$$= n(2a_1 + (n-1)d).$$

Thus

$$\boxed{S_n = \frac{n}{2}(2a_1 + (n-1)d)} \tag{2.5}$$

which can also be written as $S_n = \dfrac{n}{2}(a_1 + a_n)$, since $a_n = a_1 + (n-1)d$.

Example 1

Consider the A.P. $\{2, 4, 6, 8, \ldots\}$. Here $a_1 = 2$ and $d = 2$. Also $a_n = 2 + (n-1)2 = 2n$. Thus

$$S_n = \frac{n}{2}(2\times2 + (n-1)2) = n^2 + n.$$

This is the sum of the first n even numbers. It is probably worth checking one of the first partial sums.

Example 2 - Simple Interest

Let D be the amount of deposit and I the interest (in decimal form) per unit time period for an account which pays **simple interest**, that is, at the end of *each* time period, the interest payable is $I \times$ (initial deposit) $= ID$. Thus if a_n denotes the total amount in the account after n time periods we have

$$a_1 = D + ID$$

$$a_2 = a_1 + ID = D + 2ID$$

$$a_3 = a_2 + ID = D + 3ID.$$

$$\cdots \quad \cdots \quad \cdots \quad \cdots \quad \cdots \quad \cdots$$

This forms an A.P. with common difference $d = ID$. Hence the amount in the account after n periods is

$$a_n = a_1 + (n-1)ID$$
$$= (D + ID) + (n-1)ID$$

that is,

$$\boxed{a_n = D(1 + nI)} \tag{2.6}$$

which is the formula for simple interest.

Conversely, the amount of initial deposit, D, which yields an amount a_n after n periods of time is called the **present value** of a_n. Thus the present value of receiving an amount A, after n periods at a rate of simple interest I, is given by

$$\boxed{PV = \frac{A}{1 + nI}}. \tag{2.7}$$

Example 3

Assuming simple interest at 7% per annum, what is the present value of receiving £1000 in 4 years' time.

Solution

$$\text{P.V.} = \frac{1000}{1 + 4(0.07)} = \frac{1000}{1.28} = £781.25.$$

We now look at another sort of progression, called a geometric progression.

A **geometric progression** (G.P.) is a sequence of numbers $\{a_1, a_2, a_3, \ldots\}$ such that each number is obtained from its predecessor by multiplying by a constant factor r, called the **common ratio**.

Thus a G.P. always takes the form

$$\{a_1,\ a_2 = a_1 r,\ a_3 = a_2 r = a_1 r^2,\ \ldots,\ a_n = a_{n-1} r = a_1 r^{n-1},\ \ldots\}$$

Examples of G.P. are

$$\{3, 9, 27, 81, \ldots\}$$

$$\{-4, -2, -1, -\tfrac{1}{2}, -\tfrac{1}{4}, \ldots\}$$

$$\{64, -32, 16, -8, 4, -2, 1, -\tfrac{1}{2}, \ldots\}$$

The common ratios for these G.P.'s are 3, $\tfrac{1}{2}$, and $-\tfrac{1}{2}$ respectively.

We can find S_n, the sum of the first n terms, by writing

$$S_n = a_1 + a_1 r + \ldots + a_1 r^{n-1}$$

and

$$r S_n = a_1 r + \ldots + a_1 r^{n-1} + a_1 r^n.$$

Subtracting the two expressions gives

$$S_n(1 - r) = a_1 - a_1 r^n,$$

so that

$$S_n = \boxed{\frac{a_1(1 - r^n)}{(1 - r)}} \quad \text{provided that } r \neq 1. \tag{2.8}$$

If $r = 1$, then clearly all terms are equal and $S_n = na_1$.

Example 4

For the G.P. $\{3. 6, 12, 24, 48, \ldots\}$, $a_1 = 3$ and $r = 2$. Then using (2.8)

$$S_n = \frac{3(1 - 2^n)}{(1 - 2)} = 3(2^n - 1),$$

for example, $S_4 = 3(2^4 - 1) = 45 \ (= 3 + 6 + 12 + 24$, as expected).

Example 5 - Compound Interest
With compound interest, the rate of return is applied not only to the initial sum deposited but to any interest credited. If the initial deposit is D and the compound interest rate I, then the amount in the account after one period is

$$a_1 = D + ID = D(1+I).$$

After two periods,

$$a_2 = a_1 + Ia_1 = a_1(1 + I) = D(1 + I)^2$$

and similarly

$$a_3 = a_2 + Ia_2 = a_2(1 + I) = D(1 + I)^3.$$

Continuing in this way, it is clear that the amount in the account after n periods is given by

$$a_n = D(1 + I)^n. \tag{2.9}$$

This is the compound interest formula. Note that $\{a_1, a_2, a_3, ...\}$ forms a G.P. with first term $D(1 + I)$ and common ratio $(1 + I)$. Note also that in this example, the periods are not necessarily years, but interest could well be compounded half-yearly or even monthly.

The present value of receiving an amount A after n periods when interest is compounded at rate I is given by

$$\boxed{\text{P.V.} = \frac{A}{(1 + I)^n}} \tag{2.10}$$

Example 6
Assuming an interest rate of 7% compounded annually, find the present value of receiving £1000 in four years' time.

Solution

$$\text{P.V.} = \frac{A}{(1 + I)^n} = \frac{1000}{(1 + 0.07)^4} = \frac{1000}{1.311} = £762.90.$$

Note that this is less than the present value obtained when using simple interest, so as expected, to yield £1000 in four years' time requires a greater initial deposit, £781.75, when simple interest is paid than when interest (at the same rate) is compounded, £762.90.

We can further extend the applications of progressions to other forms of saving accounts. For instance consider an account in which a payment, say D, at the end of each period is made, and where the payments are allowed to accumulate at compound interest rate, say I. If A_n denotes the total amount in the account after n periods, then

$$A_1 = D$$

$$A_2 = D(1 + I) + D$$

$$A_3 = D(1 + I)^2 + D(1 + I) + D$$

and after n periods

$$A_n = D(1 + I)^{n-1} + D(1 + I)^{n-2} + \ldots + D(1 + I) + D.$$

If we define

$$a_1 = D, \ a_2 = D(1 + I), \ a_3 = D(1 + I)^2, \ldots, \ a_n = D(1 + I)^{n-1}$$

then $\{a_1, a_2, \ldots a_n\}$ is a G.P. with common ratio $r = 1 + I$. Also A_n is the sum of the first n terms. Then using (2.8), provided that $r \neq 1$ (that is, provided $I \neq 0$),

$$A_n = \frac{a_1(1 - r^n)}{(1 - r)} = \frac{D\{1 - (1 + I)^n\}}{1 - (1 + I)}$$

that is,

$$\boxed{A_n = \frac{D\{(1 + I)^n - 1\}}{I}}. \qquad (2.11)$$

This is the formula for the total amount in the account after n periods.

Example 7

If £20 is invested at the end of each month for 3 years at 1% interest rate per month, determine the amount in the account at the end of three years. What is the total amount paid out in interest throughout the whole period?

Solution

The monthly instalments are £20, so that by (2.11) with $n = 36$ we have

$$A_{36} = \frac{20}{0.01}\{(1 + 0.01)^{36} - 1\} = 2000(1.01^{36} - 1) = £861.54.$$

The total interest payable over the three years is

$$£(861.54 - 20 \times 36) = £(861.54 - 720) = £141.54.$$

Now consider the opposite problem where a sum of money is deposited in order to yield a fixed monthly amount over a period of years. The present value of an *annuity* is the amount of money that must be invested in order to yield a fixed income for a prescribed number of periods in the future, assuming that the money invested has interest compounded in the same period.

Suppose an annuity pays A per period over the next n periods. The present value of the annuity is the initial investment that must be made at the compound interest rate I in order to have just enough in the account to withdraw A per period for the life of the annuity.

Let D_j be that part of the initial investment that will yield A after j periods. Then the total initial investment required for an n period annuity, or present value, will be given by

$$\text{P.V.} = D_1 + D_2 + \ldots + D_n$$

$$= \frac{A}{1+I} + \frac{A}{(1+I)^2} + \ldots + \frac{A}{(1+I)^n}$$

on using formula (2.10). But the R.H.S is the sum to n terms of a G.P. with first term $\dfrac{A}{1+I}$ and common ratio $r = \dfrac{1}{1+I}$. Hence, from (2.8),

$$\text{P.V.} = \frac{A}{1+I} \left[\frac{1 - (\frac{1}{1+I})^n}{1 - \frac{1}{1+I}} \right]$$

$$= \frac{A}{1+I} \left[\frac{1 - (\frac{1}{1+I})^n}{\frac{I}{1+I}} \right] = \frac{A}{I} \left[1 - (\frac{1}{1+I})^n \right]. \qquad (2.12)$$

Example 8

Find the present value (that is, the cost) of an annuity of £250 for ten years, if compound interest is accumulated at 8% per annum.

Solution

Using formula (2.12) with $A = £250$, $I = 0.08$, and $n = 10$ gives

$$\text{P.V.} = £\frac{250}{0.08}\left[1 - \left(\frac{1}{1.08}\right)^{10}\right] = £1677.52.$$

2.3 SOLUTION TO THE CASE STUDY

Taking the figure of 7% as the rate of compound interest on money invested, we can now find the present value, evaluated at 1 Oct 1980, of an annual saving of £20 000 per annum over 16 years (see expression (2.2)). Using formula (2.12) we obtain

$$\text{P.V.}_{80} = £20\,000\left[\frac{1 - \left(\frac{1}{1.07}\right)^{16}}{0.07}\right]$$

$$= £20\,000\,\frac{[1 - 0.3387]}{0.07}$$

$$= £188\,933. \tag{2.13}$$

Against this we must set the value of the additional interest costs in years 1 to 4. The money involved could otherwise be invested by Gnome at 7% compounded annually. We now use formula (2.11) to obtain the amount after 4 years of an annuity of £40 000 (see (2.1)) per annum. We obtain

$$A_4 = £40\,000\left[\frac{(1.07)^4 - 1}{0.07}\right]$$

$$= £40\,000.\,\frac{[1.311 - 1]}{0.07}$$

$$= £177\,598. \tag{2.14}$$

Presented in terms of present values at 1 October 1980, the apparent net saving of £160 000 obtained in (2.4) appears as a saving of only £11 335 ((2.13) minus (2.14)). In 1 October 1976 terms formula (10) gives a saving

$$P.V._{76} = £11\,335 \left(\frac{1}{1.07}\right)^4$$

$$= £11\,335 \times 0.7629 = £8647.$$

Although the decision in the idealised model would be to make the issue, in real terms this saving is not enough to cover the administrative cost of calling in and reissuing a large number of bonds. The conclusion also depends heavily on the board's estimate of future interest rates and a change of only half a percent could reverse the decision. Gnome would be better advised to postpone their decision to 1980 in the hope that rates would stabilise.

Exercise

What would be the effect of taking the discount rate as 8% from 1980? Does $P.V._{80}$ in (2.13) increase or decrease with increasing discount rate?

The return on money invested is a few points less than the bank's base rate which is in turn linked to the Bank of England's minimum lending rate. In the fifteen years before 1973 this fluctuated gently between 4% and 8%, but during the oil crisis reached a peak of 13%. Since then it has declined to around 9% before rising again to 15%. Its vulnerability to external monetary pressures makes it very difficult to predict for modelling purposes. The interested reader can look up the Central Statistical Office's monthly publication *Financial Statistics* (London: HMSO) for full details of all these rates. More concise information is given in the quarterly reviews of the London clearing banks.

2.4 CASE STUDIES

2.4.1 Nominal and Effective Interest Rates

Ms Brown has £1000 to invest. If invested with the Haliford Building Society, interest will be compounded annually at 7%, but if invested with the Bradfax Building Society, interest is paid at the 'nominal' annual rate of 6.9% but compounded *monthly*. Ms Brown's problem is to know which account will, at the end of the year, have the larger value.

Invested with the Haliford B.S., at the end of the first year the interest payable is £70 and the account stands at £1070. So the 'effective' interest rate is 7%, the same as the nominal rate. But with the Bradfax B.S., at the end of the first month, the interest compounded is

$$1000 \times \left(\frac{0.069}{12}\right)$$

and the account stands at $1000[1 + \frac{0.069}{12}]$. Using the compound interest formula (2.9), the amount in the account at the end of 12 months is

$$1000(1 + \frac{0.069}{12})^{12} = £1071.22.$$

Hence the 'effective' interest rate is 7.12%, although the nominal value is 6.9%, and Ms Brown would be advised to invest with the Bradfax B.S.

2.4.2 Mr Smith's Mortgage Problems

Mr Smith has a mortgage problem. Over what period should he choose to repay his loan of £10 000? Clearly the shorter the total period of the mortgage (usually called the **term**), the larger will be the repayments. On the other hand, increases in the repayments reduce the term of the mortgage and so reduce the total amount of interest paid. Before going into detail, let us convert the results on annuities to mortgages, for a mortgage is just a form of annuity. Hence if I is the interest rate, n the number of years of the loan, A the yearly repayments, and L the total loan, formula (2.12) gives

$$A = IL/\left[1 - (\frac{1}{1+I})^n\right]. \tag{2.15}$$

Thus if Mr Smith is deciding about a 20 or 25 year term his first relevant information is the yearly repayments required. Supposing that the interest rate is 12%; we have, using (2.12)

(i) $n = 20$, $A = £1338.79$

(ii) $n = 25$, $A = £1275.00$.

If Mr Smith is having some difficulty in meeting all his other financial commitments, he might well be tempted to plump for the 25 year repayment scheme. But he really ought to look a little deeper into his problem. For the respective total amounts of interest payable over the full term of each mortgage are £16 776 and £21 875, so that over 25 years he has to pay £5099 more interest. He will probably obtain income tax relief on his interest repayments, so that if he is paying tax at the rate of 40%, he will effectively be paying £3059 extra on the 25 year loan. But that is not the end of his dilemma. For he will receive the income tax relief each year of the loan on the interest payable in *that* year. Thus the income tax relief is greatest in the first year and then decreases. Table 1 lists the interest payable and income tax relief for each year of the mortgage.

Table 1

Year	20 Year Mortgage					25 Year Mortgage				
	Outstanding Balance	Repayment	Interest Paid	Income Tax Relief	Effective Repayment	Outstanding Balance	Repayment	Interest Paid	Income Tax Relief	Effective Repayment
1	9861.21	1338.79	1200.00	480.00	858.79	9925.00	1275.00	1200.00	480.00	795.00
2	9705.76		1183.35	473.34	865.45	9841.00		1191.00	476.40	798.60
3	9531.66		1164.69	465.88	872.91	9746.92		1180.92	472.37	802.63
4	9336.67		1143.80	457.52	881.27	9641.55		1169.63	467.85	807.15
5	9118.28		1120.40	448.16	890.63	9523.54		1156.99	462.80	812.20
6	8873.68		1094.19	437.68	901.11	9391.36		1142.82	457.13	817.87
7	8599.73		1064.84	425.94	912.85	9243.32		1126.96	450.78	824.23
8	8292.91		1031.97	412.79	926.00	9077.52		1109.20	443.68	831.32
9	7949.27		995.15	398.06	940.73	8891.82		1089.30	435.72	839.28
10	7564.39		953.91	381.56	957.23	8683.84		1067.02	426.81	848.19
11	7133.32		907.73	363.09	975.70	8450.90		1042.06	416.82	858.18
12	6650.53		856.00	342.40	996.39	8190.01		1014.11	405.64	869.36
13	6109.80		798.06	319.22	1019.57	7897.81		982.80	392.12	881.88
14	5504.19		733.18	293.27	1045.52	7570.55		947.74	379.10	895.90
15	4825.90		660.50	264.20	1074.59	7204.02		908.47	363.39	911.61
16	4066.22		579.11	231.64	1107.15	6793.50		864.48	345.79	929.21
17	3215.38		487.95	195.18	1143.61	6333.72		815.22	326.09	948.91
18	2262.44		385.85	154.34	1184.45	5818.77		760.05	304.02	970.98
19	1195.14		271.49	108.60	1230.19	5242.02		698.25	279.30	995.70
20	0.0		143.42	57.37	1281.42	4596.06		629.04	251.02	1023.38
21						3872.59		551.53	220.61	1054.39
22						3062.30		464.71	185.88	1089.12
23						2154.78		367.48	146.99	1128.01
24						1138.35		258.57	103.43	1171.57
25						0.0		136.60	54.64	1220.36
TOTALS			16755.59	6710.24	20065.56			21874.95	8748.38	23125.03

If he can afford the effective repayments on the 20 year plan, but elects to take on the 25 year repayment plan, then each year he will have a certain amount of cash to invest for the first twenty years, whereas on the 20 year plan he will have cash to invest after 20 years. So the problem gets more and more complicated, and probably Mr Smith will make his judgement on short term considerations rather than estimated savings over a 25 year period! Especially in these days of volatile interest rates and uncertain government policy on tax relief, this is probably a wise policy.

2.4.3   The Multiplier

The national economy has been stagnant for several months, and there is a large pool of unemployed labour of all kinds. The national output Y_t in month t is given by the sum of consumer goods C_t and investment goods I_t. Thus we have the identity

$$Y_t = C_t + I_t. \tag{2.16}$$

In each month the consumer spending C_t is assumed to be a fixed proportion c of the previous month's national output Y_{t-1}. Hence we have

$$C_t = cY_{t-1}. \tag{2.17}$$

The fraction c is often called the **average propensity to consume** in economics textbooks. Suppose that for $t < 0$ we have

$$I_t = \text{£20m}, \quad C_t = \text{£80m}, \quad Y_t = \text{£100m}$$

(hence $c = 0.8$). Starting in month 0 the government proposes to spend £1m per month on additional public works. What is the effect on the national output? From the point of view of benefitting the economy it is not necessary that these works be for the public good. The economist J. M. Keynes in his 'General Theory of Employment, Interest and Money' suggested that the Treasury should bury old bottles filled with banknotes in disused coal mines, which would then be filled up with rubbish, men being employed to dig the notes up again. The pyramid-building of ancient Egypt was also commended. The basic idea is that people are employed who would otherwise be idle. As their income rises, so does their spending on consumer goods, which means more work for the people producing these goods, which in turn produces a rise in their income, adding further to the demand for consumer goods. We may construct a table (entries in £m):

Table 2

t	Y_{t-1}	C_t	I_t	Y_t	$Y_t\text{-}Y_{t-1}$
−1	100	80	20	100	0
0	100	80	21	101	1
1	101	80.8	21	101.8	0.8
2	101.8	81.44	21	102.44	0.64
3	102.44	81.952	21	102.952	0.512
..	.. ..	.. ..	..	.. ..	.. ..

The important column is the last one, showing increases in output over the preceding period. These rise steadily, making more money available for consumption in the following month, and will continue to do so as long as there are no labour shortages or external influences. But income cannot grow indefinitely, and we see from the table that, even after 3 periods, the increase is down to just over half its initial level. To calculate the total increase in income, notice that the entries in the last column are the terms of a G.P. with common ratio $c = 0.8$. Thus for $t = n$ the increase $Y_n\text{-}Y_{n-1}$ is given by c^n. Using formula (2.8) for the sum to n terms of a G.P. we obtain the total increase after n periods as

$$S_n = \frac{1-c^n}{1-c}. \tag{2.18}$$

Since $0 < c < 1$, as n increases c^n tends to zero. Thus for large n we can regard the numerator in (2.18) as unity and we obtain the final total increase as

$$S = \frac{1}{1-c} = \frac{1}{1-0.8} = 5.$$

Thus if £1m extra is invested monthly in public works, the total increase will be £1m $\times \dfrac{1}{1-c}$ = £5m. Thus, in the long term, Y_t will level out at £105m. The expression $1/1-c$ is often called the **multiplier**, since it multiplies the change in investment to yield the change in income. We shall return to this topic in greater detail in the chapter on difference equations.

2.4.4 The Size of the Firm

An idealized organizational structure for a manufacturing firm with three levels of administration and one level of production workers is illustrated in Fig. 2.1. The number of subordinates under one administrator is called the **span of control**, which in the example illustrated above is constant and equal to 3.

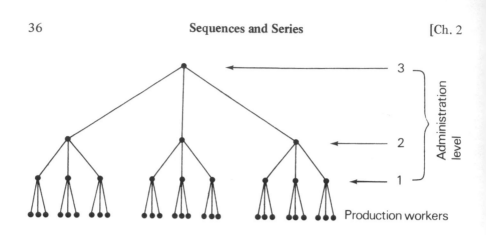

Fig. 2.1 Idealized organizational structure of a manufacturing firm.

Considering a more general model, let n denote the number of administrative levels, and a the constant span of control. Thus at level n, there will be one administrator (for example, the Chairman), at level $(n-1)$ there will be a administrators, at level $(n-2)$ there will be a^2 administrators and so on down to level 1 where there will be a^{n-1} administrators. Hence the **total number of administrators** is

$$1 + a + a^2 + \ldots + a^{n-1} = \frac{a^n - 1}{a - 1}, \tag{2.19}$$

using equation (2.8). Clearly there are a^n number of workers. Note that when $a = 3$ and $n = 3$, (2.19) gives

$$\text{number of administrators} = \frac{3^3 - 1}{3 - 1} = 13$$

$$\text{number of workers} = 3^3 = 27$$

which agrees with the illustration above.

How does the size of the firm affect earnings? In a small firm, the firm's chief administrator might well take all key decisions and be close to the production line, so that decisions taken will be efficient. But as the size of the firm increases, the barriers between the executive suites and the production line become insurmountable, and rational decision making becomes difficult as no one person can fully understand all the essential information. Administration expands, increasing the red tape and leading to higher costs per unit output. This is termed **diseconomies of scale**.

In our model above we shall consider increasing size in relation to the earnings per maker. We first assume that

Earnings = Net Revenue − Worker Costs − Administrative Costs − Fixed Costs

$$(2.20)$$

where net revenue is the capital obtained from sales of the output minus the cost of the materials used. Worker and Administrative costs will clearly depend on the size of the firm, whereas fixed costs are independent of the size.

Now

$$\frac{\text{Earnings + Fixed Costs}}{\text{Worker Costs}} = \frac{\text{Net Revenue − Worker Cost}}{\text{Worker Cost}} - \frac{\text{Administrative Cost}}{\text{Worker Cost}},$$

$$(2.21)$$

and if we assume that the fixed output of the firm is directly proportional to the number of production workers as is the worker costs, we see that the earnings, over and above fixed costs, per unit worker cost depend on the second term in (2.21), administrator cost per worker cost.

The ratio of administrators to workers for our idealized model is given by

$$\frac{\text{administrators}}{\text{workers}} = \frac{(a^n - 1)/(a - 1)}{a^n} - \frac{(1 - \frac{1}{a^n})}{(a - 1)} = \frac{1}{(a - 1)} - \frac{1}{a^n(a - 1)}.$$

As the number of administrative levels increases, the second term gets smaller and the expression tends to $1/(a - 1)$ for large n. For example if $a = 3$, the limiting value is 0.5 and the administrator/worker ratio will not exceed this value for any n. When $n = 3$, for instance, this ratio is $13/27 = 0.4815$. Let us suppose, though, that administrators at different levels receive different levels of salary, so that each administrator receives a salary b times the salary of his immediate subordinates. Under this assumption, if W is the salary of the production workers, the salaries of respective administrator levels are

$$bW, b^2W, \ldots, b^nW.$$

Thus the administrator costs, the sum of the products of the number of administrators at a level and their salary, is given by

$$a^{n-1}bW + a^{n-2}b^2W + \ldots + 1.b^nW$$

$$= a^{n-1}bW[1 + (b/a) + \ldots + (b/a)^{n-1}]$$

$$= a^{n-1}bW \frac{(1 - (b/a)^n)}{(1 - (b/a))}.$$

Since worker costs are $a^n W$, the ratio

$$\frac{\text{Administrator Cost}}{\text{Worker Cost}} = \frac{a^{n-1}bW}{a^n W} \frac{[1 - (b/a)^n]}{[1 - (b/a)]}$$

$$= \frac{(b/a)}{[1 - (b/a)]} - \frac{(b/a)^{n+1}}{[1 - (b/a)]}. \tag{2.22}$$

So under our assumptions, the ratio of 'salary increase factor' to span of control size is the relevant parameter. Normally (b/a) is less than one (for example, $a = 6$ and $b \simeq 1.5$), so that as n increases the first term becomes dominant, and approximately equal to $b/(a - b)$.

What conclusions do we reach? Firstly, an increase in b will increase the above ratio, and from (2.21), so decrease the earnings efficiency. Similarly an increase in a will decrease the ratio, improving the earnings efficiency. No surprises here! But for increasing n, the ratio (2.22), although increasing, tends to a finite limit, *independent* of the size of the firm. So serious diseconomies of scale depend very much on the size of b/a.

Of course, we must remember that these conclusions are valid only under the assumptions made concerning, for instance, the proportionality of output to workers and constant span.

2.5   PROBLEMS

1. Find the next three terms in the sequences
    (i) $2, 5, 8, 11, \ldots \ldots$
    (ii) $15, 9, 3, -3, \ldots \ldots$
    (iii) $-6, -1, 3, 6, \ldots \ldots$
    (iv) $\frac{4}{5}, \frac{5}{6}, \frac{6}{7}, \ldots \ldots$
    (v) $7, 7/2, 7/3, 7/4, \ldots \ldots$
    In each case deduce a formula for a_n, the nth term in the sequence. In (v) what does a_n tend to as $n \to \infty$?
2. Consider the sequence $\{7, 10, 13 \ldots\}$. Find the sum of the first 21 terms.
3. Find an A.P. whose fifth term is 32 and whose eleventh term is 74.
4. Find S_n for the following A.P.'s:
    (i) $\{7, 12, 17, 22, \ldots\}$
    (ii) $\{-17, -11, -5, \ldots\}$.
5. Determine a_n for an A.P. with $a_{15} = 37$, $a_{20} = 117$.
6. Write out the first seven terms of the G.P. with $a_1 = 2$, $r = 6$, and so find their sum. Evaluate formula (2.8) for S_7 and check the result.
7. Determine S_n for the G.P. $\{24, 12, 6, \ldots\}$. What happens to S_n as $n \to \infty$?
8. Find a_n for a G.P. with $a_2 = 40$, $a_5 = 2560$.

9. The number of bacteria in a culture trebles every four hours. If there are 20 bacteria now, how many will there be in 24 hours?

10. A university lecturer has a starting salary of £3500, and he receives regular annual increments of £250. What will be his salary in his eighth year?

11. A machine is bought for £12 000, and depreciation is expected to be £2400 per year. What will be its value at the end of four years?

12. A bus costs £15 000, and at the end of ten years' service is assessed to have a scrap value of £1500. Determine the depreciation rate if it is assessed as a fixed amount per year.

13. Two rival firms A and B produce cricket bats. In 1970, firm A produced 720 but has decreased its annual production by 40 each year. Firm B produced 250 in 1970 and has increased its production by 50 yearly. In what year does firm B become the larger producer?

14. An investor in the Wellford Building Society has the following two choices for a lump sum investment of £2000:
    (i) receives annual simple interest of 12% for seven years
    (ii) receives no interest but a lump sum of £900 at the end of six years and a further £900 at the end of the seventh year.
    Assuming the investor does not reinvest his interest, what option should he choose?

15. What is the 'present value' of receiving £10 000 in 10 years' time assuming simple interest of 10% per annum?

16. £100 is invested at 7% per annum compound interest. What will the value of the investment be in
    (i) 5 years' time?
    (ii) 10 years' time?
    (iii) 20 years' time?

17. What is the 'present value' of receiving £10 000 in 10 years' time, assuming interest of 10% compounded annually?

18. The accumulated value of £500 invested for seven years with interest compounded annually is £827. What is the annual rate of interest?

19. Ms Smith has £200 to invest. She wishes to increase its value to £300 as quickly as possible and has the following options available
    (i) compounded interest of 11½% paid annually
    (ii) compounded interest of 11% paid quarterly
    (iii) compounded interest of 10% paid monthly.
    Which option should she choose?

20. How long will it take to save £2000 by investing £10 per month, compound interest of 8% being added yearly after the initial investment.
    (Note that interest is paid on the first £10 for a whole year, for the next £10 for 11 months and so on.)

21. Find the cost of an annuity of £200 for 10 years if compound interest of 7% per annum is accumulated.

22. Mr Brown wishes to borrow £15 000 from the Haliford Building Society in order to buy a house. With annual compound interest of 10% determine his annual repayments if the term of the mortgage is
    (i) 20 years
    (ii) 25 years
    (iii) 33 years.
    If he elects for the 25 year term, and assuming income tax relief of 30%, what is his effective monthly repayment?

23. The John Smith Engineering Company is developing a formula to determine the 'years of return' of a machine. This is the number of years, n, that the machine must last for it to be just worth buying. Let C be the net cost of the machine (that is, actual cost minus scrap value of replaced machine), and let a be the average yearly savings in running costs. Show that the present value of the new machine, assuming compound interest of $I\%$, is

$$\frac{a}{I}(1 - \frac{1}{(1 + I)^n}).$$

Equating this to the net cost, show that the years of return is given by

$$n = \frac{\log a - \log[a - CI]}{\log(1 + I)}.$$

A particular new machine costing £8000 replaces an existing machine which has a scrap value £1200. The saving in running costs are estimated as £700 per year. Allowing interest at 7% per annum, when will the new machine have paid for itself?
(Readers unfamiliar with log should see Sec. 3.4.2.)

24. Following the national economy model in Sec. 2.4.3, suppose for $t < 0$ that $I_t = £15m$, $C_t = £85m$, and that in month $t = 0$, the Government proposes to spend £1m on additional public works. Determine the effect for the next six months on the national output.
    Repeat the analysis but with the Government spending an extra £2m on public works.

CHAPTER 3

Limits and Continuity

3.1 THE CASE OF THE BAKEWELL BEAN PROMOTION

The Bakewell Organization has spent an increasing precentage of gross income from its sale of baked beans on media advertising both in the press and on television. There has been no doubt that this effort has been successful in achieving widespread awareness of Bakewell's product. The issue that the Chairman has posed to his Marketing Director is how much *should* they spend on overall advertising. While their experience so far suggests that advertising increases sales, there is some doubt whether this effect will be maintained indefinitely.

Fitting a curve to the graph of company profits y to total advertising expenditure x has produced the formula

$$y = \frac{22x + 11}{x + 2} \qquad (3.1)$$

linking profits and advertising, where x and y are measured in £100 000s. Before presenting these results to his Chairman, the Marketing Director wishes to determine:

(a) Is the model realistic in that profit increases with advertising expenditure?
(b) Do profits increase indefinitely with advertising expenditure, or is there some fixed value which they can never exceed?

In mathematical terms, equation (3.1) says that y is a *function* of x: given a value of x, the value that y takes is determined uniquely by (3.1). Questions (a) and (b) are really about the nature of this function, and we answer them in Sec. 3.3 after developing the theory of functions in Sec. 3.2.

3.2 THE THEORY OF FUNCTIONS OF A REAL VARIABLE

A set S is any collection of well-defined objects. If s is an element or member of S we write $s \in S$. A **mapping** or function f from a set S into another set T is an association of a unique element t of T with each element s of S. We write $t = f(s)$, and say that t is the **image** of s under f. To define a function we must specify the set of elements on which it acts (the **domain** of f), the set of elements into which the domain is mapped (the **range** of f) and what happens to each element s under f.

The most useful examples of functions are those mapping the real numbers $\mathbf{R}$† into themselves. Often the domain of f is a subset S of $\mathbf{R}$, and we distinguish a special class of subsets called intervals. Let a and b be real numbers such that $a < b$. The **open interval** (a,b) is the subset of $\mathbf{R}$ consisting of those $x \in \mathbf{R}$ which satisfy $a < x < b$, that is, x lies strictly between a and b. The **closed interval** $[a,b]$ consists of those $x \in \mathbf{R}$ which satisfy $a \leqslant x \leqslant b$. Notice that the endpoints are included in the closed interval, but not in the open interval. It is also possible to have semi-infinite intervals: the subset of $\mathbf{R}$ consisting of those numbers which are greater than a, for instance, is the semi-infinite interval (a,∞). If a is to be included we write $[a, \infty)$.

Example 1

Taking the sine of an angle is an example of a function from the real numbers into themselves. If we take the angle in radians the domain is the interval $[0,2\pi]$, and the range, the set of possible values for sin s, is the interval $[-1,1]$.

The sets S and T need not be sets of numbers. For instance, S could be the set of human males, T the set of human females, and we could write $t = f(s)$ if t is the mother of s.   Then f is a function from S into T, but notice that if we write $s = g(t)$ if s is the son of t, then g fails to be function from T into S since one woman t could have several sons s_1, s_2, s_3, say, and the element $s \in S$ is not uniquely defined. Under the mapping f it is possible for different elements s_1 and s_2 of S to be associated with the same element t of T, but this does not contradict the definition of a function. In the special case when distinct elements of S are always mapped into distinct elements of T we say the mapping is one-to-one, usually written 1-1. This is equivalent to asking that $f(s_1) = f(s_2)$ imply $s_1 = s_2$. The function f is said to be **onto** if every element in T is the image under f of an element in S.

Example 2

Consider the function sin defined on $[0,\pi]$. Then sin fails to be 1-1 since sin $\pi/4 = 1/\sqrt{2} = $ sin $3\pi/4$. It also fails to be onto $[-1,1]$ since sin s takes only non-negative values for s in $[0,\pi]$. This is illustrated in Fig. 3.1.

---

† The reader unfamiliar with the real number system $\mathbf{R}$ should see Appendix I.

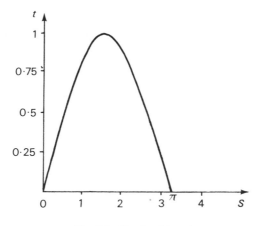

Fig. 3.1 Graph of $t = \sin s$.

A **real-valued function of a real variable** is a mapping from a subset S of $\mathbf{R}$ into $\mathbf{R}$ which associates with each real number x in S a uniquely determined real number y. We write $y = f(x)$. Recalling that a function is specified by giving its domain and its action on each element of the domain we sometimes write

$$f: \ S \rightarrow \mathbf{R}: \ x \mapsto y.$$

The **graph** of f is the subset of the plane $\mathbf{R}^2$ consisting of all ordered pairs $(x, f(x))$ where x varies over S.

Example 3

Let S be the open interval $(0, \tfrac{1}{2}\pi)$ and let the function f be given by $f(x) = \sin x$ for x in S, that is,

$$f: \ (0, \tfrac{1}{2}\pi) \rightarrow \mathbf{R}: \ x \mapsto \sin x.$$

The domain of f is $(0, \tfrac{1}{2}\pi)$. The range of f is not all of $\mathbf{R}$ but only the open interval $(0,1)$, since $0 < \sin x < 1$ for $0 < x < \tfrac{1}{2}\pi$. Thus f is not onto $\mathbf{R}$, since no element $\geqslant 1$ or $\leqslant 0$ can be the image under f of an element of S, but it is 1–1 since, for $0 < x_1 < x_2 < \tfrac{1}{2}\pi$, $\sin x_1 = \sin x_2$ implies that $x_1 = x_2$. As we saw in Example 2, if the domain of f is extended from $(0, \tfrac{1}{2}\pi)$ to $(0, \pi)$ then f is no longer 1–1.

Suppose we are given two functions $f: S \rightarrow T$ and $g: T \rightarrow U$, as illustrated in Fig. 3.2. The **composite function** (function of a function) $g \circ f$ maps $S \rightarrow U$ and is given by $(g \circ f)(x) = g(f(x))$ for each $x \in S$.

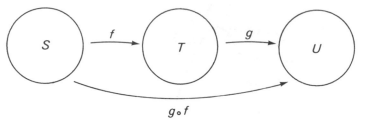

Fig. 3.2   The composite function.

Example 4

Suppose f and g are real functions of a real variable given by

$$f: \ \mathbf{R} \to \mathbf{R}: \ x \mapsto 1 + x^2$$

$$g: \ (0,\infty) \to \mathbf{R}: \ y \mapsto y^{\frac{1}{2}}.$$

Then

$$(g \circ f)(x) = g(f(x)) = g(1 + x^2) = (1 + x^2)^{\frac{1}{2}}.$$

Thus

$$g \circ f: \ \mathbf{R} \to \mathbf{R}: \ x \mapsto (1 + x^2)^{\frac{1}{2}}.$$

The graphs of the three functions f, g, and $g \circ f$ are shown in Fig. 3.3. Notice that the range of f is $[1,\infty)$ which is contained in $(0,\infty)$ the domain of g, hence the composite function can be defined for all x in $\mathbf{R}$.

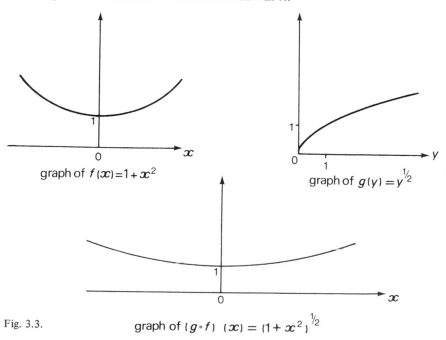

graph of $f(x) = 1 + x^2$

graph of $g(y) = y^{\frac{1}{2}}$

Fig. 3.3.

graph of $(g \circ f)(x) = (1 + x^2)^{\frac{1}{2}}$

Let S be a set of real numbers. Let a be in S or arbitrarily close to S: for instance S might be the open interval (a,b). Let $f: S \to R$. We say that the **limit** of f at a is L and write $\lim_{x \to a} f(x) = L$ if, given a real number $\epsilon > 0$, we can find a real number $\delta > 0$ such that whenever $|x - a| < \delta$ we have $|f(x) - L| < \epsilon$. Intuitively, this says that $f(x)$ is 'close' to L whenever x is 'close' to a, although $f(x)$ may never actually reach L. If we are told how close $f(x)$ has to be to L (that is, we are given ϵ) we can then say how close x must be to a for this to happen (that is, choose δ). Note that for most functions f and points a, L will be $f(a)$, and there is no need to resort to the rigorous definition to find L. In fact L is found simply by considering the limit of $f(x)$ as $x \to a$. We illustrate this in the next example.

Example 5

Consider $f: (0,1) \to R: x \mapsto (1-x)^{-1}$, that is $f(x) = \dfrac{1}{1-x}$. The function is illustrated in Fig. 3.4. What can we say about the limit of $f(x)$ as $x \to \frac{1}{2}$ for instance? (see Fig. 3.4.) Clearly, as $x \to \frac{1}{2}$, $f(x) \to f(\frac{1}{2}) = \dfrac{1}{1-\frac{1}{2}} = 2$. But what about the limit of $f(x)$ as $x \to 0$? $x = 0$ does not belong to $S = (0,1)$, but nevertheless $L = \lim_{x \to 0} f(x)$ does exist. For

$$\lim_{x \to 0} f(x) = \lim_{x \to 0} \frac{1}{1-x} = 1 \, .$$

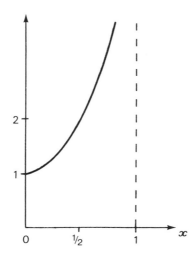

Fig. 3.4   Graph of $f(x) = (1 - x)^{-1}$.

Does this agree with our rigourous definition above? Suppose $0 < x < \delta < 1$ ($a = 0$ in the above general treatment, and x is restricted for this problem to $0 < x < 1$). Then

$$f(x) - 1 = \frac{1}{1-x} - 1 = \frac{x}{1-x} < \frac{\delta}{1-x}.$$

Also $1 - x > 1 - \delta$ so that $\dfrac{1}{1-x} < \dfrac{1}{1-\delta}$, and

$$f(x) - 1 < \frac{\delta}{1-\delta}.$$

Hence $|f(x) - 1| < \epsilon$ for $0 < x < \delta$ where $\dfrac{\delta}{1-\delta} = \epsilon$, that is, $\delta = \dfrac{\epsilon}{1+\epsilon}$. Thus, given any real number $\epsilon > 0$, by choosing $\delta = \epsilon/(1 + \epsilon)$, for $0 < x < \delta$, $|f(x) - 1| < \epsilon$ and by the definition $\lim\limits_{x \to 0} f(x) = 1$, as expected.

We may also define the **limit of f at infinity** by writing $\lim\limits_{x \to \infty} f(x) = L$ if, given $\epsilon > 0$, we can find a real number m such that whenever $x > m$ we have $|f(x) - L| < \epsilon$.

Note

This definition of limit of a function is in accord with our earlier definition [Ch. 2] of the limit of a sequence. For a sequence of real numbers $\{a_n\}$ gives rise to a function f defined on the natural numbers $\mathbf{N}$ and taking $n \in \mathbf{N}$ into the real number a_n; that is,

$$f: \mathbf{N} \to \mathbf{R}: n \mapsto a_n.$$

Thus $\lim\limits_{n \to \infty} a_n$ is simply $\lim\limits_{n \to \infty} f(n)$, since $\lim\limits_{n \to \infty} f(n) = L$ implies that, given $\epsilon > 0$, we can find $m \in \mathbf{N}$ such that for all $n > m$ $|f(n) - L| < \epsilon$, that is, $|a_n - L| < \epsilon$.

It is possible to perform algebraic operations on limits according to the following.

Theorem 1

Assume $\lim\limits_{x \to a} f(x) = L$ and $\lim\limits_{x \to a} g(x) = M$.

Then

    (i) $\lim\limits_{x \to a} \{f(x) + g(x)\} = L + M$

    (ii) $\lim\limits_{x \to a} cf(x) = cL$ for any $c \in \mathbf{R}$

    (iii) $\lim\limits_{x \to a} f(x)g(x) = LM$

    (iv) $\lim\limits_{x \to a} f(x)/g(x) = L/M$ provided that $M \neq 0$.

Proof

We shall prove assertion (i): the proof of the others is similar and may be found in any elementary analysis textbook. See, for example, Goult, Hoskins, Milner and Pratt (1973) p. 44.

Let $\epsilon > 0$. Then there are numbers $\delta_1, \delta_2 > 0$ such that

$$|f(x) - L| < \tfrac{1}{2}\epsilon \quad \text{whenever} \quad |x - a| < \delta_1$$

and $|g(x) - M| < \tfrac{1}{2}\epsilon$ whenever $|x - a| < \delta_2$.

Let $\delta = \min(\delta_1, \delta_2)$.

Then, for $|x - a| < \delta$,

$$|(f(x) + g(x)) - (L + M)| = |f(x) - L + g(x) - M|$$
$$< |f(x) - L| + |g(x) - M| < \tfrac{1}{2}\epsilon + \tfrac{1}{2}\epsilon = \epsilon.$$

Hence $\lim_{x \to a} (f(x) + g(x)) = L + M$.

Example 6

Find $\lim_{x \to \infty} \dfrac{x}{x + 1}$.

We write $\dfrac{x}{x + 1} = \dfrac{x + 1}{x + 1} - \dfrac{1}{x + 1}$

$$= 1 - \dfrac{1}{x + 1}.$$

Then by Theorem 1

$$\lim_{x \to \infty} \dfrac{x}{x + 1} = \lim_{x \to \infty} 1 - \lim_{x \to \infty} \dfrac{1}{x + 1} = 1 - 0 = 1.$$

The idea of limit leads naturally to the concept of continuity of a function. Let a be a point of the subset S of **R**, and $f: S \to$ **R**. We say that f is **continuous at the point** a if $\lim_{x \to a} f(x) = f(a)$. This will be so if, given $\epsilon > 0$, we can find a $\delta > 0$ such that whenever $|x - a| < \delta$ we have $|f(x) - f(a)| < \epsilon$. If f is continuous at every point of S we say f is **continuous on** S. This corresponds to our intuitive geometric notion of the graph of a continuous function being 'all in one piece', that is, there are no jumps or gaps in the graph (see Fig. 3.5). We may also define continuity at a by saying that these limits of f from the left and right should both exist and be equal to $f(a)$.

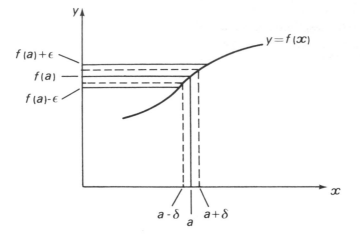

Fig. 3.5   The $\epsilon - \delta$ definition of continuity.

Example 7

The Heaviside function $H(x) = \begin{cases} 0 & x < 0 \\ \frac{1}{2} & x = 0 \\ 1 & x > 0 \end{cases}$

is discontinuous at $x = 0$, since

$$\lim_{\substack{x \to 0 \\ x < 0}} H(x) = 0, \qquad \lim_{\substack{x \to 0 \\ x > 0}} H(x) = 1$$

and neither of these is equal to $H(0)$, as shown in Fig. 3.6.
     A discontinuity of this type is known as a **jump discontinuity**.

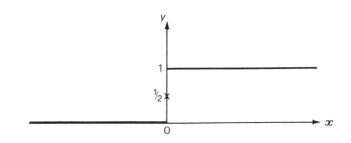

Fig. 3.6   The graph of $H(x)$.

Example 8

$f(x) = 1/x$ is discontinuous at $x = 0$.

In this case neither left nor right-hand limits of f at 0 exist, since

$$\lim_{\substack{x \to 0 \\ x < 0}} f(x) = -\infty, \qquad \lim_{\substack{x \to 0 \\ x > 0}} f(x) = +\infty.$$

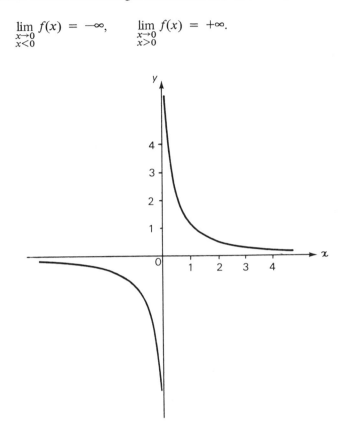

Fig. 3.7 The graph of $y(x) = 1/x$.

We say that f has an **infinite discontinuity** at 0.

Many functions such as the polynominals

$$p_n(x) = a_0 x^n + a_1 x^{n-1} + \ldots + a_{n-1} x + a_n$$

and the trigonometric functions $\cos x$, $\sin x$ are continuous over the whole real line **R**.

Let f and g both map S into **R**. Then the sum function $f + g$ also maps S into **R** and is given by

$$(f + g)(x) = f(x) + g(x) \text{ for all } x \in S.$$

The product function fg and quotient function f/g are defined similarly. Since continuity was defined via limits, Theorem 1 now gives

Theorem 2

If f and g are both continuous at a, then so are

(i) $f + g$, (ii) cf for any $c \in \mathbf{R}$, (iii) fg, (iv) f/g provided that $g(a) \neq 0$.

The need for the restriction $g(a) \neq 0$ in (iv) is clearly shown in Example 6. Continuity is also preserved under composition of mappings as follows.

Theorem 3

If f is continuous at x, and g is continuous at $f(x)$, then $g \circ f$ is continuous at x.

As an illustration of the theorem, take the functions $f(x) = 1 + x^2$ and $g(x) = x^{\frac{1}{2}}$ of Example 2. We see that the function $(g \circ f)(x) = (1 + x^2)^{\frac{1}{2}}$ is continuous on $\mathbf{R}$.

Given a function f on a set S, suppose that $f(x) = y$. If it is possible to determine x uniquely at each point y in the range of f, as a function of y, say $x = g(y)$, we say that g is the **inverse** function to f and write $g = f^{-1}$. Notice that $(f^{-1} \circ f)(x) = x$ and $(f \circ f^{-1})(y) = y$. For example, the inverse of the function $f(x) = 1 + x$ is the function $f^{-1}(y) = y - 1$.

Example 9

$f(x) = x^2$ has no inverse as a function on $\mathbf{R}$. Given any $y > 0$, we have both $f(y^{\frac{1}{2}}) = y$ and $f(-y^{\frac{1}{2}}) = y$. Thus the inverse of f does not exist as a function since it does not assign a unique value of x to each y.

There is an important class of functions for which an inverse always exists. Let S be a subset of $\mathbf{R}$ and $f : S \to \mathbf{R}$. We say that f is **monotonic increasing** (decreasing) on S if, whenever $x_1, x_2 \in S$ and $x_1 < x_2$, then $f(x_1) < f(x_2)$ ($f(x_1) > f(x_2)$).

Theorem 4

If f is monotonic on S (either increasing or decreasing) then f^{-1} exists. If f is continuous then so is f^{-1}.

For a proof of this result see Goult, Hoskins, Milner and Pratt (1973) p. 76.

3.3 SOLUTION OF THE BAKEWELL BEAN PROMOTION PROBLEM

In the language of Sec. 3.2 we now see that profit y is a function of advertising expenditure x given by

$$y = y(x) = \frac{22x + 11}{x + 2}. \tag{3.1}$$

To answer question (a) of Sec. 3.1 we must show that y is an increasing function of x. For any $x_2 > x_1$ we must show that $y(x_2) > y(x_1)$. This follows, since

$$y(x_2) - y(x_1) = \frac{22x_2 + 11}{x_2 + 2} - \frac{22x_1 + 11}{x_1 + 2}$$

$$= \frac{33(x_2 - x_1)}{(x_2 + 2)(x_1 + 2)} > 0, \text{ since } x_2 > x_1 > 0.$$

Thus as advertising increases, so does profit, although at a slower rate, for, if we let c be any positive number,

$$y(x_2 + c) - y(x_1 + c) = \frac{33(x_2 - x_1)}{(x_2 + 2 + c)(x_1 + 2 + c)} < y(x_2) - y(x_1).$$

We suspect that the answer to (b) will be that profits tend to a fixed value as advertising increases, and this is confirmed by calculating the limit of $y(x)$ as x tends to infinity. We have

$$\lim_{x \to \infty} y(x) = \lim_{x \to \infty} \frac{22x + 11}{x + 2}$$

$$= \lim_{x \to \infty} \left[\frac{22x}{x + 2} + \frac{11}{x + 2} \right]$$

$$= \lim_{x \to \infty} \frac{22x}{x + 2} + \lim_{x \to \infty} \frac{11}{x + 2}$$

$$= \lim_{x \to \infty} \left[\frac{22x + 44}{x + 2} - \frac{44}{x + 2} \right] + 0$$

$$= \lim_{x \to \infty} 22 - \lim_{x \to \infty} \frac{44}{x + 2}$$

$$= 22 - 0 = 22.$$

Thus no matter how much Bakewell advertise, profits will not exceed £2 200 000. This is borne out if we plot the graph of y against x as shown in Fig. 3.8.

This model is realistic in that, even if Bakewell succeeds in capturing the entire baked bean market, there must be an upper limit to the number of cans of baked beans that may be consumed. It is also likely in practice that, perceiving Bakewell's success, their main competitors would institute a counter advertising campaign, regaining their market share or at least stemming Bakewell's advance. In this case formula (3.1) would have to be modified accordingly.

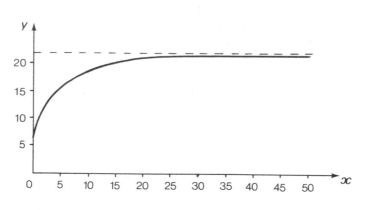

Fig. 3.8   Profit y against advertising expenditure x.

3.4   CASE STUDIES

3.4.1   Production Costs

The cost of production of any industrial commodity depends on a large number of factors: the rental and heating of the factory, the number of machines employed, the cost of raw materials, the wages paid to the workers, and the number of shifts worked. In many cases some of these factors will be fixed, for example the cost of the factory rental, while others will depend on the amount of the commodity produced, for instance the amounts of raw material inputs and the number of machines employed.

It has been found in a particular industry that the cost of production y is a function of the amount produced x given by

$$y = f(x) = 300 - x + (0.1)x^2 \qquad\qquad (3.2)$$

for amounts less than 50 units. For amounts greater than or equal to 50 units it is necessary to work a night shift which increases the fixed costs by 100, so that for $x > 50$ the function f is given by

$$y = f(x) = 400 - x + (0.1)x^2 . \qquad\qquad (3.3)$$

We may draw up Table 1.

Note that the limit of f as x tends to 50 from below is

$$\lim_{\substack{x \to 50 \\ x < 50}} f(x) = \lim_{x \to 50} (300 - x + 0.1x^2)$$

$$= 300 - \lim_{x \to 50} x + 0.1 \lim_{x \to 50} x^2$$

$$= 300 - 50 + 250 = 500 .$$

Table 3.1

x	$(0.1)x^2$	$-x + (0.1)x^2$	$f(x)$
5	2.5	−2.5	297.5
10	10	0	300
20	40	20	320
30	90	60	360
40	160	120	420
50	250	200	600
60	360	300	700
70	490	420	820
80	640	560	960

But $f(50)$ from the table is given by 600. Thus the cost function f has a jump discontinuity at $x = 50$ as may be seen from Fig. 3.9 below:

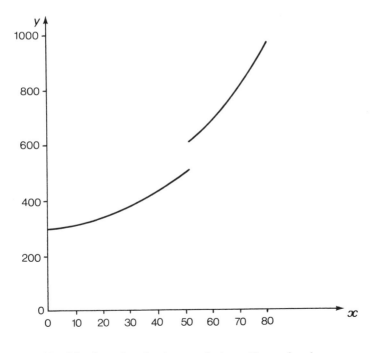

Fig. 3.9   Cost of production y against quantity produced x.

3.4.2 Continuously accruing interest: the exponential and logarithmic functions

Consider an amount of £1 invested at a rate of interest x (expressed as a decimal) compounded annually. Then formula (2.9) of Chapter 2 gives the amount in the account after one year as $(1+x)^1$. But we saw in the case of the Bradfax Building Society (Sec. 2.4.1) that the amount depends not only on the rate of interest but also on the intervals at which interest is compounded. For instance, if interest is compounded quarterly the amount after one year is $(1 + x/4)^4$, or monthly, $(1 + x/12)^{12}$, or even daily, $(1 + x/365)^{365}$. In general if there are n interest periods in the year the amount A is a function of x and n given by

$$A \equiv f(x,n) = (1 + x/n)^n. \tag{3.4}$$

To proceed further, we use the **Binomial Theorem** (see Goult, Hoskins, Milner and Pratt (1973), p. 89). If h is any positive real number and n any positive integer, then

$$(1+h)^n = 1 + nh + \frac{n(n-1)}{2!}h^2 + \frac{n(n-1)(n-2)}{3!}h^3 + \ldots + h^n.$$

Applying this result to (3.4) gives

$$f(x,n) = (1 + x/n)^n = 1 + n.\frac{x}{n} + \frac{n(n-1)}{2!}\frac{x^2}{n^2} + \frac{n(n-1)(n-2)}{3!}\frac{x^3}{n^3} + \ldots$$

$$= 1 + x + \frac{x^2}{2!}(1-1/n) + \frac{x^3}{3!}(1-1/n)(1-2/n) + \ldots$$

We see that the third and subsequent terms in this expression increase with n, and that new positive terms are added as n increases. Thus $f(x,n)$ is an increasing function of n.

On the other hand $f(x,n)$ is bounded above, since for all n

$$(1+x/n)^n < 1 + x + \frac{x^2}{2!} + \frac{x^3}{3!} + \ldots$$

$$< 1 + x + \frac{x^2}{2} + \frac{x^3}{2^2} + \ldots + \frac{x^n}{2^{n-1}}$$

$$= 1 + \frac{x(1-(x/2)^n)}{1-x/2} \quad \text{(since this is a geometric progression with common ratio } x/2)$$

$$\rightarrow 1 + \frac{2x}{2-x} \quad \text{(assuming } x < 2).$$

Hence the increasing function of n, $f(x,n)$, must tend to a certain limit as $n \to \infty$: denote this limit by e^x. That is,

$$\lim_{n \to \infty} f(x,n) = \lim_{n \to \infty} (1 + x/n)^n = e^x. \qquad (3.5)$$

It can be shown that e is an irrational number given to four decimal places by $e = 2.7183$. The limit function $\lim_{n \to \infty} f(x,n)$ is a function of x alone and hence maps the real numbers onto the positive real numbers. This function is usually known as the **exponential function**, exp.

$$\exp: \ \mathbf{R} \to (0,\infty): \ x \mapsto e^x. \qquad (3.6)$$

As $n \to \infty$ we are in the case of continuous compound interest. It follows that the amount A of a deposit D after n years of interest continuously compounded at an annual rate x is $A = De^{nx}$. Thus if we introduce into Case Study 2.4.1 a third building society offering an interest rate of 6.8% continuously compounded we see that Ms Brown's investment after one year would be worth

$$1000 \, e^{0.068} = 1000 \times 1.0704$$

$$= £1070.40$$

which is better than the higher Bradfax B.S. rate of 7% compounded annually. Because $f(x,n)$ is an increasing function of n for fixed x, the shorter the interval at which interest is compounded, the greater the amount.

The function $\exp x = e^x$ has the fundamental property that for any real numbers x_1 and x_2

$$e^{x_1 + x_2} = e^{x_1} e^{x_2} \qquad (3.7)$$

$$(e^{x_1})^{x_2} = e^{x_1 x_2}. \qquad (3.8)$$

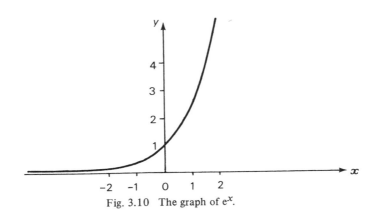

Fig. 3.10   The graph of e^x.

Since exp is a monotonic increasing continuous function (see Fig. 3.10) it has by Theorem 4 a continuous inverse, l say, defined on $(0,\infty)$. Suppose that $y_1, y_2 \in (0,\infty)$ are such that $l(y_1) = x_1$ and $l(y_2) = x_2$. Then, applying the exponential function to each side and noting that $\exp^{-1} = l$ gives

$$y_1 = e^{x_1} \quad \text{and} \quad y_2 = e^{x_2}.$$

It is easily seen that $y_1 y_2 = e^{x_1} e^{x_2} = e^{x_1 + x_2}$,

hence $l(y_1 y_2) = x_1 + x_2 = l(y_1) + l(y_2)$.

We may also verify that

$$e^0 = 1 \qquad \text{hence} \qquad l(1) = 0,$$

$$l(y^n) = nl(y), \qquad\qquad l(1/y) = -l(y).$$

$l(y)$ is usually called the **natural logarithm** of y or the logarithm of y to base e. Thus if $y = e^x$ we write $x = l(y) = \log_e y$. Natural logarithms are related to logarithms to base 10 by the formula

$$\boxed{\log_{10} y = \frac{\log_e y}{\log_e 10}} \qquad\qquad (3.9)$$

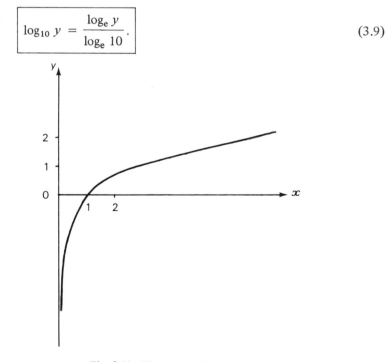

Fig. 3.11   The graph of $\log_e x$.

We conclude by restating the basic properties of the log function:

$$\log_e (y_1 y_2) = \log_e (y_1) + \log_e (y_2) \tag{3.10}$$

$$\log_e(1) = 0 \tag{3.11}$$

$$\log_e(y^n) = n \log_e y. \tag{3.12}$$

In what follows we will drop the suffix e for natural logarithms.

3.5 PROBLEMS

1. Determine whether the following functions f from S to T are (i) one-to-one (ii) onto:

   (i) $f(x) = x^2$, $S = [0, 1]$ $T = [0, 1]$
   (ii) $f(x) = x^2$, $S = [-1, 1]$ $T = [0, 1]$
   (iii) $f(x) = x^2$, $S = [0, 1]$ $T = [-1, 1]$
   (iv) $f(x) = ax + b$, $S = T = R$
   (v) $f(x) = 1/x$, $S = (0, \infty)$ $T = (0, \infty)$

2. If x and y are the temperature in Fahrenheit degrees and Celsius degrees, then

$$y = \frac{5}{9}(x - 32).$$

   Illustrate this function graphically.

3. Draw graphs of the following functions for $x \in [-2, 2]$

   (i) $x/(x^2 + 1)$,
   (ii) $x^2 - 2x + 4$,
   (iii) $3x^3 + 5x^2 - 2x - 7$.

4. In the following cases determine the composite function g of:

   (i) $g(x) = x^2$, $f(x) = 1 + x$
   (ii) $g(x) = \sin x$, $f(x) = x^2$

   (iii) $g(x) = \dfrac{1 - x}{x}$, $f(x) = \dfrac{1}{(1 + x)}$ for $x \in (0, \infty)$.

5. Show that the function

$$y = mx + c$$

   represents a straight line in the y-x plane with gradient m and passing through the point $x = 0$, $y = c$.

   Determine the equation of the straight line when

   (i) the gradient is 1 and it passes through $x = 0$, $y = -1$;
   (ii) it passes through $x = 0$, $y = 1$ and $y = 0$, $x = 1$;
   (iii) it passes through $x = 1$, $y = 1$ and $x = 2$, $y = 3$.

6. A **root** of a polynominal $f(x) = a + a_1 x + a_2 x^2 + \ldots + a_n x^n$ is defined as a value $x = \alpha$ such that $f(\alpha) = 0$.
   (i) Determine the root of the linear equation $f(x) = ax + b$.
   (ii) Show that the two roots of the quadratic equation

$$f(x) = ax^2 + bx + c$$

are given by

$$x = [-b \pm \sqrt{b^2 - 4ac}]/2a$$

7. Apply the formula in Exercise 6 to finding the roots of the following quadratic equations
   (i) $x^2 - 7x + 12$

   (ii) $x^2 - 16x + 64$

   (iii) $2x^2 + 11x + 12$.

8. Find the following limits:

   (i) $\lim\limits_{x \to 1} \left(\dfrac{x^2 - 1}{x - 1} \right)$

   (ii) $\lim\limits_{x \to 9} \left(\dfrac{3 - \sqrt{x}}{9 - x} \right)$

   (iii) $\lim\limits_{x \to \infty} \left(\dfrac{2x^2}{x^2 + 1} \right)$

   (iv) $\lim\limits_{x \to 0} \left(\dfrac{x + |x|}{x} \right)$

[The absolute value function $|x|$ is defined as $|x| = \begin{bmatrix} x \text{ if } x > 0 \\ -x \text{ if } x < 0 \end{bmatrix}$.

9. For what values of x are the following functions not continuous
   (i) $1/x$,

   (ii) $x + |x|$,

   (iii) $1/(x^2 - 1)$?

   Sketch each function, and describe the types of discontinuity in each case.

10. Determine the inverse of the function $f = \dfrac{1}{1 + x^2}, x \in [0, \infty)$.

    Explain why the function $f = \dfrac{1}{1 + x^2}, x \in R$ has no inverse.

11. The relationship in a manufacturing process between total production costs, T, and quantity produced, x, can be represented by a linear model,

$$T = F + Dx.$$

Here F and D are the fixed and direct costs respectively. Assuming that the revenue, R, is modelled by $R = px$, where p is the price, determine the gross profit, and show that the break-even point is given by

$$x = F/(p-D).$$

12. A manufacturer of cement finds that his total production costs average £1393 per day. He knows that fixed costs amount to £217 per day, and the average production is 49 tons of cement per day. The selling price is £31 per ton. (a) What is the daily revenue? (b) What is the daily gross profit? (c) What is the production and the revenue at the break-even point?

13. A manufacturer of steel strip finds that his total production cost is £120 660 per week when he is producing 1240 tons per week. The fixed costs are £67340 per week, and the selling price is £117 per ton. Find (a) the weekly revenue, (b) the weekly selling gross profit, and (c) the weekly production and total production cost at the break-even point.

14. The sales manager of a local motorcycle shop claims that the shop's sales of motorcycles will increase £6 for each additional pound spent on advertising over the local radio station. If the bike shop has averaged monthly sales of £20 000 while spending £150 a month on the commercials, then find the linear equation relating the shop's expected sales to the amount spent on the radio commercials. What is the expected sales income if £170 of air time is bought?

15. A manufacturer of rubberized fabrics has three machines which prepare fabric and five machines which rubberize it. Two types of rubberized fabric are produced; type A requires 3 minutes per yard to prepare and 6 minutes to rubberize it, whilst type B requires 11 and 17 minutes respectively. How much of each type of fabric should be produced per hour in order to keep all the machines fully occupied?

16. We can assume that the temperature, $t°$ Fahrenheit, at a point h feet above the surface of the earth is a linear function of h for limited altitudes under certain atmospheric conditions. Suppose the temperature on the surface of the earth is $70°$ and the temperature at 3 000 feet is $61°$. Find the formula for t in terms of h, and sketch the graph for those values of h between 0 and 20 000.

17. Draw a graph of the postage rate against the weight of letter posted, using the table of current charges available at your local post office. Is the relationship linear? Why do you think this is?

18. Supply and demand curves for various products can be modelled by linear equations of the form

$$S = ap - b$$
$$D = c - dp$$

when p is the price. Determine the market equilibrium price, when $S = D$.

19. The monthly supply of sugar is estimated to be 73 000 tons when the price is £32 per ton, and 101 000 tons when the price is £40 per ton. The monthly demand is estimated to be 109 000 tons at £32 per ton and 89 000 tons at £40 per ton. Assuming that the supply and demand functions are both linear, find these functions and hence determine the equilibrium price and quantity.

20. The weekly supply and demand for pig iron is assessed at six different prices, as follows:

Price (£ per ton)	15	20	25	30	35	40
Supply (thousand tons)	155	190	225	260	340	420
Demand (thousand tons)	490	380	270	230	190	150

Assuming that the supply and demand functions each consist of two straight lines, find these functions and hence determine the equilibrium price and quantity.

21. The table shows the supply and demand for butter. Make any necessary modelling steps and determine the price at which all the butter that is produced will be sold.

TABLE: Supply and demand variations with the price of butter

price/p per kg	quantity demanded/ millions of kg	quantity supplied/ millions of kg
65	30	20
70	28	20.5
75	26	21
80	23	22
85	21	23
90	20	23.5
95	18	25
100	16	26

CHAPTER 4

Turning Points and Changes: Models based on the Differential Calculus

4.1 THE CASE OF THE WONDERBIKE SELLING PRICE

An old established engineering firm, Wonder Works, has designed a stabilized children's bicycle of revolutionary design which is about to be put into production, but the board has met to discuss the recommended selling price of the Wonderbike, as the marketing division believes that this will strongly influence the number sold and thus the production ordered. The marketing director estimates that if the selling price is fixed at £50 then 5500 bicycles will be sold in the first month, whereas if the price is doubled to £100 only 1000 will be sold.

He believes that the relation between selling price x and total sales s is a linear one given by

$$s = 10\,000 - 90x. \tag{4.1}$$

This function is sketched in Fig. 4.1.

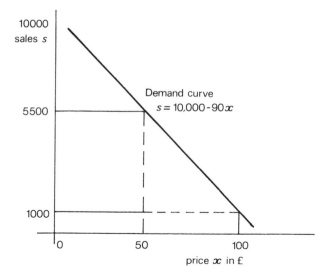

Fig. 4.1 Demand curve.

This is an example of what economists call a **linear demand curve**. The sales revenue r is given by the product of the selling price and number sold; that is,

$$r = \text{s}x$$
$$= (10\,000 - 90x)x \qquad \text{from (4.1)},$$

that is, $r = 10\,000x - 90x^2.$ (4.2)

The graph of sales revenue against selling price is shown in Fig. 4.2.

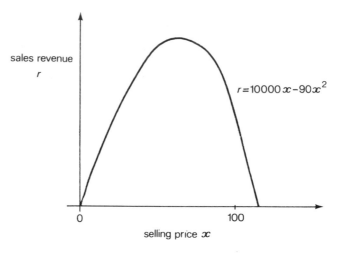

Fig. 4.2   Sales revenue curve.

The marketing director suggests that the selling price be fixed at the value x for which $r(x)$ achieves its maximum. The production manager is quick to point out that this need not maximize profits, which are obtained from sales revenue by subtracting the cost of production C which depends on the number produced (assumed to be the same as the number sold) according to the formula

$$C = 4000 \quad + \quad 70s$$
$$\text{'fixed cost' 'variable cost'}$$
$$= 4000 + 70\,(10\,000 - 90x)$$
$$= 704\,000 - 6300x \qquad (4.3)$$

as shown in Fig. 4.3.

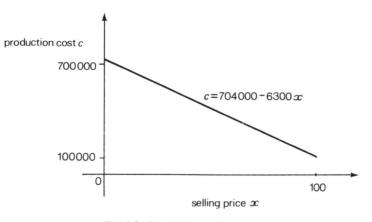

Fig. 4.3 Production cost curve.

The profit is thus given by

$$p = r - c$$

$$= 10\,000x - 90x^2 - 704\,000 + 6300x$$

using (4.1) and (4.3)

$$\boxed{p = -704\,000 + 16\,300x - 90x^2} \qquad (4.4)$$

The chairman now puts the question
    'What should the selling price x of each Wonderbike be in order to give the largest possible company profit p?'
Before answering this question we must develop some additional mathematics.

4.2 DERIVATIVES AND MAXIMA AND MINIMA OF FUNCTIONS OF A REAL VARIABLES

Recalling the definitions and notation of Sec. 3.2, let $I = [a, b]$ be an interval of the real line and consider a function $f = I \rightarrow \mathbf{R}$. Let x be an interior point of I. The function of f is **differentiable** at x if the limit $\lim\limits_{h \to 0} \dfrac{f(x+h) - f(x)}{h}$, taken over those h for which $x + h \in I$, exists as a unique finite real number. This limit, which we will denote by $f'(x)$, is called the **derivative** of f at the point x. If f is differentiable at every point in I, then f' is a function on I called simply the **derivative** of f, sometimes denoted by df/dx.

Examples

(a) If f is a constant function, say $f(x) = c$, then

$$\lim_{h \to 0} \frac{f(x+h) - f(x)}{h} = \lim_{h \to 0} \frac{c - c}{h} = 0.$$

and so $f'(x) = 0$ for all x

(b) If $f(x) = x^n$, where n is a positive integer, then

$$\frac{f'(x+h) - f(x)}{h} = \frac{(x+h)^n \quad x^n}{h}$$

$$= \frac{(nx^n + nx^{n-1}h + \tfrac{1}{2}n(n-1)x^{n-2}h^2 + \ldots + h^n) - x^n}{h}$$

(using the Binomial expansion)

$$= nx^{n-1} + h\{\tfrac{1}{2}n(n-1)x^{n-2} + \ldots + h^{n-2}\}$$

$$\to nx^{n-1} \text{ as } h \to 0;$$

so $f'(x) = nx^{n-1}.$

(c) Other important derivatives are listed below:

Function	Derivative
e^x	e^x
$\log x$	$1/x$
$\sin x$	$\cos x$
$\cos x$	$-\sin x$

The geometrical significance of the derivative soon becomes clear. For, if we represent the function $y = f(x)$ on a graph (see Fig. 4.4), we see that

$$\frac{f(x + h) - f(x)}{h} = \frac{QN}{PN} = \tan \theta$$

where θ is the angle QPN. As we take the limit as $h \to 0$, $Q \to P$ and the line segment PQ becomes closer and closer to a tangent line at the point P. In fact in the limit

$$\lim_{h \to 0} \frac{f(x + h) - f(x)}{h} = \text{slope of tangent at point P.}$$

So f' geometrically is just the slope of the tangent to the curve $y = f(x)$ at any point x.

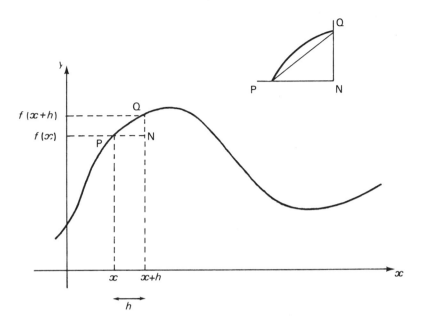

Fig. 4.4 Geometrical interpretation of the derivative.

In mathematical terms, we can think of the derivative as a linear mapping on the set of functions on I. Our justification for this is provided by:

Theorem 1
Let α, β be real numbers and f, g real valued functions differentiable on I. Then

$$(\alpha f + \beta g)'(x) = \alpha f'(x) + \beta g'(x) \qquad (4.5)$$

Proof
Using the definition $(\alpha f + \beta g)'(x) = \lim_{h \to 0} \dfrac{(\alpha f + \beta g)(x + h) - (\alpha f + \beta g)(x)}{h}$

the result follows from the corresponding results on limits contained in Theorem 1 (i) and (ii) of Sec. 3.2.

Example
The derivative of $x + x^3$ is given by $1 + 3x^2$; this is seen from Theorem 1 with $f = x$, $g = x^3$ and $\alpha = \beta = 1$.

This deals with the derivative of a sum: there are corresponding results for products and quotients.

Theorem 2

If f, g are differentiable at x then so is the product fg, and

$$(fg)'(x) = f(x)g'(x) + f'(x)g(x). \tag{4.6}$$

Proof

$$\{f(x + h)g(x + h) - f(x)g(x)\}/h =$$

$$\{f(x + h)g(x + h) - f(x) + h)g(x)\}/h + \{f(x + h)g(x) - f(x)g(x)\}/h$$

$$= f(x + h)[g(x + h) - g(x)]/h + g(x)\{f(x + h) - f(x)\}/h.$$

Letting $h \to 0$ gives the required result.

Example

If $f = x^2$, $g = \sin x$, then by Theorem 2

$$\frac{d}{dx}(x^2 \sin x) = x^2 \cos x + 2x \sin x$$

since $\qquad f' = 2x,\ g' = \cos x.$

Theorem 3

If f, g are differentiable at x and $g(x) \neq 0$, then f/g is differentiable at x and

$$(f/g)'(x) = (g(x)f'(x) - g'(x)f(x))/g(x)^2 \tag{4.7}$$

Proof

Consider first the function $1/g$. Then

$$\{1/g(x + n) - 1/g(x)\}/h = -\frac{g(x + h) - g(x)}{h} \cdot \frac{1}{g(x + h)g(x)}$$

Taking the limit as $h \to 0$ yields

$$(1/g)'(x) = -g'(x)/g(x)^2.$$

The result now follows by applying Theorem 2 to the product $f.(1/g)$.

Examples

(a) If $f = \sin x$, $g = \cos x$, we can apply Theorem 3 to find the derivative of $\tan x$; for

$$\frac{d}{dx}(\tan x) = \frac{d}{dx}\frac{\sin x}{\cos x} = (\cos x. \cos x - (-\sin x)\sin x)/\cos^2 x$$

$$= \frac{1}{\cos^2 x} = \sec^2 x.$$

(b) If $f(x) = x^{-n}$, where n is a positive integer, then $f'(x) = -nx^{-n-1}$, which can be derived from Theorem 3 with $f = 1, g = x^n$.

Another idea introduced in Sec. 3.2 was the **composition** of a function. If f is defined at x and g at $f(x)$, then the composed function $g \circ f$ is given by $(g \circ f)(x) = g(f(x))$. The derivative of such a function is given by $\cdots$

Theorem 4
If f is differentiable at x, and g is differentiable at $f(x)$, then $g \circ f$ is differentiable at x and

$$(g \circ f)'(x) = g'(f(x))f'(x). \tag{4.8}$$

Proof
An equivalent definition of differentiable is that

$$f(x + h) = f(x) + f'(x)h + \phi(h)$$

where $\phi(h) \to 0$ as $h \to 0$.
Let $k = k(h) = f(x + h) - f(x)$ and let $y = f(x)$. Then

$$g(f(x + h)) - g(f(x)) = g(y + k) - g(y)$$
$$= g'(y)k + k\psi(k)$$

where $\psi(k) \to 0$ as $k \to 0$, since g is differentiable at y. Hence

$$\frac{g(f(x + h)) - g(f(x))}{h} = g'(f(x)) . \frac{f(x + h) - f(x)}{h} + \frac{f(x + h) - f(x)}{h} \psi(k(h)).$$

Since $k(h) \to 0$ as $h \to 0$, taking the limit as $h \to 0$ we obtain

$$(g \circ f)'(x) = g'(f(x)) . f'(x).$$

Note
Using the classical notation dg/dx for $g'(x)$, if we put $y = f(x)$ and $u = g(y)$, this theorem may be expressed as

$$\frac{du}{dx} = \frac{du}{dy}\frac{dy}{dx} \qquad \text{usually known as the \textbf{chain rule}.}$$

Example
To evaluate $\dfrac{d}{dx}(e^{x^2})$, we can put $g(x) = e^x$, $f(x) = x^2$,

then $g \circ f = e^{x^2}$, and $g' = e^x$, $f' = 2x$, so that $\dfrac{d}{dx}(e^{x^2}) = e^{x^2} . 2x$.

A function f has a *maximum* at the point x_0 if the value of f at x_0 is greater than the value of f at any point x near to x_0, that is, $f(x_0) > f(x)$ for all x near x_0. Similarly, we say that f has a *minimum* at x_0 if $f(x_0) < f(x)$ for all x near x_0.

A typical maximum is shown in Fig. 4.5.

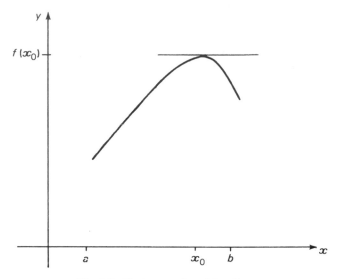

Fig. 4.5   Maximum value of function.

We see that at a maximum the tangent to $y = f(x)$ is parallel to the x-axis. The gradient of the tangent changes from positive to negative as x increases through x_0. Recalling the geometrical interpretation of the derivative as the gradient of the tangent we see that at a *maximum* x_0 of f we have

(i) $f'(x_0) = 0$
(ii) $f'(x_0)$ decreases steadily with x.

If we define the **second derivative** of f at x, $f''(x)$ by

$$f''(x) = (f'(x))' = \lim_{h \to 0} \frac{f'(x+h) - f'(h)}{h}$$

then (ii) is equivalent to: (ii)' $f''(x_0) < 0$.
Similar considerations show that at a *minimum* we also have $f'(x_0) = 0$, but in this case $f''(x_0) > 0$.

   In the case when both $f'(x_0) = 0$ and $f''(x_0) = 0$ but $f'''(x_0) \neq 0$ we obtain a **point of inflexion**. For example if $f(x) = x^3$, then $f'(x) = 3x^2$ and $f''(x) = 6x$. Both f' and f'' vanish at $x = 0$. The graph is shown in Fig. 4.6.

4.3 SOLUTION TO THE WONDERBIKE SELLING PRICE PROBLEM

We now recognise that equation (4.4) gives the profit p as a function of the selling price x, and that the Chairman's question, in mathematical terms, is
   'What is the maximum of the function

$$p(x) = -704\,000 + 16\,300x - 90x^2?'$$

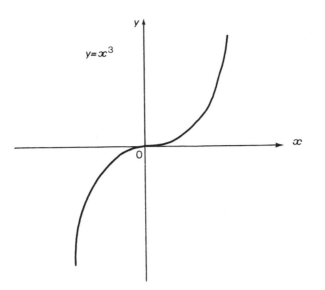

$y = x^3$

Fig. 4.6   The function $y = x^3$.

Using the results of Sec. 4.2 we have

$$p'(x) = 16\,300 - 180x,$$
$$p''(x) = -180.$$

Thus $p'(x) = 0$ when $x = 16\,300/180 = 90.56$, and since $p''(x) < 0$ for all x, this must give a maximum of p. In real terms, this means that the selling price of the Wonderbike should be £90.56 to maximize profits.

Economists often calculate this optimal selling price by applying the

Fundamental Principle of Economics

Profit is maximum when marginal revenue (defined by dr/dx) is equal to the marginal cost (defined to be dc/dx).

We check that this procedure gives the same result. From (4.2)

$$r(x) = 10\,000x - 90x^2$$

and from (4.3)

$$c(x) = 704\,000 - 6300x.$$

Then

$$r'(x) = 10\,000 - 180x$$
$$c'(x) = -6300.$$

Hence maximum profit occurs when $r'(x) = c'(x)$. That is,

$$10\,000 - 180x = -6300$$

$$180x = 16\,300$$

or $x = 90.56$ as before.

The idea behind the economists' method can be seen by superimposing Figs 4.2 and 4.3. The maximum profit occurs when the tangents to the sales revenue and production cost curves are parallel. When that occurs, the vertical distance between the two curves, that is, the profit, is greatest; see Fig. 4.7.

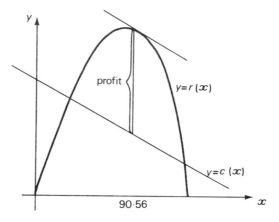

Fig. 4.7   Illustration of maximum profit.

4.4 CASE STUDIES

4.4.1 The economics of production – diminishing returns

We regard production as the transformation of given inputs (men, machines, material commodities) into one or more outputs, for example

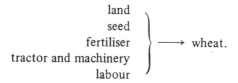

Sometimes this process can be represented by an input-output matrix, (see Ch. 8), but only where the relationship is linear. In general, production is represented by a non-linear function f mapping a vector of inputs $(x_1, x_2, \ldots x_n)$ into a vector of outputs $(y_1, \ldots y_m)$. In the example above $x_1 =$ acres of land, $\ldots, x_5 =$ man hours of labour and there is only one output y measured in tons of wheat. In order to represent this function graphically it is usual to regard only one of the inputs as variable and all the others fixed. Thus we may write a production function of one variable as

$$y = f(x).$$

The graph of a typical production function is shown in Fig. 4.8, denoted by the letters TP for **total product** curve. We also show the **average product** curve (AP) obtained by plotting y/x against x.

The **marginal product** MP is defined to be the ratio of the change in total output Δy resulting from a small change Δx in input, to the change in input Δx. We have

$$\text{MP} = \frac{\Delta y}{\Delta x} = \frac{f(x + \Delta x) - f(x)}{\Delta x} \rightarrow f'(x)$$

as $\Delta x \rightarrow 0$. Hence $\text{MP} = dy/dx$, and this is also plotted in Fig. 4.8.

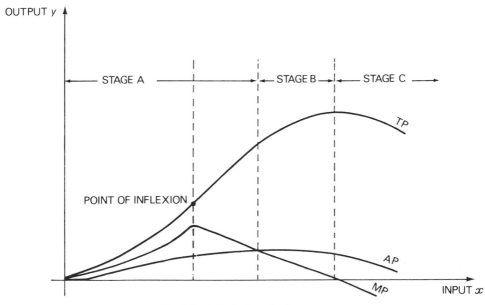

Fig. 4.8 A typical production curve.

The law of **diminishing returns** (or variable proportions) asserts that in a given state of technology, increasing one input to production while keeping the other inputs constant will yield increasing returns per unit added until a point is reached beyond which further additions to the variable input will give diminishing returns per unit added. To return to our agricultural example, if fertilizer has not been used previously, the output of wheat will rise with each ton of fertilizer applied, until a point is reached where the extra fertilizer has little effect and may eventually poison the soil.

We see this effect in Fig. 4.8 if we examine the relationship between the total and marginal product curves. While the TP curve $y = f(x)$ is concave, the MP curve $y = f'(x)$ is rising. It reaches its maximum at the point of inflexion of the TP curve where it changes from concave to convex. This is the point at which diminishing returns set in. When the TP curve reaches its maximum, $MP = f'(x) = 0$, and beyond this point $f(x)$ is decreasing, with $f'(x) < 0$. This is the point of negative returns.

From the graph we also observe a relationship between the average and marginal product curves. While $MP > AP$, AP is increasing, but when $MP < AP$, AP is decreasing. We may confirm this mathematically as follows:

$$\frac{d}{dx}(AP) = \frac{d}{dx}(y/x) = (x\frac{dy}{dx} - y)/x^2$$

(using Theorem 3 of Sec. 4.2)

$$> 0 \quad \text{if and only if} \quad x\frac{dy}{dx} - y > 0$$

$$\text{that is, if and only if} \quad \frac{dy}{dx} > \frac{y}{x}.$$

But this last inequality simply says that $MP > AP$. Hence AP is increasing if and only if $MP > AP$.

It is usual to classify three distinct stages of production, shown in Fig. 4.8.

Stage A: zero input to input giving maximum of AP

Stage B: input giving maximum of AP to input giving zero MP (which, as we have seen, corresponds to maximum TP)

Stage C: inputs giving negative MP.

In stage A the fixed inputs are too high relative to the variable input x, and we may increase output y by increasing x or decreasing the other inputs. In stage C the opposite situation applies, and we can increase y by decreasing x or increasing the other inputs. It is therefore best to operate in stage B, the exact point of operation depending on the relative costs of the variable and fixed inputs. For instance, if labour is the variable input, and it is cheap relative to the price of land, as is the case in underdeveloped countries, the farmer will operate at the end of stage B. In developed countries, with high labour costs, it is more efficient to operate at the beginning of stage B.

These stages may also be distinguished by the **elasticity of production** parameter E, defined to be the ratio of the percentage change in output to a small percentage change in input. We have

$$E = \frac{\Delta y}{y} \bigg/ \frac{\Delta x}{x} = \frac{x}{y} \cdot \frac{\Delta y}{\Delta x} \rightarrow \frac{x}{y} \frac{dy}{dx} \quad \text{as} \quad \Delta x \rightarrow 0$$

$$= MP/AP.$$

Thus we see that in

Stage A: $MP > AP$ and $E > 1$
Stage B: $AP > MP > 0$ and $0 < E < 1$
Stage C: $AP > 0 > MP$ and $E < 0$.

4.4.2 Drug Concentration in the Bloodstream

The concentration in the bloodstream, $x = x(t)$, of a particular group of drugs approximately obeys a law of the form

$$\boxed{x(t) = c(e^{-at} - e^{-bt})}$$

where a, b, c, $(a < b)$ are constants for a given dosage of a particular drug, and where the drug has been injected into the body at time $t = 0$. We require to know the general characteristics of the drug concentration in the body for time $t > 0$.

We first note the behaviour at $t = 0$ and as $t \rightarrow \infty$.
At $t = 0$, $x = 0$, and as $t \rightarrow \infty$, $x \rightarrow 0$. Also for $t > 0$, since $a < b$, $-at > -ab$ and so $e^{-at} > e^{-ab}$. Thus for all $t > 0$, $x > 0$. Clearly x must have a maximum somewhere in the range $0 < t < \infty$. To find this maximum, we put $dx/dt = 0$.

That is,

$$\frac{dx}{dt} = c(-ae^{-at} - (-b)e^{-bt}) = 0$$

that is,

$$e^{(b-a)t} = b/a.$$

Taking logs,

$$(b-a)t = \log[b/a]$$

that is,

$$t = \frac{1}{b-a} \log(b/a).$$

Also

$$\frac{d^2x}{dt^2} = c(a^2e^{-at} - b^2e^{-bt})$$

$$= ce^{-bt}(a^2e^{(b-a)t} - b^2)$$

$$= ce^{-bt}(a^2 \cdot \frac{b}{a} - b^2) \quad \text{when} \quad e^{(b-a)t} = b/a$$

$$= ce^{-bt}b(a - b) < 0.$$

Clearly, we have a maximum value at $t = (1/(b - a)) \log(b/a)$ and the actual maximum concentration level is given by

$$x_{max} = ce^{-bt}(e^{(b-a)t} - 1)$$

$$= ce^{-(b/(b-a))\log(b/a)}(\frac{b}{a} - 1)$$

$$= c\frac{(b-a)}{a}e^{\log(a/b)(b/(b-a))}$$

that is,

$$x_{max} = c\frac{(b-a)}{a}(\frac{a}{b})^{b/(b-a)}.$$

The behaviour of the concentration is illustrated in Fig. 4.9. The figure shows that as time increases the concentration increases as more of the injected drug is absorbed into the bloodstream. This concentration eventually reaches a maximum level after which the level of concentration decays gradually, tending to zero as $t \to \infty$.

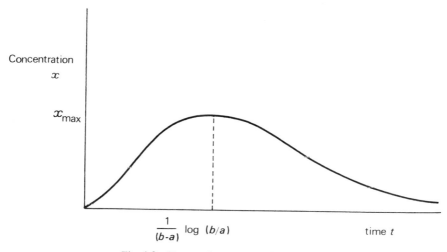

Fig. 4.9 Changes in concentration with time.

4.4.3 The Kertz Leasing Company

The Kertz Leasing Company leases fleets of new cars to large corporations. They charge £1000 per car per year, but for contracts with a fleet size of more than 10 cars the rental fee per car is discounted by 1% for each car in the contract. The company wishes to know how many cars leased to a single corporation in one year will produce maximum income?

If T denotes total income for a contract with a fleet size x, then

$$T = \begin{cases} 1000x & \text{if } 0 \leqslant x \leqslant 10 \\ (1000 - (1/100) \times 1000x)x & \text{if } x > 0, \end{cases}$$

since for $x > 10$, the rental for each car is reduced by 1% of £1000 for every car in the contract. There will also be an upper bound, say $x = 75$, to the maximum fleet size. So the problem is to determine the fleet size x which maximizes T. For $0 \leqslant x \leqslant 10$, T is just a linear increasing function and has no maximum in this range. But for $x > 10$,

$$T = 1000x - 10x^2$$

and $$\frac{dT}{dx} = 1000 - 20x$$

$$= 0 \text{ when } x = 50:$$

also $$\frac{d^2T}{dx} = -40,$$

and so $x = 50$ gives a maximum value to T. To sum up, a leasing of a fleet size of 50 will yield a maximum revenue. The situation is illustrated in Fig. 4.10.

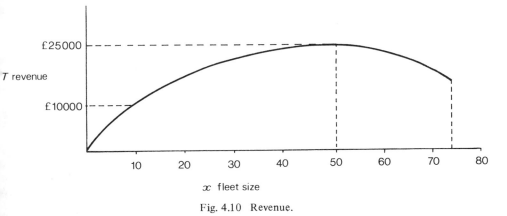

Fig. 4.10 Revenue.

But this answer is not really what the company wants to know. A fleet size of 50 will maximize the revenue from one corporation, but will it maximize the company's profit? Almost certainly not. For each car leased, it is estimated that over a year, the value of a car depreciates by £500 so that the total loss in value of fleet size of x cars is $500x$. Hence the profit made by Kertz on a fleet size of x cars is given by

$$P = \begin{cases} 1000x - 500x & \text{if} \quad 0 \leqslant x \leqslant 10 \\ (1000 - 10x)x - 500x & \text{if} \quad 10 < x \leqslant 75 \end{cases}$$

that is,

$$P = \begin{cases} 500x & \text{if} \quad 0 \leqslant x \leqslant 10 \\ 500x - 10x^2 & \text{if} \quad 10 < x \leqslant 75. \end{cases}$$

We must look for the fleet size x which maximizes this profit function. Clearly it does not occur in the range $0 \leqslant x \leqslant 10$. But for $x > 10$,

$$\frac{dP}{dx} = 500 - 20x$$

$$= 0 \text{ when } x = 25.$$

Also $\dfrac{d^2P}{dx^2} = -20$, so $x = 25$ gives a maximum value to the profit function. The situation is illustrated in Fig. 4.11.

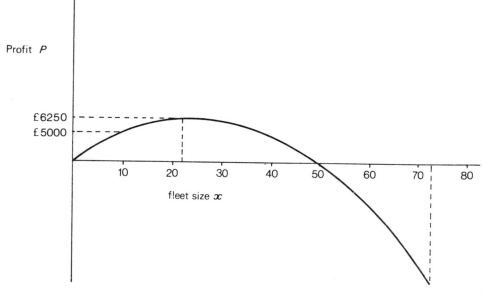

Fig. 4.11 Profit.

It should be noted that the fleet size for maximum revenue, $x = 50$, in fact gives no profit at all, and the maximum fleet size, $x = 75$, gives a considerable loss. So the company would be well advised to either

    (i) reduce the maximum fleet size to say 40; or

    (ii) change the discount rate for x larger than 30, say.

4.5 PROBLEMS

1. Differentiate the following functions

    (i) $3x^2 + 2x - 7$

    (ii) $(x^2 + 1)(x^2 - 1)$

    (iii) $2\sin x + 5\cos x$

    (iv) $\frac{1}{2}(1+x^2)\sin x$

    (v) $\sin^2 x$

    (vi) $(1+x^2)/(1-x^2)$

    (vii) $(1+\cos x)/(1-\cos x)$

    (viii) $\sin(4x)$

    (ix) $(1 + 4x^3)^3$

    (x) e^{x^3}

    (xi) $\log(1+x)$

    (xii) $x^2\log x^2$

2. Find the first and second derivatives of the following functions

    (i) $(1+x^2)^2$

    (ii) $x^2 + 4x + 1$

    (iii) $\sin(2x)$

    (iv) $\log(1+e^x)$

    (v) $(1-x)/(1+x^2)$

3. Find maximum and minimum points for the following functions

    (i) x^2

    (ii) $x^2 - 4x + 7$

    (iii) $x^3 - 12x$

    (iv) $x^3 - 3x^2 - 9x + 3$.

    In each case sketch the functions.

4. For the following functions, determine the first and second derivatives. Determine the intervals on which the function is increasing, and also determine maximum and minimum points and points of inflexion. Sketch the curves of these functions.

    (i) $x(x + 1)(x + 2)$

    (ii) $4/(4+x^2)$

    (iii) $(1 + x)/(1 + x^2)$.

5. The production function for a certain product is given by

$$y = \frac{A x^2}{(1 + x^3)}.$$

Sketch this curve for $x > 0$ and determine the marginal product and average product curves. Also determine the elasticity of production and find the appropriate ranges for Stages A, B, and C as defined in Sec. 4.4.1.

6. Referring to the case study of Sec. 4.4.3, suppose the 1% discount when the number of cars is in excess of 10, is given only to those cars in excess of 10. Determine the total income function, and find what fleet size yields maximum revenue.

   Assuming that each car depreciates by £500 in the year, find the profit function and again determine the optimum fleet size.

7. An open box is made from a rectangular piece of tin 10 metres long and 8 metres wide by cutting pieces 'x' metres square from each corner and bending up the sides. Express the volume, V cubic metres, of the box in terms of x. What value of x produces a box of maximum value, and what is this value?

8. Determine the rectangle which has maximum area inside for a given total perimeter length.

9. There are many variables which affect a person's reaction to a drug, e.g. blood pressure and body temperature. The strength of the reaction will also depend on the quantity of the drug taken and this can be modelled by

$$y = f(x) = x^2(a - x)^3 ,$$

Where a is a positive constant. Show that this reaction is at a maximum when $x = \dfrac{2a}{5}$.

10. A population of fruit fly grows according to the equation

$$p(t) = 100 + \frac{40 t^{\frac{1}{2}}}{(20 + t)},$$

where t is the time in days. What is the initial population and at what time is the maximum population reached?

11. An estate office handles a large property with 200 flats. When the rent of each flat is £200 per month, all flats are occupied. Experience has shown that for each £10 per month increase in rent, five flats become vacant. It is also relevant that the cost of servicing a rented flat is £20 a month. What rent should the office charge in order to maximize profit? How much is that maximum profit? How many flats will be rented at that maximum profit?

12. A steel company knows that if it charges £x a ton it can sell $(300 - x)$ tons in a single order. There is a charge of £120 to manufacture each ton and a total cost of £5000 which is spread equally among each of the $(300 - x)$ tons produced in a single batch. How much should the company charge per ton to maximize its revenue, what is that revenue, and how many tons are sold at the maximum revenue?

13. A manufacturer can sell x items per week at a selling price of

$$p(x) = 200 - 0.1x$$

pence per item, and it costs

$$c(x) = 50x + 10\,000$$

pence to produce the batch of x items. How many items should he produce in a single batch to maximise the profit?

14. In a certain truck factory the total cost of producing x trucks per week is

$$C = f(x) = x^2 + 75x + 1000.$$

How many trucks should be produced to maximize the profit if the number produced is limited by a production capacity of fifty per week and the sale price per truck is

$$s = g(x) = \begin{cases} \dfrac{5}{3}(125 - x) & \text{if } x \leqslant 25, \\[2mm] \dfrac{500}{3} & \text{if } 25 < x \leqslant 50? \end{cases}$$

15. Suppose that a company making a certain item knows that its cost function is

$$C = f(x) = \frac{x^3}{3} - 17x^2 - 111x + 50$$

and its revenue function is

$$R = g(x) = x(100 - x).$$

Find the quantity of output that minimizes the cost.
What is the marginal cost at the value of x which minimizes the cost?
Find the quantity of output that maximizes the profit.
What is the maximum profit?

16. A dealer has an approximately constant demand rate of r per year for one of his products. He orders the product from the manufacturer in a batch size of quantity x, say, and he wishes to know the optimum batch size in order to minimize his costs.

    His costs arise from

    (i) a set up cost of each order of amount c_1,

    (ii) a storage cost of c_2 per unit stock per unit time.

The average stock held is $x/2$ and the number of orders per year will be r/x giving a total yearly cost as

$$F = \frac{r}{x}c_1 + c_2\frac{x}{2}.$$

Show that for minimum total costs, the optimum batch size is given by

$$x = \sqrt{2rc_1/c_2}.$$

(This is known as the **economic order quantity** – E.O.Q.)

CHAPTER 5

Growth and Decay: Models based on First Order Differential Equations

5.1 THE CASE OF CUSPIC CONTAINERS

Cuspic Containers of London have built up production of a new type of moulded plastic container over the last few years, and at present have 2500 moulding machines producing them. Surveys indicate that demand for their product will double over the next 10 years, and management has decided to expand the plant steadily year by year, spreading the purchase of new machines out over each year. As a rough guide they intend to purchase 100 new machines over the first year, 200 over the second year, 300 over the third year, and so on until the tenth year when they anticipate buying 1000 new machines.

This planned expansion will exceed the required capacity of 5000 at the end of year ten; but management must allow for a drop in productivity of the older machines, which become increasingly out of service for repair, and for the replacement of the oldest and most unreliable machines when they are beyond economic repair. From experience they expect that this rate of decay in productivity, δ, will be about 5% of the plant capacity per year. This parameter δ is very important, because a bad estimate could lead to serious under- or over-expansion. They therefore require a model which will predict the current plant capacity x, in terms of the time t (which we will measure in years) and the decay factor δ.

The plant capacity x will increase by units of whole machines, but because the numbers are large for given δ we approximate the real situation by regarding $x = x(t)$ as a continuous function of the continuous variable t. The rate of plant expansion may then be formulated as dx/dt which will decay at a rate $-\delta x$. On the other hand, new machines are being added. The added capacity after t years will be

$$100 + 200 + 300 + \ldots + 100t = 100(1 + 2 + \ldots + t).$$

The formula (2.5) given in Chapter 2 gives the sum of this arithmetic progression:

$$= \frac{100t(t+1)}{2}$$

$$= 50t^2 + 50t.$$

From the preceding chapter we know that the rate at which capacity is added will be the derivative of this, namely $100t + 50$.

Since the net rate of plant expansion is the rate of adding capacity less the rate of decay we obtain

$$\boxed{\frac{dx}{dt} = 100t + 50 - \delta x} \qquad (5.1)$$

A problem of this type, where we have to determine an unknown function x from an equation involving x, dx/dt and a given function, is a **first order differential equation**. To solve our problem we must first consider how to find the solution of such equations.

5.2 THEORY OF FIRST ORDER ORDINARY DIFFERENTIAL EQUATION

A first order ordinary differential equation is a relation between the derivative of an unknown function $x(t)$, where t is a real variable, the function x itself, the independent variable t, and given functions of t. Denoting dx/dt by $\dot{x}$,[†] we assume that in some domain D we can express x as a function of t and x, namely

$$\boxed{\dot{x} = f(t,x)} \qquad (5.2)$$

where f is a given function on the subset D (assumed open and connected) of R^2 taking values in R. A function $x = \phi(t)$ which when substituted in (5.2) reduces it to an identity for each t in some interval (a,b) is called a **solution** of (5.2) **over the interval** (a,b).

If f is continuous on D, each solution $x = \phi(t)$ will define a smooth curve in D called an **integral curve** of the equation. Through each point (t,x) of D there will pass an integral curve whose gradient at that point is given by $f(t,x)$. Which curve we choose as our solution will depend on the initial data given. This is illustrated in Fig. 5.1.

[†] By convention differentiation with respect to t is denoted by a dot, and not by a prime.

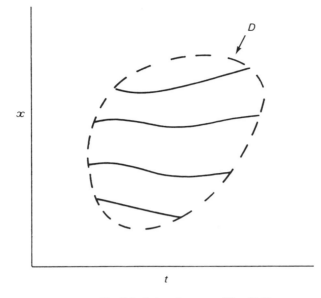

Fig. 5.1   Integral curves of Eq. (5.2).

Example 1

Consider the special case where the unknown function $x(t)$ does not appear in the equation; that is,

$$\dot{x} = f(t) \tag{5.3}$$

where f is continuous on (a,b). The domain D may be taken as the infinite strip $\{(t,x): a < t < b, \ -\infty < x < \infty\}$. Consider the family of curves K_α given by

$$\phi(t,\alpha) = \alpha + F(t)$$

where α is any real number and

$$F(t) = \int_{t_0}^{t} f(s) \, ds, \ a < t < b, \ \text{for some given } t_0 \text{ in } (a,b).$$

Each member ϕ of K_α satisfies $\dot{\phi} = f(t)$ and $\phi(t_0,\alpha) = \alpha$. Thus the integral curves of Eq. (5.3) are simply translations of the curve $x = F(t)$ as shown in Fig. 5.2. If we are given the value α_0 that the solution must take at $t = t_0$ we obtain the unique solution

$$\phi(t,\alpha_0) = \alpha_0 + F(t).$$

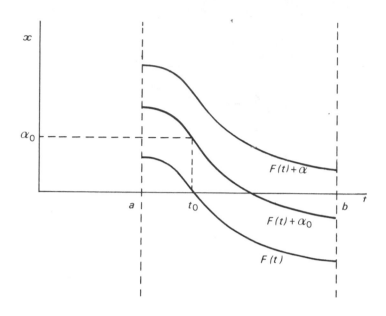

Fig. 5.2   Integral curves for Example 1.

Example 2

To obtain a specific example, take $f(t) = t$ in Example 1. Since this is a continuous function for $-\infty < t < \infty$, we need not specify the domain D: it is the whole plane R^2. The most general solution of

$$\dot{x} = t \tag{5.4}$$

is $x = \phi(t,\alpha) = \alpha + \tfrac{1}{2}t^2 .$

Thus the integral curves of Eq. (5.4) are the family of parabolae shown in Fig. 5.3. If we require the solution which is zero when $t = 0$, then we must choose the integral curve passing through the point (0,0), namely $\phi(t) = \tfrac{1}{2}t^2$.

These are special cases of the more general result now given.

Theorem

Given the equation (5.2), $\dot{x} = f(t,x)$, where f is defined on some domain D in R^2, if f and $\partial f / \partial x$ are continuous in D, then at each point (t_0, x_0) of D there is a unique solution $x = \phi(t)$ of (5.2) satisfying the **initial condition** $\phi(t_0) = x_0$, and defined in some open set containing (t_0, x_0). (For a proof of this theorem, see Sanchez (1968) page 8.)

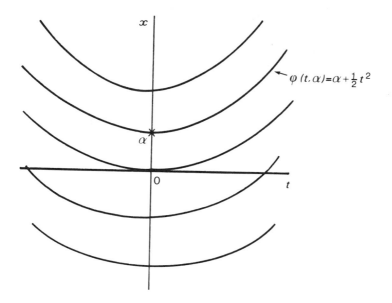

Fig. 5.3   Integral curves for Example 2.

Having satisfied ourselves as to the existence and uniqueness of a solution with the given initial condition, we turn to the important practical problem of constructing this solution explicitly. There are still many equations of first order for which this cannot be done, but if the equation is linear (that is, only $x(t)$ and no power or other function of x appears in (5.1)) a number of techniques may be applied, and we now review these.

The **homogeneous equation** is given by

$$\boxed{\dot{x} = p(t)x} \tag{5.5}$$

where p is a continuous function of t on (a,b). We allow a to be $-\infty$ or b to be $+\infty$. It is easily verified by differentiation that the solution of (5.5) satisfying the initial condition $x(t_0) = x_0$ is given by

$$x(t) = x_0 \exp \int_{t_0}^{t} p(s)\,ds \ . \tag{5.6}$$

If we are given no initial condition, we have the general solution x, where x_0 can take on any value. If $p(t)$ is equal to a constant p on (a,b) we have the very simple case of constant coefficients and the solution is

$$x(t) = x_0\, e^{p(t-t_0)}. \tag{5.7}$$

The **non-homogeneous equation** is given by

$$\dot{x} = p(t)x + q(t) \qquad (5.8)$$

where p and q are continuous functions of t on (a, b). Let $x(t)$ be the general solution of the associated homogeneous equations (5.5) (the **complementary function**) and let $y(t)$ be any solution of (5.8) (the **particular integral**) which is usually obtained by trial or guessing. We can show that the general solution of (5.8) is given by $x(t) + y(t)$; for $x(t)$ is a solution of (5.4) and we have

$$\frac{dx}{dt} = p(t)x(t).$$

Similarly, since $y(t)$ is a solution of (5.8),

$$\frac{dy}{dt} = p(t)y(t) + q(t).$$

Adding, and using the linearity of the derivative, we have

$$\frac{d}{dt}(x + y) = p(t)(x(t) + y(t)) + q(t)$$

and the result follows.

Although it is almost always easier to find the particular integral by inspection, there is a result which gives an explicit construction for the solution of (5.8). If $x = \phi(t)$ is the solution of (5.5) satisfying $\phi(0) = 1$, then the solution of (5.8) satisfying $x(0) = x_0$ is given by

$$x(t) = \phi(t)x_0 + \int_0^t \phi(t-s)q(s)\,ds.$$

This is proved in Sanchez, page 27.

5.3 THE SOLUTION OF THE CUSPIC CONTAINERS PROBLEM

We have the inhomogeneous problem

$$\frac{dx}{dt} + \delta x = 100t + 50$$

with initial condition $x(0) = 2500$.

The functions $f(t,x) = 100t + 50 - \delta x$ and $\partial f / \partial x$ are continuous over the whole plane R^2, and so we are assured of the existence and uniqueness of a solution to this problem. In subsequent problems we shall not mention the domain D, unless a solution fails to exist over R^2.

The homogeneous equation $dx/dt + \delta x = 0$ has solution $x = Ke^{-\delta t}$, where K is an arbitrary constant; this is the complementary function. We now seek a particular solution of the inhomogeneous problem. Since the right-hand side is a linear function of t, we try $\alpha t + \beta$ as a solution, where α and β are real constants. Substituting this in the equation gives

$$\alpha + \delta(\alpha t + \beta) = 100t + 50.$$

Since this holds for all $t \geqslant 0$, the coefficient of t and the constant coefficient must be the same on each side of the equation. This gives

$$\alpha\delta = 100$$

$$\alpha + \beta\delta = 50$$

which we can solve for α,β in terms of δ to obtain the particular integral

$$\frac{100}{\delta}t + \frac{50\delta - 100}{\delta^2}.$$

The general solution is thus given by

$$x(t) = Ke^{-\delta t} + \frac{100}{\delta}t + \frac{50\delta - 100}{\delta^2}.$$

The arbitrary constant K is determined by the initial condition which gives

$$2500 = x(0) = K + \frac{50\delta - 100}{\delta^2}.$$

Therefore, introducing the subscript δ to emphasize that the solution depends on the given rate of decay, we have

$$x_\delta(t) = \{2500 + \frac{(100 - 50\delta)}{\delta^2}\}e^{-\delta t} + \frac{100}{\delta}t + \frac{50\delta - 100}{\delta^2}. \qquad (5.9)$$

Taking the management's expected rate of decay $\delta = 0.05$ we obtain

$$x_{.05}(t) = 41500e^{-0.05t} + 2000t - 39000.$$

$$x_{.05}(8) = 4817$$

Thus

$$x_{.05}(9) = 5460.$$

The solution is illustrated in Fig. 5.4. The target will be met about the middle of year 8 if the rate of decay is 5%. The solutions for $\delta = 0.03$ and 0.07 are also illustrated.

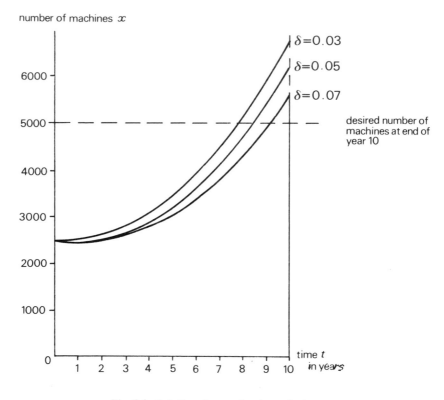

Fig. 5.4   Solutions for varying decay factors.

5.4 CASE STUDIES

5.4.1 The National Debt and Gross National Product

The Gross National Product (GNP) is defined as the sum of final products such as consumption goods and gross investment (which is the increase in inventories plus gross production of buildings and equipment). We assume that the GNP is increasing continuously at a rate of 2% per annum.

For various reasons the Government has a deficit in its spending which becomes part of the National Debt. Government policy is to keep deficit spending a constant proportion K of the increasing GNP. It seems possible that the national debt may outstrip the increasing GNP.

Writing the National Debt as D and GNP as Y, we have a pair of first order differential equations

$$\frac{dY}{dt} = 0.02Y \tag{5.10}$$

$$\frac{dD}{dt} = KY . \tag{5.11}$$

Eq. (5.10) is the special case of Sec. 5.2 with $p = 0.02$: the general solution is $ce^{0.02t}$ where c is an arbitrary constant. If the GNP in year 0 is Y_0 we have

$$Y(t) = Y_0 e^{0.02t}.$$

Substituting in (5.11) gives

$$\frac{dD}{dt} = KY_0 e^{0.02t}$$

which may be integrated directly to give

$$D = \frac{KY_0}{(0.02)} e^{0.02t} + d,$$

where d is an arbitrary constant.

If the initial national debt is D_0 we find

$$d = D_0 - \frac{KY_0}{(0.02)}$$

and

$$D(t) = D_0 + \frac{KY_0}{(0.02)} (e^{0.02t} - 1).$$

We may now construct the ratio D/Y.

$$\frac{D(t)}{Y(t)} = \frac{K}{0.02} + \left[\frac{D_0}{Y_0} - \frac{K}{0.02} \right] e^{-0.02t} \rightarrow \frac{K}{(0.02)} \quad \text{as} \quad t \rightarrow \infty.$$

Thus in the long term the ratio of national debt to GNP tends to a constant level. The rate at which it tends to this level depends on the rate of growth of GNP: the larger the rate of growth, the more quickly the ratio reaches this constant level (recall the properties of the exponential function). In many industrialized nations it is common practice for the National Debt to be several times larger than the GNP. For instance the British National Debt has been between 2 and 3 times the GNP in 1946, 1923, and as early as 1818 (see Samuelson (1973) page 368).

5.4.2 Population Growth

Charles Darwin delayed writing *The Origin of Species* for more than 20 years after he had convinced himself of the truth of evolution, because he could not explain what caused evolution. His explanation was eventually obtained after reading *An Essay on the Principle of Population*, which had been written by Thomas Malthus in 1798. At the time when Malthus was writing, the industrial revolution and related scientific discoveries had caused a boom in the European population. He was writing as a prophet of doom, and in his essay he coined the phrase 'the struggle for existence', which led to Darwin's natural selection theory for evolution.

Malthus in fact formulated the first population model. In mathematical terms, consider a small time interval, δt, in which births and deaths are assumed to be proportional to the total population size and to the time interval. Thus if $N = N(t)$ is the population size, in a time interval δt there are

$$\text{births} = \alpha N \delta t, \quad \text{deaths} = \beta N \delta t$$

where α and β are assumed to be constants. Thus the increase in population size in time δt is given by

$$\delta N = \alpha N \delta t - \beta N \delta t = (\alpha - \beta) N \delta t.$$

Writing $\gamma = \alpha - \beta$, dividing by δt and taking the limit as $\delta t \to 0$ gives

$$\boxed{\frac{dN}{dt} = \gamma N \ .} \tag{5.12}$$

We have already met this differential equation in Sec. 5.2, and it has solution

$$N = N_0 \ e^{\gamma t}$$

where N_0 is the population size at $t = 0$. Depending on the sign of γ there is exponential growth, steady state, or exponential decay, as illustrated in Fig. 5.5. Malthus also considered food and land resources and deduced that these could grow only linearly, which would inevitably lead to some form of crisis. He was in fact incorrect at that time, probably because of the discovery and development of land resources in America and to a lesser extent Australia.

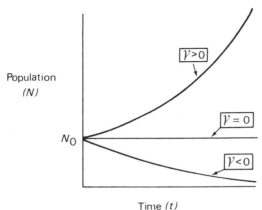

Fig. 5.5   Malthusian population model: exponential growth or decay.

This 'crowding' consideration can, however, be introduced into the mathematical model itself. The simplest resulting model is achieved by adding a term to the right-hand side of (5.12) which will depress the rate of growth when N becomes increasingly large; that is,

$$\frac{dN}{dt} = \gamma N - \eta N^2 \tag{5.13}$$

where η is a positive constant.

This first order differential equation is not linear, since it contains an 'N^2' term, but it can readily be solved by writing

$$\int \frac{dN}{(N - \eta N^2/\gamma)} = \int \gamma \, dt$$

that is,

$$\int \left[\frac{1}{N} + \frac{(\eta/\gamma)}{(1 - \eta N/\gamma)} \right] dN = \gamma t + K.$$

Integrating the left-hand side, we have

$$\log N - \log(1 - \eta N/\gamma) = \gamma t + \log C$$

writing the arbitrary constant K as $\log C$. Thus

$$\log\{\frac{N}{C(1 - \eta N/\gamma)}\} = \gamma t$$

giving

$$\frac{N}{C(1 - \eta N/\gamma)} = e^{\gamma t},$$

and solving for N,

$$N = Ce^{\gamma t}/[1 + C\eta e^{\gamma t}/\gamma].$$

If the initial population size is N_0, then the constant C is given by

$$C = \frac{N_0}{(1 - \eta N_0/\gamma)}$$

and so

$$\boxed{N = \kappa N_0\, e^{\gamma t}/(\kappa + N_0\{e^{\gamma t} - 1\})} \tag{5.14}$$

where $\kappa = \gamma/\eta$. The behaviour of the solution now depends on the sign of $N_0 - \kappa$, where N_0 is the initial population size. For $N_0 < \kappa$ there appears to be at first exponential growth, but as the crowding term becomes more dominant, the rate of increase diminishes, and tends to zero as $t \to \infty$, and with $N \to \kappa$. This illustrates the familiar sigmoid population growth, which is observed in many types of population. A typical curve is illustrated in Fig. 5.6.

Do either of the above models adequately describe the world human population? Fig. 5.7 sketches the human population size, and it is certainly apparent that we have growth of the same sort! Whether the maximum sustainable population has been reached is a topical question. Clearly there are crowding effects that will at some stage inhibit the population growth on a world wide scale. Perhaps the most important factors will occur from limitations to energy or from pollution effects.

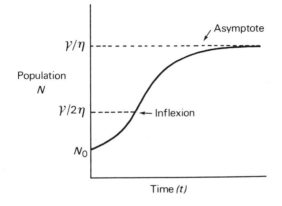

Fig. 5.6   Population model with crowding term: sigmoid population growth.

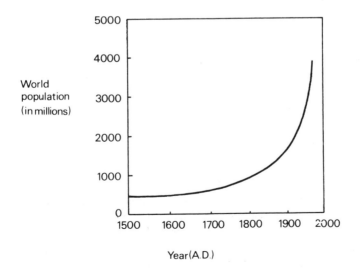

Fig. 5.7   Growth of world human population.

The second model, (5.13), has been used to predict the population of the United States. In 1845, Verhulst proposed equation (5.13) with

$$\gamma = 0.03134$$

$$\eta = 1.5887 \times 10^{-10}$$

and $N(1790) = 3.9 \times 10^6$.

In Table 1, Verhulst's predictions are compared with the actual population numbers in millions of people. There is a remarkable correlation between the predicted and observed data.

Table 1: Population of USA

Year	Observed N	Predicted N
1790	3.9	3.9
1800	5.3	5.2
1810	7.2	7.2
1820	9.6	9.8
1830	12.9	13.1
1840	17.1	17.5
1850	23.2	23.2
1860	31.4	30.4
1870	38.6	39.4
1880	50.2	50.2
1890	62.9	62.8
1900	76.0	76.9
1910	92.0	92.0
1920	106.5	109.4
1930	123.2	123.9

5.4.3 Drug Distribution in the Body

The study of 'dose–response' relationships plays an important role in pharmacology. We consider here the problem of determining the dosage required so that the body concentration of the drug tends towards a certain value.

Introducing mathematical terminology, let $y = y(t)$ be the quantity of the drug present in the patient's body at time t. Initially, at time $t = 0$ say, the patient is given a dose, say y_0, of the drug. As a first approximation we assume that the drug disappears from the body according to the law

$$\frac{dy}{dt} = -ky \quad , \tag{5.15}$$

the value of the constant k depending on the particular drug used (some forms of penicillin, for example Benzylpenicillin, roughly obey (5.15)). Solving (5.15) gives

$$y = y_0 e^{-kt}. \tag{5.16}$$

After a set interval, T say, an equal amount of the drug, y_0, is added so that the concentration at time T is

$$y(T) = y_0 + y_0 e^{-kT}.$$

Similarly, as $t \to 2T$, the concentration will approach $(y_0 + y_0 e^{-kT})e^{-kT}$, and after adding another dose y_0, the concentration at time $2T$ is

$$y(2T) = y_0 + (y_0 + y_0 e^{-kT})e^{-kT} = y_0(1 + e^{-kT} + e^{-2kT}).$$

In the same way, after another dose at time $3T$, the concentration is given by

$$y(3T) = y_0(1 + e^{-kT} + e^{-2kT} + e^{-3kT}),$$

and continuing in this way, at time nT (n being a positive integer)

$$y(nT) = y_0(1 + e^{-kT} + e^{-2kT} + e^{-3kT} + \ldots + e^{-nkT}).$$

This is a geometric progression and can be summed to give

$$y(nT) = y_0 \frac{(1 - e^{-(n+1)kT})}{(1 - e^{-kT})}.$$

For large n, it is clear that

$$y \to \frac{y_0}{(1 - e^{-kT})}$$

so that if the dosage level is required to approach the level y_c, we must have

$$y_c = \frac{y_0}{(1 - e^{-kT})}.$$

For a given time interval T, the required dosage is given by

$$\boxed{y_0 = (1 - e^{-kT})y_c.} \tag{5.17}$$

The accumulation of the drug is illustrated in Fig. 5.8.

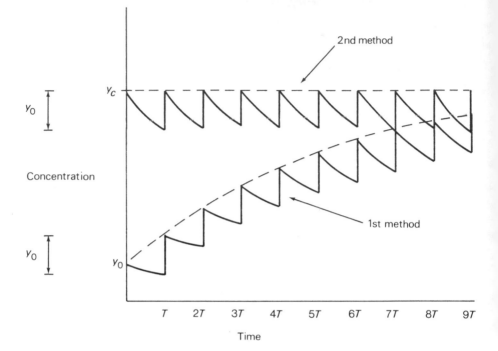

Fig. 5.8 Comparison of accumulation methods.

Clearly one of the disadvantages of this accumulation is its slowness in approaching the limiting value y_c. A second method is to start with an initial booster dose y_c, so that at the end of the first interval, T, the concentration is given by $y_c e^{-kT}$. We now add a dose, say y_1, which returns the level to y_c,

that is $y_1 + y_c e^{-kT} = y_c,$

giving $y_1 = y_c(1 - e^{-kT}) = y_0.$

Thus we continue giving doses y_0 at time intervals T after the initial dose y_c. The accumulation is illustrated in Fig. 5.8.

This second method has the advantage of bringing the body concentration straight to the required level, but this can also be a disadvantage, as a large *initial* dose can have side effects on the body. One common method is to give the patient an initial dose twice as large as the regular dose, y_0, and then continue with doses y_0.

5.4.4 Dating Archaeological Samples

One accurate method of dating archaeological samples is the method of Carbon 14 dating, discovered by W. Libby about 1949. The atmosphere is continuously bombarded by cosmic rays, producing neutrons which combine with nitrogen to produce C^{14}, sometimes called radiocarbon. C^{14} decays radioactively. In living tissues, the rate of absorption of C^{14} balances the rate of disintegration of C^{14}. When an organism dies it ceases to absorb C^{14} though disintegration continues. Assuming that cosmic ray bombardment has remained constant, the original rate of disintegration of C^{14} in a sample is the same as the rate measured today.

Let $N(t)$ be the amount of C^{14} present in a sample such as charcoal at time t, and N_0 the amount at time $t = 0$ when the sample was found. Radioactive decay obeys the equation

$$\boxed{\frac{dN}{dt} = -\lambda N} \tag{5.18}$$

where the constant λ is called the **decay constant** of the substance. Solving (5.18) we have

$$N(t) = N_0 e^{-\lambda t}. \tag{5.19}$$

The present rate, $R(t)$, of disintegration of C^{14} in the sample is given by

$$R(t) = -\frac{dN}{dt} = \lambda N_0 e^{-\lambda t}$$

and the original rate of disintegration is $R(0) = \lambda N_0$. Thus

$$\frac{R(t)}{R(0)} = e^{-\lambda t},$$

giving

$$\boxed{t = \frac{1}{\lambda} \log \frac{R(0)}{R(t)}}. \tag{5.20}$$

In the sample we can measure $R(t)$, and noting that $R(0)$ must equal the rate of disintegration of the C^{14} in a comparable amount of living wood, we can use (5.20) to determine t.

The constant λ is usually given in terms of the **half-life** of the substance, which is defined as the time required for half a given quantity of radioactive atoms to decay. From (5.19), this time, τ, is determined from

$$\frac{N_0}{2} = N_0 e^{-\lambda\tau}$$

that is, $\tau = \dfrac{1}{\lambda} \log 2 = \dfrac{0.6931}{\lambda}.$

For carbon 14, the half-life is 5568 years.

As an example, consider the Lascaux Cave in France, where charcoal gave an average count in 1950 of 0.97 disintegrations per minute per gram, whereas living wood gave 6.68 disintegrations. From (5.20), the probable age of the paintings in the Lascaux Cave is given by

$$t = \frac{5568}{0.6931} \log \left(\frac{6.68}{0.97}\right) \simeq 10\,540 \text{ years.}$$

5.4.5 Response of Sales to Advertising

Here we introduce a model for sales response to advertising, first developed by Vidale and Wolfe (1957). Let $S(t)$ be the sales rate at time t. If at time τ, say, all advertising ceases, we would clearly expect the sales rate to decrease, and we suppose that the decline is proportional to the level of sales. Thus for $t > \tau$,

$$\frac{dS}{dt} = -\lambda S, \tag{5.21}$$

λ being the decay constant.

A second important parameter is the **saturation constant**, M, which represents the upper limit of sales rate which the company may obtain, no matter how much is spent on advertising. There is clearly some upper limit, for there are only a limited number of prospective purchasers and there are usually competitive firms. Thus if $R = R(t)$ is the change in sales rate per unit spent on advertising, then

$$R = 0 \text{ when } S = M.$$

One other parameter needed is the zero sales response constant, r, defined by

$$S = 0 \text{ when } R = r.$$

Clearly a unit increase in advertising would have greater effect at a low sales level rather than near $S = M$. In fact, we use a linear model to describe the relationship between sales and the change in sales rate due to advertising, that is,

$$\frac{R}{r} + \frac{S}{M} = 1. \tag{5.22}$$

Now combining the effect of advertising and the decay effect, we have, for $0 < t < \tau$,

$$\frac{dS}{dt} = AR - \lambda S$$

where $A = A(t)$ is the advertising rate. Thus, from (5.22),

$$\boxed{\frac{dS}{dt} = Ar\frac{(M-S)}{M} - \lambda S \ .} \tag{5.23}$$

This simple model does in fact provide a good model for much experimental data.

Before solving (5.23), it is interesting to note that the model predicts *constant* sales if $dS/dt = 0$, that is, if

$$A = \lambda SM/r(M-S) = (\frac{\lambda M}{r})/(\frac{M}{S} - 1).$$

Thus the closer sales, S, are to the saturation level, M, the more advertising is required to maintain a constant sales level.

Returning to the more general problem, suppose we choose an advertising strategy

$$A(t) = \begin{cases} A, \text{ constant } 0 < t < \tau \\ 0 \qquad\qquad t > \tau \end{cases} \tag{5.24}$$

If a is the total advertising expenditure, then $A = a/\tau$. Thus on $0 < t < \tau$, we must solve

$$\frac{dS}{dt} + bS = C \tag{5.25}$$

where $b = \frac{ar}{\tau M} + \lambda$ and $C = \frac{ar}{\tau}$. This is a first order linear differential equation of the type discussed in Sect. 5.2. The complementary function, which is the solution of

$$\frac{dS}{dt} + bS = 0,$$

is given by $S = \kappa e^{-bt}$, κ being a constant. A particular integral is readily seen to be $S = C/b$, so that the general solution is

$$S = \kappa e^{-bt} + \frac{C}{b}.$$

If, at $t = 0$, $S = S_0$, then $S_0 = \kappa + C/b$, and

$$S(t) = \frac{C}{b}(1 - e^{-bt}) + S_0 e^{-bt}. \tag{5.26}$$

For $t > \tau$, (5.21) holds, and

$$\int \frac{1}{S} dS = \int (-\lambda) \, dt$$

that is, $\log S = -\lambda t + \log k,$

giving $S = k e^{-\lambda t}.$ \hfill (5.27)

At $t = \tau$, $S = S(\tau)$, as given by (5.26), so that substituting into (5.27) gives

$$S(\tau) = k e^{-\lambda \tau}$$

that is, $k = e^{\lambda \tau} S(\tau).$

Hence the predicted sales rate is

$$S(t) = \begin{cases} \dfrac{C}{b}(1 - e^{-bt}) + S_0 e^{-bt} & 0 < t < \tau \\ S(\tau) e^{\lambda(\tau - t)} & t > \tau \end{cases} \tag{5.28}$$

This is indicated in Fig. 5.9.

As expected, the best returns on advertising revenue are to be found at the beginning of the campaign. In the illustration above, the maximum sales rate occurs at $t = \tau$. For fixed total advertising revenue a, the value of $S(\tau)$ depends on τ and so depends on whether the advertising campaign is short or protracted. What sort of campaign to mount will of course depend on the objectives to be met. In some cases, it may be more advantageous to have a slow beginning with a steady build-up in sales, whilst for some products the big initial push may be appropriate.

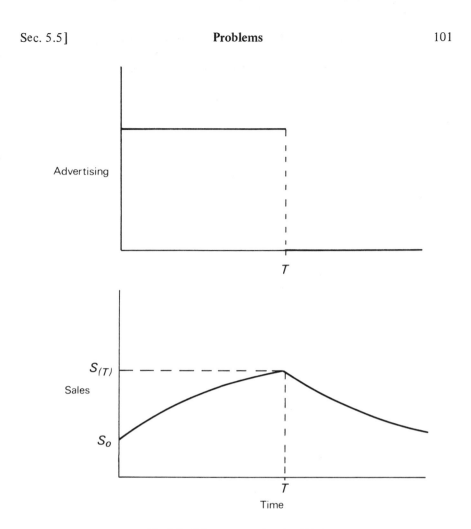

Fig. 5.9 Sales response to advertising.

5.5 PROBLEMS

1. Find the general solution of the following differential equations:

    (i) $\dfrac{dx}{dt} = -x/t$

    (ii) $\dfrac{dx}{dt} = x \tan t$

    (iii) $at\, \dfrac{dx}{dt} = bx \ (a \neq 0).$

In (i) find the solutions which satisfy (a) $x(1) = 1$, (b) $x(1) = 2$. Sketch the integral curves.

2. Find the general solution of the following linear first order differential equations:

(i) $$\frac{dx}{dt} - x = e^{2t}$$

(ii) $$t\frac{dx}{dt} + x = \sin t$$

(iii) $$t\frac{dx}{dt} + x = 2t.$$

In (iii) find the solution which satisfies $x(1) = 2$.

3. Show that multiplying the differential equation

$$\frac{dx}{dt} + p(t)x = q(t)$$

by $e^{\int p(t)dt}$, reduces it to

$$\frac{d}{dt}\{xe^{\int p(t)dt}\} = q(t) e^{\int p(t)dt}.$$

Hence solve the equation and show that

$$x(t) = e^{-\int p(t)dt}\{\int q(t)e^{\int p(t)dt} dt + c\}$$

where c is a constant. Identify the complementary function and particular integral. [The term $e^{\int p(t)dt}$ is called an **integrating factor**.]

4. Use the method of solution described in Question 3 to solve

$$\frac{dx}{dt} + \frac{2x}{t} = 4t.$$

(Show that the integrating factor is t^2.)

5. Separable equations are defined to be of the form.

$$\frac{dx}{dt} = \frac{f(t)}{g(x)}$$

where f is a function of t alone, g is a function of x alone. Show that the solution of this equation is of the form

$$\int g(x) \, dx = \int f(t) \, dt + c$$

where c is a constant.

6. Use the method described in Question 5 to solve the following differential equations:

(i) $$\frac{dx}{dt} = -\frac{4t}{9x}$$

(ii) $$\frac{dx}{dt} = -2xt$$

(iii) $$\frac{dx}{dt} = 1 + t + x^2 + tx^2$$

(iv) $$x^2 \frac{dx}{dt} = \cos^2 t.$$

In (iv) find the complete solution when $x(0) = 0$.

7. A generalization of the Verhulst population model described in Sec. 5.4.2 is to take a crowding term of the form $(-\eta N^{\alpha})$ where α is a positive constant (>1). Using this formulation, solve the model for N.

Using the U.S.A. population data for 1790 to 1820, find values for the parameters N_0, γ, η, and α. Use these values to predict the population for 1830 to 1930.

What conclusions can you make regarding this model?

8. An alternative derivation of Verhulst's population model (Eq. (5.13)) is to assume that at any particular time there is a limiting value, say N_{∞}, to the population that can be sustained by the governing technology. The rate of change of population is assumed to be proportional to
(i) the present population level $N(t)$; and
(ii) the degree of unsaturation of the population

$$\frac{(N_{\infty} - N(t))}{N_{\infty}} \quad \text{at time } t.$$

Show that these assumptions lead to an equation of the form (5.13). What is the appropriate value for N_{∞} in the problem in Sec. 5.4.2?

9. The value of N_{∞} determined in Question 8 is appropriate only up to 1930. The U.S.A. population data from 1950 onwards are given below. Use the

Verhulst model with the data for 1950, 1960, 1970 to predict the level of the U.S.A. population up to 2000. What is the new value of N_∞?

Date	Population ($\times 10^6$)
1950	150.7
1960	179.3
1970	203.2

10. The Irish population data from 1780 to 1920 are given below. Illustrate the data on a graph. Potato famines occurred in the 1840s. Using the Verhulst model with different values of N_∞, one for up to 1840, one for after 1850, to explain the changes in population.

Date	Population ($\times 10^6$)
1780	4.0
1790	4.6
1800	5.2
1810	5.9
1820	6.7
1830	7.6
1840	8.2
1850	6.9
1860	5.8
1870	5.4
1880	5.2
1890	4.7
1900	4.5
1910	4.4
1920	4.4

11. A patient is given a dosage y_0 of a drug at regular intervals of time, T. The body concentration of the drug approximately obeys the law.

$$\frac{dy}{dt} = -ke^y \quad (k \text{ is a positive constant}).$$

Show that the concentration, y_1, just before the second dosage is given by

$$y_1 = -\log(kT + e^{-y_0})$$

and the concentration, y_2, just before the third dosage, is given by

$$y_2 = -\log\{kT(1 + e^{-y_0}) + e^{-2y_0}\}.$$

Evaluate y_3 and y_4 in the same way, and hence deduce that

$$y_n = -\log\{kT(1 + e^{-y_0} + \ldots + e^{-(n-1)y_0}) + e^{-ny_0}\}.$$

If the concentration is required to tend to the value y_c as the number of doses becomes large, show that the required time interval, T, is given by

$$T = \frac{e^{-y_c}}{k}(1 - e^{-y_c}).$$

12. The famous round table in the Great Hall of Winchester Castle has recently been under study in order to determine its probable date of manufacture. For the carbon dating technique the appropriate value for the number of disintegrations per minute per gram is 6.08, whereas living wood gave 6.68 disintegrations. Show that the table was not in fact King Arthur's celebrated round table.

13. Using the Vidale and Wolfe model described in Sec. 5.4.5, determine the predicted sales rate for an advertising strategy of the form (with $\lambda = 0$)

$$A(t) = \begin{cases} \dfrac{2a}{\tau}(1 - t/\tau) & 0 < t < \tau \\ 0 & t > \tau. \end{cases}$$

Compare the *total* sales in the period $[0,\tau]$ using this advertising strategy rather than the one described in Sec. 5.4.5.

What conclusions can you make concerning an optimal advertising policy given that the total advertising expenditure for the campaign is a?

14. The von Bertalanffy fish growth model is described by the differential equation

$$\frac{dw}{dt} = \alpha w^{3/2} - \beta w$$

where $w = w(t)$ is the weight of the fish, α and β are positive constants. Determine the predicted growth of a fish and illustrate your predictions.

15. Seasonal plant growth can be modelled by

$$\frac{dx}{dt} = a x \sin bt \,.$$

Determine the predicted behaviour of x, the size of the plant, if at $t = 0$, $x = x_0$.

16. The quantity of a drug being infused into the bloodstream, Q, is given approximately by

$$\frac{dQ}{dt} = a - bQ \,.$$

Here the term 'a' represents the rate of infusion, and 'bQ' the removal rate due to natural body reaction. Find the level of the drug in the body at time t. What does this level tend to as $t \to \infty$.

17. In a chemical reaction, the concentration, x, of the new substance formed is modelled by

$$\frac{dx}{dt} = k (m - x) (n - x) \qquad\qquad (m > n) \,.$$

If $x(0) = 0$, find $x(t)$ for all $t > 0$. What happens to the concentration as $t \to \infty$?

18. The spread of an epidemic can be modelled by

$$\frac{dx}{dt} = ax (b - x) \,,$$

where x is the number of infectives, b the saturation level, and a is a positive constant. Find the solution of this differential equation if $x = x_0$ at $t = 0$. What does x tend to as $t \to \infty$?

19. During the early stages in the growth of a cell, the rate of increase of the cell's weight can be modelled by an equation of the form

$$\frac{dw}{dt} = cw^\alpha \qquad\qquad (0 < \alpha < 1) \,.$$

Find the weight predicted by this model if the cell starts with approximately zero weight. Show that w is proportional to $t^{1/(1-\alpha)}$. What happens to the model if $\alpha \to 1$.

20. The population growth of a species is given by the differential equation

$$\frac{dx}{dt} = rx\,(k - x^2), \ r \text{ and } k \text{ positive constant} .$$

If at $t = 0$, $x = x_0$, find an equation that x satisfies. Hence show that as $t \to \infty$, $x \to k$.

CHAPTER 6

Cycles and Oscillations: Models based on Second Order Differential Equations

In the last chapter we saw that the solution of the first order linear differential equation with constant coefficients either grew or decayed with increasing time. For the second order linear equation with constant coefficients we shall see that a third possibility, that of an oscillating solution, can occur.

6.1 CONTROL OF THE ECONOMY BY GOVERNMENT SPENDING

A simplified model for a national economy is

National Output (GNP) = Consumption + Investment + Government Spending.
$\qquad Y \qquad\qquad\qquad C \qquad\qquad I \qquad\qquad\qquad G$

This says that the incomes generated by the production of goods and services can only go towards purchasing these goods and services, towards investment, or towards government spending. For simplicity we are assuming that there is no foreign trade in this model economy, although this can be accommodated by introducing imports and exports into the basic equation.

It is usually found in real economics that C and I are internal to fluctuations in Y, while G is an external influence that may possibly offer some means of 'controlling' the economy in the sense of lessening the effect of recessions or damping down booms. It was one of the main postulates of J. M. Keynes in 1936 that the greatest single factor affecting expenditure on personal consumption was the level of national income. The economic policies pursued in the post-war period by the Western nations were Keynesian in nature, although in recent years the alternative monetarist approach has been gaining ground in some countries. We therefore assume that

$\qquad C = kY$

where k is a constant between 0 and 1, usually known as the propensity to consume. It follows that the total demand D for goods and services in the economy is given by

$$D = (1 - s)Y + I + G \qquad (6.1)$$

where $s = 1 - k$ is the propensity to save. In practice, output cannot respond instantaneously to changes in demand. It may be necessary to commission new plant or hire more workers, for instance. Let l be the speed of response of output to demand. Then

$$\frac{dY}{dt} = l(D - Y). \qquad (6.2)$$

Substituting for D from (6.1) we obtain

$$\frac{dY}{dt} + lsY = l(I + G). \qquad (6.3)$$

If output is constant, $dY/dt = 0$ and Y takes its equilibrium value $\bar{Y} = \frac{1}{s}(I + G)$, assuming that I and G remain constant with time. We know from the preceding chapter that the solution of (6.3) satisfying the given initial condition $Y(0) = Y_0$ is $Y = \bar{Y} + (Y_0 - \bar{Y})e^{-lst}$. Notice that since both l and s must be positive in the long term, $Y \to \bar{Y}$ as $t \to \infty$. The term $\frac{1}{s} = \frac{1}{1 - k}$ is usually called the **multiplier.**

But in this model we are not taking I to be constant. We assume that I is proportional to the rate of change of output, Taking into account the speed of response of investment to rate of change of output, according to the equation

$$\frac{dI}{dt} = m(a\frac{dY}{dt} - I). \qquad (6.4)$$

The constant a is often called the **accelerator**. We may now rewrite (6.3) as, denoting dY/dt by $\dot{Y}$,

$$I = \frac{1}{l}\dot{Y} + sY - G. \qquad (6.5)$$

Remembering that Y, C, and I are varying with t, but that G is assumed constant, differentiation with respect to t gives

$$\dot{I} = \frac{1}{l}\ddot{Y} + s\dot{Y}. \qquad (6.6)$$

Substituting the expression (6.5) and (6.6) into (6.4), we obtain the second order differential equation

$$\ddot{Y} + (ls + m - mla)\dot{Y} + mlsY = mlG$$

or

$$\boxed{\ddot{Y} + \alpha\dot{Y} + \beta Y = mlG} \tag{6.7}$$

on introducing the new constants $\alpha = ls + m - mla$ and $\beta = mls$. In planning its economic policy, the Government of the day would like to know:

(1) Given the constants m, l, a, s (which can be found from economic data) and the initial values of Y and I, can a solution of Eq. (6.7) be found to give the national output Y at time t?

(2) Does the national output grow, decay, or oscillate either finitely or infinitely?

(3) How does the level of government spending G affect Y? Is it possible to alter the behaviour of the economy by changing G?

6.2 THE SECOND ORDER LINEAR DIFFERENTIAL EQUATION WITH CONSTANT COEFFICIENTS

Following the notation of Sec. 5.2, a **second order differential equation** is a relation between the first and second derivatives of an unknown function x of a real variable t, the function $x(t)$ itself, and certain given functions of t, namely

$$\boxed{\ddot{x} = f(t, x, \dot{x}).} \tag{6.8}$$

A function $\phi(t)$ which, when substituted for x in (6.8), reduces it to an identity for each t in some interval (a,b), is called a **solution** of (6.8) **over the interval** (a,b).

The **linear homogeneous second order differential equation** is a special form of this relation, namely

$$\boxed{\ddot{x} + \alpha(t)\dot{x} + \beta(t)x = 0} \tag{6.9}$$

where α and β are continuous on (a,b). Under given **initial conditions**, for example $x(a)$, $\dot{x}(a)$ prescribed, or **boundary conditions**, for example $x(a)$, $x(b)$ prescribed, it is a standard result (Sanchez (1968) p. 29) of differential equation theory that (6.9) has a unique solution satisfying such conditions.

The idea of linear independent functions must be introduced. A set of functions $\phi_1(t) \ldots \phi_n(t)$ is **linearly independent** on (a,b) if there exist no constants $c_1 \ldots c_n$, not all zero such that

$$c_1\phi_1(t) + \ldots + c_n\phi_n(t)$$

is identically zero on (a,b). It can be proved that Eq. (6.9), without end conditions, has exactly two linearly independent solutions on (a,b), say $\phi_1(t)$ and $\phi_2(t)$, and any other solution $x(t)$ may be written as a linear combination of these. That is,

$$x(t) = A\phi_1(t) + B\phi_2(t)$$

where A and B are constants. If we are given end conditions on $x(t)$, these will enable us to determine A and B explicitly. To test whether two solutions $\phi_1(t)$, $\phi_2(t)$ are linearly independent we consider the **Wronskian** of ψ_1 and ϕ_2 given by

$$W(\phi_1,\phi_2)(t) = \dot{\phi}_1(t)\phi_2(t) - \phi_1(t)\dot{\phi}_2(t).$$

If the Wronskian does not vanish for any t in (a,b), then $\phi_1(t)$ and $\phi_2(t)$ are linearly independent.

For example, we can easily check by differentiating twice that $\phi_1(t) = \cos t$ and $\phi_2(t) = \sin t$ are solutions of

$$\ddot{x} + x = 0.$$

In this case

$$W(\phi_1,\phi_2)(t) = (-\sin t)\sin t - \cos t \cos t$$
$$= -(\sin^2 t + \cos^2 t) = -1 \text{ for all } t.$$

Hence the Wronskian does not vanish for any t, and the solutions $\phi_1(t) = \cos t$ and $\phi_2(t) = \sin t$ are linearly independent.

Eq. (6.9) with non-zero right-hand side; that is,

$$\boxed{\ddot{x} + \alpha(t)\dot{x} + \beta(t)x = f(t),} \qquad (6.10)$$

where f is a given function of t on (a,b), is called the **non-homogeneous linear equation**. Given two linearly independent solutions $\phi_1(t)$ and $\phi_2(t)$ of (6.9), it is possible to construct an explicit solution of (6.10) by the method of **variation of parameters** (Sanchez (1968) p. 34). Since finding explicit solutions of (6.9) can be extremely difficult, we restrict attention to the case when α and β are not functions of t, but real constants.

We consider the second order linear homogeneous equation with constant coefficients

$$\ddot{x} + \alpha\dot{x} + \beta x = 0 \qquad (6.11)$$

and the corresponding non-homogeneous equation

$$\ddot{x} + \alpha\dot{x} + \beta x = f(t). \qquad (6.12)$$

Since constant functions are continuous over the whole line **R**, there is no need to specify an interval (a,b) in (6.11). Eq. (6.12) will hold over any interval of continuity of f, which may be the whole line.

The solution of (6.11) may always be constructed by the following process. Let D denote the differentiation operator given by $Dx = \dot{x}$. Then

$$D^2x = D(Dx) = D(\dot{x}) = \ddot{x},$$

and we may rewrite (6.11) in the form

$$D^2x + \alpha Dx + \beta x = 0$$

or $$L(D)x = 0$$

where L is the quadratic operator given by

$$L(D) = D^2 + \alpha D + \beta.$$

It follows from the linear properties of differentiation that $L(D)$ is a **linear operator** in the sense that

$$L(D)(Ax + By) = AL(D)x + BL(D)y$$

for any constants A, B and any twice differentiable functions x, y. Given equation (6.11), the quadratic

$$L(p) = p^2 + \alpha p + \beta$$

is called the **characteristic polynomial** of (6.11).

Theorem
The function $x(t) = e^{\lambda t}$ is a solution of (6.11) if and only if λ is a root of the characteristic polynomial $L(p)$.

Proof
$$\begin{aligned}
L(D)x(t) &= L(D)(e^{\lambda t}) \\
&= D^2(e^{\lambda t}) + \alpha D(e^{\lambda t}) + \beta e^{\lambda t} \\
&= \lambda^2 e^{\lambda t} + \alpha\lambda e^{\lambda t} + \beta e^{\lambda t} \\
&= (\lambda^2 + \alpha\lambda + \beta)e^{\lambda t} = L(\lambda)e^{\lambda t}
\end{aligned}$$

and the right-hand side is identically zero if and only if $L(\lambda) = 0$; that is, λ is a root of $L(p)$.

Since $L(p)$ is a quadratic with real coefficients, there are three possibilities:
(1) $L(p)$ has distinct real roots λ_1, λ_2.
(2) $L(p)$ has complex conjugate roots $\lambda = \mu + iv$ and $\bar{\lambda} = \mu - iv$.†
(3) $L(p)$ has equal real roots $\lambda_1 = \lambda_2 = \lambda$.

Corollary 1

If $L(p)$ has distinct real roots λ_1 and λ_2, then the functions $x_1(t) = e^{\lambda_1 t}$ and $x_2(t) = e^{\lambda_2 t}$ are linearly independent solutions of (6.11). Hence the general solution of (6.11) is

$$x(t) = A e^{\lambda_1 t} + B e^{\lambda_2 t}.$$

Proof

$x_1(t)$ and $x_2(t)$ are solutions by the theorem. To show that they are linearly independent consider the Wronskian.

$$W(x_1, x_2)(t) = e^{\lambda_1 t}(\lambda_2 e^{\lambda_2 t}) - \lambda_1 e^{\lambda_1 t} e^{\lambda_2 t}$$

$$= (\lambda_2 - \lambda_1) e^{(\lambda_1 + \lambda_2)t}$$

$$\neq 0 \text{ since } \lambda_1, \lambda_2 \text{ are distinct.}$$

Example 1

Find the solution of $\ddot{x} - 3\dot{x} + 2x = 0$ satisfying $x(0) = 1$, $\dot{x}(0) = 0$.

Solution

We have $L(p) = p^2 - 3p + 2 = (p - 1)(p - 2)$.
Hence $L(p)$ has distinct roots $\lambda_1 = 1$, $\lambda_2 = 2$, and the general solution is $x(t) = A e^t + B e^{2t}$.

This satisfies $x(0) = 1$ if $A + B = 1$

and $\dot{x}(0) = 1$ if $A + 2B = 0$.

Solving these simultaneous equations gives $A = 2$, $B = -1$. Hence the required solution is $x(t) = 2e^t - e^{2t}$.

Corollary 2

If $L(p)$ has complex conjugate roots $\lambda = \mu + iv$, $\bar{\lambda} = \mu - iv$, then the functions $x_1(t) = e^{\mu t} \cos vt$ and $x_2(t) = e^{\mu t} \sin vt$ are linearly independent solutions of (6.11). The general solution is $x(t) = C e^{\mu t} \sin (vt + \omega)$ where C and ω are arbitrary constants called the **amplitude** and **phase**.

† For readers unfamiliar with complex numbers, see Appendix I.

Proof

It follows from the theorem that the functions

$$z_1(t) = e^{(\mu+iv)t} = e^{\mu t}(\cos vt + i \sin vt)$$

and $$z_2(t) = e^{(\mu-iv)t} = e^{\mu t}(\cos vt - i \sin vt)$$

are solutions. Since the equation (6.11) is linear and homogeneous, any linear combinations of z_1 and z_2 will also be solutions, in particular

$$x_1(t) = \tfrac{1}{2}(z_1(t) + z_2(t)) = e^{\mu t} \cos vt$$

and $$x_2(t) = \tfrac{1}{2}(z_1(t) - z_2(t)) = e^{\mu t} \sin vt.$$

A simple calculation shows that

$$W(x_1, x_2)(t) = e^{\mu t}\{v \cos^2 vt + v \sin^2 vt\} = v e^{\mu t} \neq 0 \text{ for } v \neq 0 \text{ and } \mu \text{ real.}$$

Hence $x_1(t)$, $x_2(t)$ are linearly independent solutions.

The general solution is $x(t) = A e^{\mu t} \cos vt + B e^{\mu t} \sin vt$ for arbitrary constants A and B. If we set $C = (A^2 + B^2)^{1/2}$ and $\omega = \tan^{-1}\frac{A}{B}$ and use the trigonometric product formula we obtain

$$x(t) = C \sin (vt + \omega).$$

Example 2

Find the solution of $\ddot{x} + x = 0$ (harmonic oscillator) satisfying $x(0) = 1$, $\dot{x}(0) = 0$.

Solution

We have $L(p) = p^2 + 1$ with complex conjugate roots $\lambda = i$, $\bar{\lambda} = -i$. Hence $\mu = 0$, $v = 1$ and Corollary 2 gives the general solution

$$x(t) = C \sin (t + \omega).$$

This satisfies $x(0) = 1$ if $C \sin \omega = 1$

and $\dot{x}(0) = 0$ if $C \cos \omega = 0$.

These equations give $\omega = \pi/2$, $C = 1$.

Hence the required solution is $x(t) = \sin(t + \pi/2) = \cos t$.

Corollary 3

If $L(p)$ has equal real roots $\lambda_1 = \lambda_2 = \lambda$ (say), then the functions $x_1(t) = e^{\lambda t}$, $x_2(t) = te^{\lambda t}$ are linearly independent solutions of (6.11). The general solution is

$$x(t) = (A + Bt)e^{\lambda t}.$$

Proof

We know by the theorem that $x_1(t)$ is a solution.

$$L(D)x_2(t) = D^2(te^{\lambda t}) + \alpha D(te^{\lambda t}) + \beta te^{\lambda t}$$

$$= \lambda^2 te^{\lambda t} + 2\lambda e^{\lambda t} + \alpha \lambda te^{\lambda t} + \alpha e^{\lambda t} + \beta te^{\lambda t}$$

$$= L(\lambda)te^{\lambda t} \text{ since } \lambda = -\alpha/2 \text{ for equal roots}$$

$$= 0 \text{ for all } t \text{ since } L(\lambda) = 0.$$

Hence $x_2(t)$ is also a solution.

To check linear independence we have

$$W(x_1, x_2)(t) = e^{\lambda t}(e^{\lambda t} + \lambda te^{\lambda t}) - te^{\lambda t}(\lambda e^{\lambda t})$$

$$= e^{2\lambda t} \neq 0 \text{ for any finite } t \text{ and real } \lambda.$$

Example3

Find the solution of $\ddot{x} - 2\dot{x} + x = 0$ satisfying $x(0) = 2$, $x(1) = 0$.

Solution

We have $L(p) = p^2 - 2p + 1$ with repeated real root $\lambda = 1$. Corollary 3 gives the general solution

$$x(t) = (A + Bt)e^t.$$

This satisfies $x(0) = 2$ if $A = 2$.
With $A = 2$, the solution satisfies $x(1) = 0$ if

$$(2 + B)e = 0; \text{ that is, } B = -2.$$

Hence the required solution is $x(t) = 2(1 - t)e^t$.

We now turn to the problem of solving the non-homogeneous equation (6.10). If we know the linearly independent solutions, say $\phi_1(t)$ and $\phi_2(t)$, of the associated homogeneous equation (6.11), then by using the method of 'variation of parameters' it is possible to deduce a formula for the solution. This formula, though, is rather cumbersome in practice, and we prefer to work more directly, using the following result.

Lemma

If ϕ_1 and ϕ_2 are linearly independent solutions of (6.11) $L(D)x = 0$, then all solutions of (6.12) $L(D)x = f(t)$ are of the form

$$x(t) = A\phi_1(t) + B\phi_2(t) + y(t) \tag{6.13}$$

where A and B are constants and $y(t)$ is one particular solution of (6.12).

Proof

$$\begin{aligned} L(D)x &= L(D)(A\phi_1 + B\phi_2 + y) \\ &= AL(D)\phi_1 + BL(D)\phi_2 + L(D)y, \text{ since L is a linear operator,} \\ &= 0 + 0 + f(t), \text{ since } \phi_1, \phi_2 \text{ satisfy } L(D)x = 0 \text{ and } L(D)y = f, \\ &= f(t). \end{aligned}$$

Thus x as given by (6.13) is a solution of (6.12). Are all solutions of this form? Suppose $z(t)$ is any solution of (6.12), and consider the difference $z(t) - y(t)$.

$$\begin{aligned} L(D)(z - y) &= L(D)z - L(D)y, \text{ since L is linear,} \\ &= f - f, \text{ since both are solutions of (6.12)} \\ &= 0. \end{aligned}$$

Thus $(z - y)$ is a solution of the associated homogeneous equation (6.11), and x will be of the form

$$z - y = A\phi_1 + B\phi_2$$

that is, $$z = A\phi_1 + B\phi_2 + y,$$

and this gives the result.

Remark

To find the solution of (6.12) we need
(i) two linearly independent solutions of (6.11)
(ii) one particular solution of (6.12) which we obtain by inspection or inspired guesswork!

Example 4

Solve $\ddot{x} - 3\dot{x} + 2x = e^t$ subject to $x(0) = 1$ and $\dot{x}(0) = 0$.

Solution

We know from Example 1 that e^t and e^{2t} are linearly independent solutions of the corresponding homogeneous equation

$$\ddot{x} - 3\dot{x} + 2x = 0.$$

For a particular solution we try γte^t (we do not try e^t since this makes the left-hand side zero). Substituting this in the non-homogeneous equation shows that it is a solution when $\gamma = -1$. By the preceding Remark, the general solution is

$$z(t) = Ae^t + Be^{2t} - te^t$$
$$= (A - t)e^t + Be^{2t}.$$

This satisfies $x(0) = 1$ if $A + B = 1$

and $\dot{x}(0) = 0$ if $(A - 1) + 2B = 0$

that is,
$$A + 2B = 1.$$

Hence $A = 1, B = 0$, and the required solution is

$$x(t) = (1 - t)e^t.$$

Finally, we remark that the second order equation may sometimes be more conveniently considered as a pair of first order equations. If we set $y(t) = \dot{x}(t)$ the second order equation

$$\ddot{x}(t) + \alpha(t)\dot{x}(t) + \beta(t)x(t) = f(t) \tag{6.14}$$

may be written as two first order equations:

$$\dot{x} = y$$

$$\dot{y} = -\beta x - \alpha y + f.$$

This is particularly effective where $\alpha(t) = 0$; for instance, in Example 2, $\ddot{x} + x = 0$ becomes

$$\dot{x} = y$$

$$\dot{y} = -x$$

and it is immediately obvious that $x(t) = A \cos t + B \sin t$ is a solution since

$\dfrac{d}{dt}$ (sin t) = cos t and $\dfrac{d}{dt}$ (cos t) = $-$ sin t. Valuable information about the

behaviour of the solutions can often be obtained by plotting them in the (x,y), that is, $(x,\dot{x})$ plane. This is known as **phase plane analysis.**

6.3 SOLUTION OF THE CASE STUDY

We now recognize the equation for national output

$$\ddot{Y} + \alpha\dot{Y} + \beta Y = mIG \qquad (6.15)$$

as being of the same type as (6.12) whose solutions have been fully explored. The characteristic polynominal for (6.15) is $L(p) = p^2 + \alpha p + \beta$ with roots

$$\lambda_1 = \frac{-\alpha + \sqrt{\alpha^2 - 4\beta}}{2}, \lambda_2 = \frac{-\alpha - \sqrt{\alpha^2 - 4\beta}}{2}.$$ Recalling that $\beta = mIs$, it is easily

seen that a particular solution of (6.7) is the constant G/s. We now distinguish three distinct cases.

Case 1

λ_1, λ_2 real and distinct. This occurs when $\alpha^2 > 4\beta$. Corollary 1 applies, and the general solution of (6.15) is

$$Y(t) = Ae^{\lambda_1 t} + Be^{\lambda_2 t} + G/s.$$

The arbitrary constants A and B may be determined from the initial values of Y and I, since the initial value of I determines the initial value of $\dot{Y}$ via (6.5).

If at least one of λ_1 or λ_2 is positive, the national output will grow exponentially with increasing time. On the other hand if both λ_1 and λ_2 are negative, national output will decay exponentially to the level G/s.

Case 2

$\lambda_1 = \lambda_2 = \lambda$. This occurs when $\alpha^2 = 4\beta$. Using Corollary 3, the general solution of (6.15) is

$$Y(t) = (A + Bt)e^{\lambda t} + G/s.$$

This case is similar to Case 1. The national output will either grow or decay exponentially depending on the sign of λ $(= -\alpha/2)$.

Case 3

λ_1, λ_2 complex conjugate, say $\lambda_1 = \mu + iv$

$$\lambda_2 = \mu - iv,$$

where $\mu = -\alpha/2$ and $\nu = \sqrt{4\beta - \alpha^2/2}$. This occurs when $\alpha^2 < 4\beta$. Corollary 2 applies, and the general solution of (6.15) is

$$Y(t) = Ce^{\lambda t} \sin (\nu t + \omega) + G/s$$

where C and ω are arbitrary constants which may be determined from the initial values of Y and I.

In this case the level of national output will oscillate, being damped (that is, oscillations decreasing in amplitude and dying out with increasing time) if $\alpha > 0$ or undamped (amplitude of oscillations growing with time) if $\alpha < 0$.

To obtain a specific example, consider an economy where it has been found that

$$s = 0.25, \ a = 0.8, \ m = 1, \ l = 2$$

and where output Y and investment I were initially zero. Then

$$\alpha = ls + m - mla = 0.5 + 1 - 1.6 = -0.1$$

$$\beta = mls = 0.5.$$

A quick check shows that $\alpha^2 - 4\beta = 0.01 - 2 = -1.99$, and we are in case 3. Hence the general solution is

$$Y(t) = Ce^{0.05t} \sin (0.7055\, t + \omega) + 4G.$$

Notice that

$$\dot{Y}(t) = Ce^{0.05t}\{0.05 \sin (0.7055\, t + \omega) + 0.7055 \cos (0.7055t + \omega)\}$$

Hence

$$Y(0) = C \sin \omega = 4G$$

and

$$\dot{Y}(0) = C\{0.05 \sin \omega + 0.7055 \cos \omega\}.$$

The given initial condition $Y(0) = 0$ implies

$$\sin \omega = -4G/C \tag{6.16}$$

By (6.5), $I(0) = 0$ implies $\dfrac{1}{l} \dot{Y}(0) + sY(0) = G,$

that is, $C\{0.05 \sin \omega + 0.7055 \cos \omega\} = 2G$

which on using (6.16) becomes

$$-0.2G + 0.7055C \cos \omega = 2G$$

or
$$\cos \omega = \frac{2.2G}{0.7055C}. \qquad (6.17)$$

Dividing (6.16) by (6.17) gives $\tan \omega = -1.283$ which may be solved to give $\omega = -0.9088$ radians. Thus $\sin \omega = -0.7887$, and substituting in (6.16) gives $C = 5.072G$. Hence the required solution is

$$\boxed{Y(t) = 5.072Ge^{0.05t} \sin (0.7055t - 0.9088) + 4G.}$$

This function performs undamped oscillations about the equilibrium level $\bar{Y} = 4G$ as shown in Fig. 6.1. This model is realistic in reflecting the cyclical behaviour of booms and slumps found in modern economies, but has the obvious drawback that $Y(t)$ can be negative for certain values of t. In practice, governments would intervene before this stage was reached, and would create a floor level for $Y(t)$ by increasing expenditure on, say, public works, to maintain output in a slump. Varying government expenditure violates one of the assumptions of our model, and a more complicated model with variable $G(t)$ is necessary to describe this situation fully. An alternative treatment of a similar problem using difference equations will be given in Chapter 7.

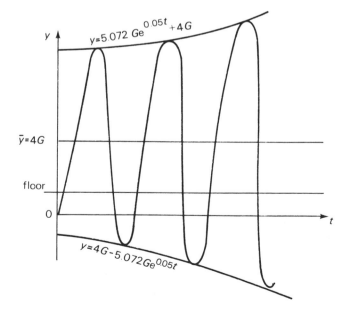

Fig. 6.1   Variation of national output.

6.4 CASE STUDIES

6.4.1 Pricing policy for optimum inventory level

Many manufacturers carry a certain basic stock or inventory of their product to meet any sudden unexpected demand from customers. This is obviously limited by the available storage capacity. The inventory level will tend to fall in periods of high demand, but because there is a time lag in adjusting production to demand, the inventory will tend to rise as demand slackens. If the level is too low, there is a risk of losing customers whose demands cannot be met quickly, but a high inventory will tie up too much working capital.

The Bedford Brick Company has fixed an optimum level L_0 (in thousands) for its holding of unsold bricks. It proposes to maintain inventory as near to this level as possible by adopting the following pricing policy. If inventory level is above L_0, the price of bricks is decreased, with the result that sales increase and inventory falls. If inventory is below L_0 the price is raised, discouraging buyers and increasing the inventory. Therefore the price in tens of pounds per thousand bricks at time t, $p(t)$, is changed in proportion to the difference between inventory level $L(t)$ (in thousands) and the optimum level L_0. This mathematically can be described by

$$\frac{dp}{dt} = -\gamma(L(t) - L_0) \qquad (6.18)$$

where γ is a positive constant of proportionality.

In forecasting sales S, given in units of a thousand bricks, the company uses the formula

$$S = 250 - 30p - 8\frac{dp}{dt} \qquad (6.19)$$

(notice that S increases when $dp/dt < 0$), and in determining the production level Q (also in thousands) they use

$$Q = 120 - 4p. \qquad (6.20)$$

While this policy will undoubtedly maintain the inventory about the optimun level, there is concern in the company that it may necessitate frequent large changes in price, causing alarm and confusion which will discourage customers in the long term. A more careful analysis of the longterm behaviour of $p(t)$ with regard to its stability is therefore required.

It is always true that the change in inventory is equal to the difference between the quantities of bricks produced and sold; that is, $dL/dt = Q(t) - S(t)$.

Differentiating (6.18) with respect to t then gives

$$\frac{d^2p}{dt^2} = -\gamma\frac{dL}{dt} = -\gamma(Q(t) - S(t))$$

$$= -\gamma(-130 + 26p + 8\frac{dp}{dt}) \quad \text{on using (6.19) and (6.20).}$$

Hence we seek conditions under which the solution of

$$\boxed{\ddot{p} + 8\gamma\dot{p} + 26\gamma p = 130\gamma} \qquad (6.21)$$

remains bounded or tends to a limit as t becomes large. It is obvious by inspection that a particular solution of (6.21) is $p = 5$. To obtain the general solution we consider the characteristic polynominal $\lambda^2 + 8\gamma\lambda + 26\gamma$. This has roots $\lambda = -4\gamma \pm \sqrt{(16\gamma^2 - 26\gamma)}$. Remember $\gamma > 0$. If $8\gamma > 13$, both roots are real, distinct, and negative (since $\sqrt{(16\gamma^2 - 26\gamma)} < 4\gamma$) and we are in Case 1 of Sec. 6.2 with solution

$$p(t) = Ae^{\lambda_1 t} + Be^{\lambda_2 t} + 5$$

where $\lambda_1, \lambda_2 < 0$. Hence the solution $p(t)$ decays exponentially to the fixed level $p(t) = 5$, and the pricing policy is stable. If $8\gamma = 13$, we have a repeated real root $\gamma = -4\gamma$, and the general solution (by Corollary 3 of Sec. 6.2) is

$$p(t) = (A + Bt)e^{-4\gamma t} + 5$$

which again decays exponentially to the equilibrium level since $e^{-4\gamma t} \to 0$ faster than any power of t (see Ch. 3). If $8\gamma < 13$, we have complex conjugate roots, and Corollary 2 of Sec. 6.2 gives the general solution

$$p(t) = Ce^{-4\gamma t}\sin(\sqrt{(26\gamma - 16\gamma^2)}t + \omega) + 5.$$

As $t \to \infty$, the dominant factor is $e^{-4\gamma t}$. The term $\sin(\sqrt{(26\gamma - 16\gamma^2)}t + \omega)$ gives oscillations of period $\dfrac{2\pi}{\sqrt{(26\gamma - 16\gamma^2)}}$, but these are damped by $e^{-4\gamma t}$, and $p(t) \to 5$ as $t \to \infty$. Thus again the pricing policy is stable. See Fig. 6.2.

Thus the fears of Bedford Brick about possible instabilities of price were groundless, but the speed with which the price settles down to its limit and the manner in which it approaches that limit both depend crucially on the choice of the constant of proportionality γ in the pricing policy equation (6.18).

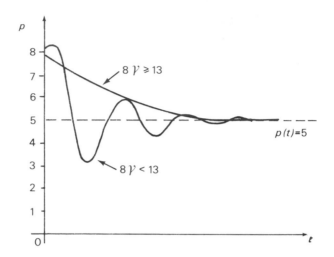

Fig. 6.2   Graphs of p against t in the cases of exponential decay and damped oscillation.

6.4.2   Interacting Species

As an illustration of the way in which different species can interact we will look at an idealized situation, one in which foxes and rabbits are living in a constant isolated area which has an abundance of food for the rabbit population. On the other hand the foxes are dependent on eating the rabbits for their food. If we let

$$x(t) = \text{number of rabbits at time } t$$

$$y(t) = \text{number of foxes at time } t.$$

then we first make the assumption that

$$\frac{dx}{dt} = \alpha x \quad \text{when } y = 0$$

and

$$\frac{dy}{dt} = -\eta y \text{ when } x = 0,$$

where α, η are positive constants. Thus the rabbits will grow exponentially in the absence of foxes, and the foxes will decay exponentially in the absence of rabbits. But how do they interact? Let us suppose that in a small time interval δt the number of kills of rabbits due to foxes is proportional to $xy\,\delta t$. This implies that for a fixed fox population, the number of kills will increase as the availability of rabbits increases, and for a fixed rabbit population, the number of kills will increase with an increasing number of foxes.

Hence if δx is the increase in the rabbit population in time δt,

$$\delta x = \alpha x \, \delta t - \beta xy \, \delta t$$

where β is the positive constant of proportionality. Dividing by δt and letting $\delta t \to 0$ gives

$$\boxed{\dot{x} = \alpha x - \beta xy.} \tag{6.22}$$

Similarly for foxes, the assumption that their increase depends on the number of rabbit kills gives

$$\boxed{\dot{y} = \gamma xy - \eta y,} \tag{6.23}$$

where γ is a positive constant. So the fox/rabbit interacting species model is described by Eqs. (6.22) and (6.23).

These are, of course, first order differential equations, but by using D for d/dt we can rewrite them as

$$\frac{1}{x}Dx = \alpha - \beta y \tag{6.24}$$

$$\frac{1}{y}Dy = \gamma x - \eta, \tag{6.25}$$

and substituting for y from (6.24) into (6.25) gives, after some manipulation,

$$xD^2x + (1 - \gamma x^2 + \eta x)Dx = x^2\alpha(\gamma x - \eta). \tag{6.26}$$

This is a second order differential equation of the form (6.8), but it is not of the form (6.9) and so is non-linear. The techniques we developed in Sec. 6.2 are not applicable to non-linear differential equations, and so we return to (6.22) and (6.23) and reformulate the problem by considering y as a function of x; that is, dividing (6.23) by (6.22) gives

$$\dot{y}/\dot{x} = \frac{\gamma xy - \eta y}{\alpha x - \beta xy}$$

that is

$$\frac{dy}{dx} = \frac{y(\gamma x - \eta)}{x(\alpha - \beta y)}$$

or

$$\int (\frac{\alpha}{y} - \beta)dy = \int (\gamma - \frac{\eta}{x})dx.$$

Integrating both sides gives

$$\alpha \log y - \beta y = \gamma x - \eta \log x + \log K$$

where $\log K$ is the arbitrary constant. Then

$$\log (y^\alpha x^\eta / K) = \gamma x + \beta y,$$

that is,

$$\frac{y^\alpha x^\eta}{K} = e^{\gamma x + \beta y}$$

$$\boxed{\frac{y^\alpha}{e^{\beta y}} \frac{x^\eta}{e^{\gamma x}} = K, \quad \text{constant}.}$$

(6.27)

This expression is a relationship between x and y, and to see what solution we have obtained, we need to look at the trajectories in the x-y plane defined by (6.27). This is the phase plane as defined at the end of Sec. 6.2. Some typical trajectories are shown in Fig. 6.3 for

$$\alpha = 4, \beta = 2, \gamma = 1, \eta = 3.$$

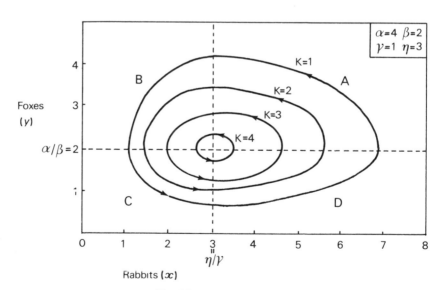

Fig. 6.3 Predicted population curves.

The trajectories have four distinct phases:
(A) Rabbits are in abundance, and the foxes increase, thus reducing the rabbit size.

(B) There is now insufficient food for the foxes, so they now decrease as well as the rabbits.

(C) There are so few foxes that the rabbits begin to increase again.

(D) Now there are sufficient rabbits for the foxes also to increase.

One point to be stressed is that at no stage do either of the populations die out. For a given initial starting point (x_0, y_0), which will determine K and hence a unique trajectory, the phase point (x, y) moves through the four stages, returning after some time interval, to the initial point, and the cycle starts again.

Of course the model is very simple and can be criticized in many ways. For instance, a crowding term, x^2 or y^2, in each of the equations (6.22) and (6.23), would make the model more realistic. Nevertheless, it does illustrate some of the characteristics to be expected in a predator-prey situation. Fig. 6.4 is a sketch of the continuous trajectory obtained from a laboratory experiment with a predatory mite, Typhlodromus, and its prey, a plant mite, Eotetranychus.

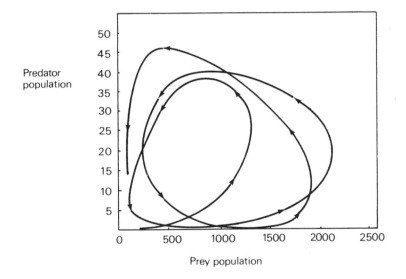

Fig. 6.4   Experimental population curves.

6.5 PROBLEMS

1. Verify that $x_1 = e^t$ and $x_2 = e^{2t}$ are solutions of the differential equation

$$\ddot{x} - 3\dot{x} + 2x = 0.$$

Show that x_1 and x_2 are linearly independent functions. Hence write down the general solution of the differential equation.

2. Solve the following homogeneous differential equations:

   (i) $\ddot{x} + \dot{x} - 2x = 0$

   (ii) $\ddot{x} - 2\dot{x} + 5x = 0$

   (iii) $\ddot{x} + 25x = 0$

   (iv) $\ddot{x} + 2\dot{x} + 4x = 0$

   (v) $\ddot{x} - 2\dot{x} + x = 0$.

   Find the complete solution in (i) when $x(0) = 1$, $x(1) = 0$, and in (v) when $x(0) = 2$, $x(1) = .2$.

3. By trying a solution of the form $x = t^m$, where m is to be determined, solve the differential equation

$$t^2\ddot{x} + t\dot{x} - x = 0.$$

4. Verify that $x = e^t$ is a solution of

$$\ddot{x} + x = 2e^t$$

   and hence find the general solution.

5. Verify that $x = te^t$ is a solution of

$$\ddot{x} - x = 2e^t$$

   and find the complete solution which satisfies $x(0) = 1$, $x(1) = 1$.

6. Find the general solution of the following differential equations:

   (i) $\ddot{x} - 3\dot{x} + 2x = 10t$

   (ii) $\ddot{x} + 4x = e^{-t}$

   (iii) $\ddot{x} + 2\dot{x} + x = 2t^2$

   (iv) $\ddot{x} - x = \sin t$

   (v) $\ddot{x} + x = \sin t$.

7. (a) Show that a particular solution of

$$\ddot{x} + \omega^2 x = F_0 \cos(\alpha t) \qquad (\alpha \neq \omega)$$

   is given by $\dfrac{F_0 \cos(\alpha t)}{(\omega^2 - \alpha^2)}$. What happens as $\alpha \to \omega$?

(b) Show that a particular solution of

$$\ddot{x} + \omega^2 x = F_0 \cos (\omega t)$$

is given by $\dfrac{F_0 t}{2\omega} \sin (\omega t)$. Illustrate this solution graphically.

This example illustrates the phenomenon of resonance, which occurs when the 'natural' frequency ω equals the 'forcing' frequency α. The system still oscillates, but the amplitude of the oscillations increases indefinitely.

8. Show that the second order differential equation

$$\ddot{x} + x = 0$$

can be converted to two first order differential equations, namely

$$\dot{x} = y, \quad \dot{y} = -x.$$

Hence show that $\dfrac{dy}{dx} = -\dfrac{x}{y}$, and solve for y as a function of x. Illustrate the solutions in the x-y plane graphically.

9. Using the model for the national output described in Sec. 6.1, that is

$$\ddot{Y} + \alpha\dot{Y} + \beta Y = mlG,$$

with parameters given by

$$s = 0.5, \quad a = 0.4, \quad m = 0.1, \quad l = 2,$$

determine the solution given that output Y and investment I were initially zero. Sketch the form of the solution.

10. A general pricing policy model is given by

$$S(t) = a_1 - b_1 p - c_1 \dot{p}$$
$$Q(t) = a_2 - b_2 p - c_2 \dot{p}$$

where S and Q are the sales forecast and production forecast respectively, $p = p(t)$ is the price, and $a_1, a_2, b_1, b_2, c_1, c_2$ are positive constants. The pricing policy is given by

$$\dot{p} = -\gamma(L(t) - L_0)$$

where γ is a positive constant, L is the inventory level, and L_0 the desired optimum inventory level. The inventory changes according to

$$\dot{L} = Q - S.$$

Show that the forecast price is determined from

$$\ddot{p} + \gamma(c_1 - c_2)\dot{p} + \gamma(b_1 - b_2)p = \gamma(a_1 - a_2)$$

and hence deduce that if $c_1 > c_2$, $b_1 > b_2$, the price is tending to a stable value as t increases.

11. A model of species competing for their food supply is given by

$$\dot{x} = ax - by$$
$$\dot{y} = cy - dx$$

where x, y are the two species populations, and a, b, c, d are positive constants. Show that x satisfies

$$\ddot{x} - (a + c)\dot{x} + (ac - db)x = 0$$

and deduce that x has a solution of the form

$$x = Ae^{\alpha_1 t} + Be^{\alpha_2 t}$$

where α_1, α_2 are positive constants, and A and B are arbitrary constants. Also find the solution for y.

The values of the parameters for two competing species are estimated by $a = c = 2$, $b = d = 1$. If at $t = 0$, $x = 100$ and $y = 200$, determine the time when one species is eliminated.

12. A model of species cooperation is given by

$$\dot{x} = -ax + by$$
$$\dot{y} = -cy + dx^-$$

Show that unless $bd \geqslant ac$, both populations tend to extinction. Find the solution when $a = 2$, $b = 4$, $c = 2$, $d = 4$ and determine what the limiting populations for x and y are if initially $x = 100$, $y = 200$.

13. The buying behaviour of the public towards a particular product is modelled by

$$\frac{dB}{dt} = b(M - \beta B)$$

$$\frac{dM}{dt} = a(B - \alpha M) + cA$$

where $B = B(t)$ is the level of buying, $M = M(t)$ is a measure of the public motivation or attitude towards the product, and $A = A(t)$ is the advertising policy. The parameters a, b, c, α, β are all assumed positive.

Deduce that

$$\ddot{B} + (b\beta + a\alpha)\dot{B} + ab(\alpha\beta - 1)B = cA$$

and that for constant advertising, the buying level tends to a limiting value. When $\alpha = \beta = 2$, $a = b = 1$, $c = 1$ and

$$A(t) = \begin{cases} 100 \text{ units for } 0 < t < 10 \\ 0 \qquad \text{ for } t > 10 \end{cases}$$

determine the complete forecast for the buying behaviour, when at $t = 0$, $B = M = 0$.

14. A mathematical model for epidemics with removals is given by

$$\frac{dx}{dt} = -\beta x^2 y$$

$$\frac{dy}{dt} = \beta x^2 y - \gamma y$$

$$\frac{dz}{dt} = \gamma y$$

where x, y, and z are the number of susceptibles, infectives, and removals respectively, and γ and β are positive constants. Show that the **threshold density of susceptibles*** is $\rho^{\frac{1}{2}}$, where $\rho = \gamma/\beta$.

The total population size is n, and initially $x = x_0$, $y = y_0$, and $z = 0$ where $y_0 < x_0$. Show that

$$\frac{dz}{dt} = \gamma\{n - z - x_0/(1 + zx_0/\rho)\}.$$

Assuming that $y \to 0$ as $t \to \infty$, deduce that the value of z as $t \to \infty$ follows from

$$(1 + x_0 z/\rho)(n - z) = x_0,$$

---

*This is the critical value of x which determines whether or not there is an epidemic.

and for $x_0 > \rho^{1/2}$, show that this value is given approximately by $x_0 - \rho/x_0$. Also show that dz/dt has a maximum value when $z = \rho^{1/2} - \rho/x_0$. Without actually solving for z as a function of t, sketch graphs of z and dz/dt against t. If $x_0 = \rho^{1/2} + v$ where $v < \rho^{1/2}$, show that the total epidemic size is given approximately by $2v$.

CHAPTER 7

Step by Step: Difference Equations

7.1 A NATIONAL ECONOMY MODEL FOR JEDESLAND

The planners in the Treasury of Jedesland have developed a model to describe (in a simplified form) the economy of Jedesland. The national income, T say, is used in three ways, namely for consumer expenditure on goods and services, C say, for private investment in industry, I say, and for government expenditure, G say. Thus we write

$$T_k = C_k + I_k + G_k \quad (k = 0, 1, 2, \ldots) \tag{7.1}$$

where the suffix k denotes the value of the quantity in the kth time period.

The model was further developed, using the following assumptions.

(i) The consumer expenditure is affected favourably by the national income. The larger the national income, the more is spent on goods and services, but in the following time period. Thus we write

$$C_k = A T_{k-1} \tag{7.2}$$

where A is a positive constant.

(ii) Private investment is stimulated not by the actual level of consumer expenditure but by its change. So if consumer expenditure increases from one time period to the next, private investment will increase. Thus we assume

$$I_k = B(C_k - C_{k-1}) \tag{7.3}$$

where B is a positive constant.

(iii) Government expenditure is assumed constant, say G.

With these assumptions, equation (7.1) reduces to

$$T_k = AT_{k-1} + B(C_k - C_{k-1}) + G$$
$$= AT_{k-1} + BAT_{k-1} - BAT_{k-2} + G$$

that is,

$$\boxed{T_k - A(1 + B)T_{k-1} + BAT_{k-2} = G.}$$ (7.4)

So what does their model predict?

Clearly we must start with some initial values, say $T_0 = 2$ and $T_1 = 3$. Then for given values of the constants A and B and G, we can successvely apply (7.4) for $k = 2, 3, 4 \ldots$, which will predict $T_2, T_3, \ldots$. For instance, if $A = \frac{1}{2}$, $B = 1$, and $G = 1$, then, applying (7.4),

$$T_2 = 3.0 \qquad\qquad T_7 = 1.875$$
$$T_3 = 2.5 \qquad\qquad T_8 = 2.0$$
$$T_4 = 2.0 \qquad\qquad T_9 = 2.0625$$
$$T_5 = 1.75 \qquad\qquad T_{10} = 2.0625$$
$$T_6 = 1.75 \qquad\qquad T_{11} = 2.03125.$$

The solution is plotted in Fig. 7.1.

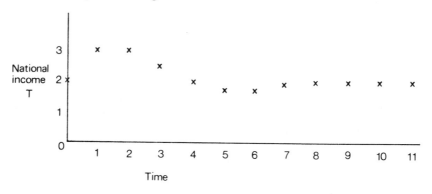

Fig. 7.1   Variation in national income.

It looks fairly clear that the national income will stabilize at the level of two units.

Unfortunately the Treasury has some doubts over the best values for A and B that will make the model a realistic one, and the planners would like to be able to predict future trends without actually specifying the values of A and B. For example, does the national income always stabilize at 2 units, no matter what values A and B have or what initial levels, T_0 and T_1, are used? One quick calculation soon yields one of the answers. For if $A = 0.8$ and $B = 2.0$ (with

$G = 1$ as before) and with $T_0 = 2$, $T_1 = 3$, we obtain

T_2	$= 5.0$	T_6	$= 24.661$
T_3	$= 8.2$	T_7	$= 30.887$
T_4	$= 12.68$	T_8	$= 35.671$
T_5	$= 18.312$	T_9	$= 37.191.$

The economy is booming (apparently) and clearly not stabilizing at 2 units. But is it stabilizing at all? If we continue the calculations

$$T_{10} = 33.186$$
$$T_{11} = 21.140$$
$$T_{12} = -1.362.$$

A disaster has occurred! By now the Jedesland Premier would already be knocking at the doors of the I.M.F. and courting some prosperous country for help.

This situation must be avoided. We would clearly have a greater under-standing of the economy if we could solve (7.4) in general. Specific examples illustrate specific types of predictions, but we would clearly like to understand the situation more fully. (For an alternative treatment of this problem, using a second order differential equation model, see Chapter 6.)

7.2 DIFFERENCE EQUATIONS – THEORY

7.2.1 Linear First Order

The linear first order constant coefficient difference equation is written as

$$\boxed{x_{k+1} = Ax_k + B} \qquad (k = 0, 1, 2, \ldots) \qquad (7.5)$$

where A, B are constants ($A \neq 0$). We can soon find the solution of (7.5) by continued application of the formula; that is,

$$x_1 = Ax_0 + B,$$

$$x_2 = Ax_1 + B = A(Ax_0 + B) + B = A^2x_0 + B(1 + A)$$

$$x_3 = Ax_2 + B = A^3x_0 + B(1 + A + A^2);$$

continuing in this way,

$$x_k = A^kx_0 + B(1 + A + A^2 + \ldots + A^{k-1})$$

$$= A^kx_0 + B\frac{(1 - A^k)}{(1 - A)}, \qquad (A \neq 1).$$

summing the geometric progression on the right hand side. If $A = 1$, then

$$x_k = x_0 + nB.$$

Thus we can summarize the solution as

$$x_k = \begin{cases} A^k x_0 + B\dfrac{(1 - A^k)}{(1 - A)} & (A \neq 1) \\[2ex] x_0 + kB & (A = 1) \end{cases} \qquad (7.6)$$

Although it is a simple matter to find the solution, it is of interest to note that the actual behaviour of the solution is most certainly dependent on x_0 and A and B. We first note that if $x_0 = B/(1-A)$, then $x_0 = x_1 = x_2 = \ldots = x_k = \ldots$. If $A > 1$, and $x_0 \neq B/(1-A)$, then the solutions grow unbounded. This is illustrated in Fig. 7.2.

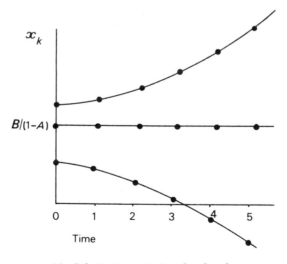

Fig. 7.2 Typical solutions for $A > 1$.

Now if $0 < A < 1$, then it is clear from (7.6) that as $k \to \infty$, $x_k \to B/(1 - A)$. Typical solutions are illustrated in Fig. 7.3.

If $-1 < A < 0$, an oscillating type of behaviour is obtained (see Fig. 7.4) and similarly for $A < -1$, with amplitude increasing. Note that the continuous lines drawn through the sequence of points have no real meaning, but are only sketched to emphasize the behaviour of the *discrete* sequences of points, x_k, $k = 0, 1, 2, \ldots$.

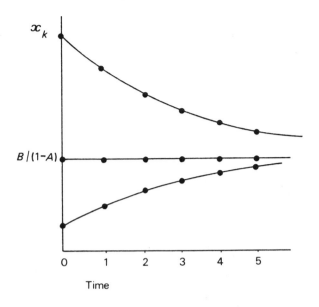

Fig. 7.3   Typical solutions for $0 < A < 1$.

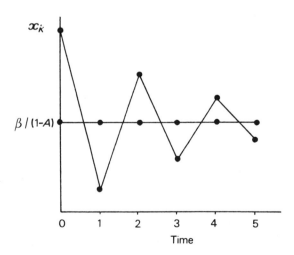

Fig. 7.4   Typical solutions for $-1 < A < 0$.

So in spite of the simplicity of the solution, the actual forms are very varied and dependent on both the initial value, x_0, and the parameters A and B.

7.2.2 Linear n^{th} Order

We shall in fact focus our attention on $n = 2$, but we first define the general n^{th} order linear difference equation as

$$\boxed{x_{k+n} + a_1 x_{k+n-1} + \ldots + a_n x_k = \phi(k)} \quad (k = 0,1,2,\ldots) \quad (7.7)$$

where $a_1, a_2, \ldots a_n$ are constants and ϕ is a function of k. For example, the linear second order difference equation takes the form

$$x_{k+2} + a_1 x_{k+1} + a_2 x_k = \phi(k) \qquad (k = 0,1,2,\ldots)$$

which alternatively can be written as

$$x_k + a_1 x_{k-1} + a_2 x_{k-2} = \phi(k-2) = \psi(k), \text{ say.}$$

We note that the governing equation of the economy discussed in Sec. 7.1 is of this form with 'x' replaced by 'T', $a_1 = -A(1 + B)$, $a_2 = BA$, and $\psi = G$, constant.

We can simplify the notation in (7.7) by defining an operator E by

$$Ex_n = x_{n+1} \tag{7.8}$$

that is, $Ex_2 = x_3$, $Ex_{n+k} = x_{n+k+1}$, etc.; then we also have

$$E^2 x_n = E(Ex_n) = Ex_{n+1} = x_{n+2}$$

that is, $E^2 x_2 = x_4$, $E^2 x_{n+k} = x_{n+k+2}$, etc.; and (7.7) can now be rewritten as

$$(E^n + a_1 E^{n-1} + \ldots + a_{n-1} E_1 + a_n) x_k = \phi(k) \quad (k = 0,1,2,\ldots) \tag{7.9}$$

The expression in the bracket on the left-hand side is a polynominal in the operator E and, calling it L(E), we have the somewhat simpler looking difference equation

$$L(E)x_k = \phi(k). \tag{7.10}$$

As yet we have got no nearer actually solving the equation, but the notation introduced above does enable us to prove the following important results.

Theorem

Let $\chi(k)$ be any solution of (7.10). Then the general solution of (7.10) takes the form

$$x_k = f(k) + \chi(k) \tag{7.11}$$

where $f(k)$ is the general solution of

$$L(E)x_k = 0. \tag{7.12}$$

Proof

The proof follows on the same lines as that given in Chapter 6 for differential operators.

So to solve (7.10) we must find
   (i) one particular solution of $L(E)x_k = \phi(k)$,
   (ii) the general solution of the associated homogeneous difference equation
   $L(E)x_k = 0$.
We will first concentrate on (ii) and in particular take the case $n = 2$, so that we are looking for the general solution of

$$\boxed{x_{k+2} + a_1 x_{k+1} + a_2 x_k = 0} \tag{7.13}$$

7.2.3 Homogeneous Second Order

By analogy with linear differential equations, the general solution of (7.13) will be of the form

$$x_k = A_1 u_1(k) + A_2 u_2(k) \tag{7.14}$$

where $u_1(k)$, $u_2(k)$ are distinct solutions of (7.13), and A_1, A_2 are arbitrary constants.

Let us try looking for u_1 and u_2 by assuming a solution of the form $x_k = \lambda^k$, where λ is a constant to be determined. Substituting into (7.13),

$$\lambda^{k+2} + a_1\lambda^{k+1} + a_2\lambda^k = 0$$

$$\lambda^k(\lambda^2 + a_1\lambda + a_2) = 0.$$

Now $\lambda^k = 0$ implies $\lambda = 0$, and we have the trivial solution $x_k = 0$. On the other hand, if

$$\lambda^2 + a_1\lambda + a_2 = 0 \tag{7.15}$$

we obtain two roots, and possibly two solutions as illustrated in the following examples.

Example 1

Solve the difference equation

$$x_{k+2} - 5x_{k+1} + 6x_k = 0$$

given that $x_0 = 1$, $x_1 = 2$.

Solution
Assuming $x_k = \lambda^k$ gives

$$\lambda^k(\lambda^2 - 5\lambda + 6) = 0$$

that is

$$(\lambda^2 - 5\lambda + 6) = 0$$

that is

$$(\lambda - 3)(\lambda - 2) = 0$$

Thus $\lambda = 2$ or 3 and we have two distinct solutions 2^k and 3^k. Hence the general solution is given by

$$x_k = A_1 2^k + A_2 3^k \qquad (k = 0, 1, 2, \ldots)$$

Applying the conditions $x_0 = 1$, $x_1 = 2$ gives

$$1 = A_1 2^0 + A_2 3^0 = A_1 + A_2$$
$$2 = A_1 2 + A_2 3.$$

Solving $A_1 = 1$ and $A_2 = 0$ leads to the complete solution

$$x_k = 2^k \qquad (k = 0, 1, 2, \ldots)$$

(Check: $x_0 = 2^0 = 1$, $x_1 = 2^1 = 2$.)

In the above example, the auxiliary equation, (7.15), has real distinct roots. The next two examples illustrate the other possibilities.

Example 2
Find the general solution of

$$x_{k+2} - 4x_{k+1} + 4x_k = 0.$$

Solution
With $x_k = \lambda^k$, we obtain

$$\lambda^2 - 4\lambda + 4 = 0$$

that is

$$(\lambda - 2)^2 = 0;$$

and so we only obtain one root, $\lambda = 2$, and one solution 2^k. A second solution is in fact given by $x_k = k2^k$. Let us check this.

$$x_{k+2} - 4x_{k+1} + 4x_k = (k + 2)2^{k+2} - 4(k + 1)2^{k+1} + 4k2^k$$
$$= 2^k\{4(k + 2) - 8(k + 1) + 4k\}$$
$$= 0.$$

Hence the general solution is given by

$$x_k = A_1 2^k + A_2 k 2^k = (A_1 + kA_2)2^k. \quad (k = 0, 1, 2, \ldots)$$

Note

In general, if a root $\lambda = \lambda_1$, say, is repeated in (7.15), then the general solution is

$$x_k = (A_1 + kA_2)\lambda_1^k.$$

This is the analogous situation to that of homogeneous linear differential equations with repeated roots where the general solution is of the form $(A_1 + tA_2)e^{\lambda t}$.

Example 3

Solve the difference equation

$$x_{k+2} - 2x_{k+1} + 4x_k = 0.$$

Solution

The auxiliary equation is

$$\lambda^2 - 2\lambda + 4 = 0$$

which has complex roots $\lambda = 1 \pm \sqrt{3}i$. It is more convenient to express this in polar form, $\lambda = re^{\pm i\theta}$. Now

$$\lambda = 2(\tfrac{1}{2} \pm \tfrac{\sqrt{3}}{2}i) = 2e^{\pm i\pi/3},$$

so we take $\lambda_1 = 2e^{i\pi/3}$, $\lambda_2 = 2e^{-i\pi/3}$, and the general solution is of the form

$$x_k = A_1(2e^{i\pi/3})^k + A_2(2e^{-i\pi/3})^k$$
$$= A_1 2^k e^{i\pi k/3} + A_2 2^k e^{-i\pi k/3}$$
$$= 2^k[A_1\cos\left(\tfrac{\pi k}{3}\right) + A_1 i \sin\left(\tfrac{\pi k}{3}\right) + A_2 \cos\left(\tfrac{-\pi k}{3}\right) + A_2 i \sin\left(\tfrac{-\pi k}{3}\right)];$$
$$= 2^k[(A_1 + A_2)\cos\left(\tfrac{\pi k}{3}\right) + (A_1 - A_2)i \sin\left(\tfrac{\pi k}{3}\right)].$$

Rewriting the arbitrary constants as

$$B_1 = A_1 + A_2$$

$$B_2 = (A_1 - A_2)i,$$

we obtain the general solution as

$$x_k = 2^k [B_1 \cos\left(\tfrac{\pi k}{3}\right) + B_2 \sin\left(\tfrac{\pi k}{3}\right)]. \quad (k = 0, 1, 2, \ldots)$$

7.2.4 Particular Solutions

We now turn to problem (1) of finding solutions of $L(E)x_k = \phi(k)$, that is, finding one particular solution, sometimes called a particular integral. As with differential equations, this problem is more complex than solving the associated homogeneous difference equation. We just illustrate some of the techniques in the following two examples.

Example 4

Find a particular solution of

$$x_{k+2} - 5x_{k+1} + 6x_k = k^2.$$

Solution

Since the R.H.S. is a polynomial of degree 2 in k we first try for a solution of the form

$$x_k = ak^2 + bk + c$$

where a, b, and c are constants to be determined. Now if

$$x_k = ak^2 + bk + c,$$

$$x_{k+1} = a(k + 1)^2 + b(k + 1) + c, \quad \text{and}$$

$$x_{k+2} = a(k + 2)^2 + b(k + 2) + c;$$

and substituting into the difference equation gives

$$a(k + 2)^2 + b(k + 2) + c$$
$$- 5\{a(k + 1)^2 + b(k + 1) + c\} + 6\{ak^2 + bk + c\} = k^2$$

which on grouping the coefficients of k and k^2 becomes

$$k^2(2a - 1) + k(- 6a + 5b) + (- a - 3b + 2c) = 0.$$

For this equation to be satisfied for $k = 0, 1, 2, \ldots$, we must have

$$\left.\begin{array}{r} 2a - 1 = 0 \\ - 6a + 2b = 0 \\ - a - 3b + 2c = 0 \end{array}\right\} \quad a = \tfrac{1}{2}, \ b = \tfrac{3}{2}, \ c = \tfrac{5}{2}.$$

and so

$$x_k = \tfrac{1}{2}(k^2 + 3k + 5)$$

is one particular solution.

[Note that the general solution of this difference equation can now be written as

$$x_k = A_1 2^k + A_2 3^k + \tfrac{1}{2}(k^2 + 3k + 5),$$

using the result from the theorem in Sec. 7.2.2 and Example 1, Sec. 7.2.3.]

Example 5

Find a particular solution of

$$x_{k+1} - 2x_k = 3^k k^2.$$

Solution

This time we look for a solution of the form

$$x_k = 3^k(ak^2 + bk + c)$$

so that

$$x_{k+1} = 3^{k+1}[a(k + 1)^2 + b(k + 1) + c].$$

Thus

$$\begin{aligned} x_{k+1} - 2x_k &= 3^{k+1}[a(k + 1)^2 + b(k + 1) + c] - 2 \cdot 3^k(ak^2 + bk + c) \\ &= 3^k\{k^2(3a - 2a) + k(6a + 3b - 2b) + (3a + 3b + 3c - 2c)\} \\ &= 3^k\{k^2 a + k(6a + b) + (3a + 3b + c)\} \end{aligned}$$

and this we require equal to $3^k k^2$. Comparing coefficients

$$a = 1, \ b = -6, \ c = 15,$$

and so we have the particular solution

$$x_k = 3^k(k^2 - 6k + 15).$$

Note

The method of finding particular solutions employed in the above two examples is one essentially of trial and error, and clearly an intelligent guess for the form of the solution is required. It is not always quite as straightforward as in the examples above. For instance, the required form of a particular solution for

$$x_{k+1} - 3x_k = 3^k k^2$$

is given by

$$x_k = 3^k(ak^3 + bk^2 + ck + d).$$

That is, the polynominal in k in the bracket is *one* degree higher than the polynominal on the R.H.S. of the difference equation.

There are in fact more precise methods for finding particular solutions, but they tend to be very cumbersome and involved. [See, for example, Read (1972) Chapter 15.]

7.3 JEDESLAND'S NATIONAL ECONOMY

We return now to the problem posed in Sec. 7.1, namely what sort of behaviour is predicted by the model for Jedesland's economy given by

$$T_k - A(1 + B)T_{k-1} + BAT_{k-2} = G \quad (k = 2, 3, 4, \ldots)$$

where A, B and G are constants. We can rewrite this difference equation as

$$\boxed{T_{k+2} - A(1 + B)T_{k+1} + BAT_k = G} \quad (k = 0, 1, 2, \ldots) \quad (7.16)$$

and we note that it is second order and linear and of the form (7.10). So we must find one particular solution and the solution of the associated homogeneous equation

$$T_{k+2} - A(1 + B)T_{k+1} + BAT_k = 0 \quad (k = 0, 1, 2, \ldots) \quad (7.17)$$

For a particular solution of (7.16), try

$$T_k = a, \text{ constant.}$$

Then $T_{k+1} = T_{k+2} = a$, and to satisfy (7.16), we require

$$a(1 - A(1 + B) + BA) = G.$$

If $A \neq 1$, $a = G/(1 - A)$. For the general solution of (7.17), we put $T_k = \lambda^k$, giving

$$\lambda^2 - A(1 + B)\lambda + BA = 0$$

and

$$\lambda = \frac{A}{2}(1 + B) \pm \frac{1}{2}\{A^2(1 + B)^2 - 4AB\}^{\frac{1}{2}}.$$

If $A^2(1 + B)^2 < 4AB$, then

$$\lambda = \frac{A}{2}(1 + B) \pm \frac{i}{2}\{4AB - A^2(1 + B)^2\}^{\frac{1}{2}}$$

which is of the form $\lambda = re^{\pm i\theta}$, where $r = \frac{1}{2}\{A^2(1 + B)^2 + 4AB - A^2(1 + B)^2\}^{\frac{1}{2}}$, that is, $r = \sqrt{(AB)}$ and, following the analysis of Example 3 in Sec. 7.2.3, we have solutions of the form

$$T_k = (AB)^{k/2}[A_1\cos(k\theta) + A_2\sin(k\theta)]$$

where θ is determined from λ and r and A_1, A_2 are arbitrary constants. The complete solution is then

$$\boxed{T_k = (AB)^{k/2}[A_1\cos(k\theta) + A_2\sin(k\theta)] + \frac{G}{(1 - A)}.} \qquad (7.18)$$

What happens as k increases? The square bracket expression is clearly bounded for all k (since both sin and cos functions are bounded). The last terms remain constant, and so all depends on the value of AB. If $AB < 1$, $(AB)^{k/2} \to 0$ as $k \to \infty$, whereas if $AB > 1$, $(AB)^{k/2}$ increases without limit as k increases. Thus in the case $A^2(1 + B)^2 < 4AB$, we can summarize the two possible results as

(i) $AB < 1$, then $T_k \to \dfrac{G}{(1 - A)}$ as $k \to \infty$ and the ecomony is stable.

(ii) $AB > 1$, then T_k increases without limit while oscillating and the economy is unstable.

Let us check with the results found in Sec. 7.1. In the first numerical example we took $A = \frac{1}{2}$, $B = 1$, so that $A^2(1 + B)^2 - 4AB = -1 < 0$, $AB = \frac{1}{2} < 1$, and the economy is stable by (i) above, and for $G = 1$, tends to 2 as $k \to \infty$, and this checks with the numerical results obtained. Similarly in the second example $A = 0.8$ and $B = 2.0$ so that $A^2(1 + B)^2 - 4AB = -0.64$ and $AB = 1.6 > 1$, and by (ii) above the economy will oscillate in an unstable manner, which again checks with the numerical results.

Although we have not analysed all possible ranges of values for the parameters A and B, it is clear that the economy is predicted as stable when

$$A^2(1 + B)^2 - 4AB < 0 \quad \text{and} \quad AB < 1.$$

that is,

$$\boxed{\tfrac{1}{4}A^2(1 + B)^2 < AB < 1}. \tag{7.19}$$

7.4 CASE STUDIES

7.4.1 A simple population model

Let us consider the growth of a single species of life in a closed environment, where the population of the species is measured at equal intervals of time. Let N_k denote the species population at the end of the kth period. Our problem is a very basic one. Given the population at a number of initial periods (for example, N_0 and N_1) can we predict the future changes in the population?

Of course this problem is very complex. We would need to know what sort of species is under study, its reproductive characteristics, whether it is limited by some predator, and many other factors. But as in all mathematical modelling, it is often a sound policy to consider first the simplest type of model, and this we will do. Our major assumption is to suppose that during any period the number of births and deaths during that period are proportional to the population at the start of the period. For example, in the $(k+1)^{\text{st}}$ period, we take the excess of births over deaths as

$$a N_k$$

where a is a constant.

But the population change during the period is $N_{k+1} - N_k$ giving

$$N_{k+1} - N_k = a N_k,$$

that is,

$$\boxed{N_{k+1} = (1 + a)N_k} \qquad (k = 0, 1, 2, \ldots). \tag{7.20}$$

This is a first order linear difference equation, and, using the theory from Sec. 7.2.1, we have the solution

$$\boxed{N_k = (1 + a)^k N_0} \qquad (k = 0, 1, 2, \ldots) \qquad (7.21)$$

Suppose we also know N_1, the population after the first period. This information will enable us to determine the parameter a introduced in the model. For, using (7.21) with $k = 1$, gives

$$N_1 = (1 + a)N_0$$

that is,

$$a = \frac{N_1}{N_0} - 1. \qquad (7.22)$$

As a simple example take the USA population in 1890 and 1900, so that we are using a 10-year period. Now from population data

$$N_0(1890) = 62.9 \times 10^6$$

$$N_1(1900) = 76.0 \times 10^6,$$

giving

$$a = \frac{76.0}{62.9} - 1 = 0.208,$$

and the predicted population is given by (7.21) as

$$N_k = (1.208)^k N_0 \qquad (k = 2, 3, \ldots).$$

Table 1 summarizes the results up to 1940.

Table 1   USA population

Time	USA Population	Predicted
1890	62.9×10^6	62.9×10^6
1900	76.0×10^6	76.0×10^6
1910	92.0×10^6	91.8×10^6
1920	105.7×10^6	110.9×10^6
1930	122.8×10^6	133.9×10^6
1940	131.7×10^6	161.8×10^6

Clearly, our mathematical model, although giving a reasonable prediction for 1910, is soon far from adequate, and for predictions past 1910 a more complex model is required. Such a model would have to incorporate limitations to unlimited growth which our first model gives. For some species, food and land may be limited, for others energy resources might be inadequate or pollution might play a significant role in reducing the population growth. One simple model, which is an extension of our first one, and which sums up these sentiments, is given by

$$N_{k+1} - N_k = (a - bN_k)N_k$$

that is,

$$N_{k+1} = (1 + a - bN_k)N_k \quad . \tag{7.23}$$

Here the excess of births over deaths in the $(k+1)^{st}$ period is given by $(a - bN_k)N_k$, so an extra term is added which has a negative effect on the growth particularly as N_k becomes large. (7.23) is a non-linear difference equation and is difficult to solve. In the Problems, a number of investigations into the properties of solutions of (7.23) are set.

7.4.2 The Cobweb Model of Supply and Demand

Let x denote the price of a certain article and let $S = S(x)$ and $D = D(x)$ denote the supply and demand functions for that product; that is, S and D denote the amounts of an article that will be supplied and demanded if the price is x. As the price increases, the demand obviously decreases, whereas the opposite is true of the supply curve. Typical curves for S and D are illustrated in Fig. 7.5.

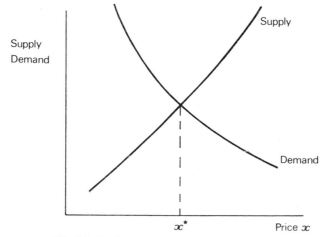

Fig. 7.5 Typical supply and demand curves.

The price, $x = x^*$, at which the two curves intersect, is where supply and demand exactly balance, that is, $S(x^*) = D(x^*)$, and we call this **market equilibrium**. In practice we do not usually achieve this, and we have a dynamic situation in which excess demand affects supply, and so on. We shall develop a mathematical model to express these ideas and to explore their outcome.

We first divide our period into equal intervals and let x_n denote the price of the article at time $t = n$. Our first assumption is that the manufacturer bases his supply at time $t = n$ on the price at time $t = n - 1$, that is, supply at time $t = n$ is $S(x_{n-1})$. We next assume that the price will adjust so that demand equals supply, so that the new price x_n will be determined by

$$D(x_n) = S(x_{n-1}). \tag{7.24}$$

The new supply, at time $t = n + 1$, is then $S(x_n)$, and the new price is determined from

$$D(x_{n+1}) = S(x_n) \tag{7.25}$$

and so on.

The exact way in which the prices change will of course now depend on the functions S and D. Taking the simplest possible forms for S and D, namely linear, we assume that

$$S(x) = a(x - \alpha) + \beta \tag{7.26}$$

$$D(x) = -b(x - \alpha) + \beta \tag{7.27}$$

so that (α,β) is the point of intersection of S and D, that is, $x^* = \alpha$ and $S(x^*) = D(x^*) = \beta$. From (7.25)

$$-b(x_{n+1} - \alpha) + \beta = a(x_n - \alpha) + \beta$$

that is, $\boxed{bx_{n+1} + ax_n = (a + b)\alpha}$.   (7.28)

This is a first order linear difference equation, and from (7.6), with $'A' = -\dfrac{a}{b}$, $'B' = \dfrac{(a + b)\alpha}{b}$,

$$x_n = (-a/b)^n x_0 + \frac{(a + b)\alpha}{b} \frac{[1 - (-a/b)^n]}{[1 - (-a/b)]}$$

that is, $\boxed{x_n = (-a/b)^n (x_0 - \alpha) + \alpha}$ $(n = 1, 2, \ldots)$.   (7.29)

Let us see what sort of behaviour is now predicted. If $(a/b) < 1$, we have a stable situation in which $x_n \to \alpha$ as $n \to \infty$, whereas for $(a/b) > 1$, as n becomes large, x_n oscillates with ever increasing magnitude and the situation is described as unstable or 'explosive'. So the predicted behaviour depends critically on the ratio a/b, which is the ratio of the slopes of the supply and demand curves. For $(a/b) < 1$, a typical development is illustrated in Fig. 7.6.

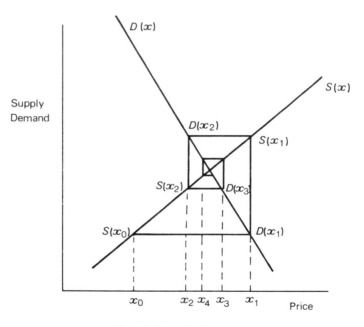

Fig. 7.6 Price development.

Since $S(x_0) = D(x_1)$, $S(x_1) = D(x_2)$, etc., it is easy to construct the 'cobweb' diagram which shows clearly that $x_n \to \alpha$ as n becomes large.

Of course this is a very simplified model, both in the original assumptions and in the assumed form for S and D. The price alternately increases and decreases, which would soon be noticeable to the supplier, who might well then decide to base his supply on the average value of the last two prices, that is, $\frac{1}{2}(x_{n-1} + x_{n-2})$. then, arguing as before,

$$D(x_n) = S(\tfrac{1}{2}(x_{n-1} + x_{n-2}))$$

and

$$D(x_{n+1}) = S(\tfrac{1}{2}(x_n + x_{n-1}))   \text{etc.}$$ (7.30)

We leave this model as an exercise for the reader.

7.4.3 Prices and Inventory

We finish this chapter with an analogous problem to that of the Bedford Brick Company discussed in Chapter 6, except that our model is now discrete rather than continuous. Suppose an industrial company operates a price policy which increases its prices if the value of the inventory, I, at the end of a period, falls below a fixed level, say $\bar{I}$, the increase being proportional to the difference $\bar{I}-I$. Similarly, prices are lowered when $I > \bar{I}$. Is this pricing policy stable?

To analyse the model, let x_k denote the price in period k, and I_k the inventory value at the end of period k, then

$$x_{k+1} - x_k = C(\bar{I} - I_k), \tag{7.31}$$

C being the constant of proportionality. Similarly

$$x_{k+2} - x_{k+1} = C(\bar{I} - I_{k+1})$$

giving

$$x_{k+2} - 2x_{k+1} + x_k = - C(I_{k+1} - I_k). \tag{7.32}$$

Now $(I_{k+1} - I_k)$ is the change in inventory in period $(k+1)$ which will be the difference between supply, S, and demand, D, in that period, that is,

$$I_{k+1} - I_k = S_{k+1} - D_{k+1},$$

so that

$$x_{k+2} - 2x_{k+1} + x_k = - C(S_{k+1} - D_{k+1}). \tag{7.33}$$

As in Sec. 7.4.2, we make the simplest assumptions about S and D, so that

$$S = a(x - \alpha) + \beta$$

$$D = - b(x - \alpha) + \beta.$$

Then (7.32) becomes

$$x_{k+2} - 2x_{k+1} + x_k = - C[(a + b)x_{k+1} - a\alpha - b\alpha]$$

that is,

$$\boxed{x_{k+2} + [C(a + b) - 2]x_{k+1} + x_k = C(a + b)\alpha}. \tag{7.34}$$

We want to know how x_k behaves as $k \to \infty$; that is, does x_k tend to an equilibrium value?

From our theory, the form of the solution is

x_k = 'particular solution' + 'general solution of associated homogeneous equation',
and for a particular solution try $x_k = A$, constant. To satisfy (7.34) we require

$$A[1 + C(a + b) - 2 + 1] = C(a + b)\alpha,$$

that is, $A = \alpha,$

and a particular solution is $x_k = \alpha$ ($k = 1, 2, \ldots$). We now consider the solution of the associated homogeneous equation

$$x_{k+2} + [C(a + b) - 2]x_{k+1} + x_k = 0. \tag{7.35}$$

Looking for solutions of the form $x_k = \lambda^k$, we have

$$\lambda^2 + [C(a + b) - 2]\lambda + 1 = 0,$$

giving

$$\lambda = -\gamma \pm \sqrt{\gamma^2 - 1}$$

where $\gamma = \frac{1}{2}[C(a + b) - 2]$. The actual solutions clearly depend on the value of γ. Now $\gamma = -1 + \frac{1}{2}C(a + b)$ so that $\gamma > -1$. Let us consider the two possibilities.

$1 > \gamma > -1$: In this case the roots are complex.

$$\lambda = -\gamma \pm i\sqrt{1 - \gamma^2}$$
$$= -e^{\pm i\theta}$$

where $\cos \theta = \gamma$. Thus we have the solution

$$x_k = A_1 e^{ki\theta} + A_2 e^{-ki\theta}$$

which we can write as

$$x_k = B_1 \cos(k\theta) + B_2 \sin(k\theta).$$

The complete solution is then

$$\boxed{x_k = B_1 \cos(k\theta) + B_2 \sin(k\theta) + \alpha} \quad (k = 1, 2, \ldots) \tag{7.36}$$

which means that the price oscillates regularly about the equilibrium price α.

$\gamma > 1$: In this case we have two real roots, namely

$$\lambda_1 = -\gamma - \sqrt{\gamma^2 - 1}$$

$$\lambda_2 = -\gamma + \sqrt{\gamma^2 - 1}$$

and the full solution is

$$\boxed{x_k = A_1\lambda_1^k + A_2\lambda_2^k + \alpha} \qquad (k = 1, 2, \ldots) \qquad (7.37)$$

But $\lambda_1 = -\gamma - \sqrt{\gamma^2 - 1} < -\gamma < -1$, and so λ_1^k will increase in magnitude while oscillating, and we have an explosive situation.

Thus for a stable pricing policy, we require $1 > \gamma > -1$ or $0 < \gamma + 1 < 2$, that is, $0 < \frac{1}{2}C(a + b) < 2$. Since C, a, and b are all positive constants, this reduces to

$$C < 4/(a + b). \qquad (7.38)$$

So, provided that the constant of proportionality is less than $4/(a + b)$ the policy is stable.

7.5 PROBLEMS

1. Find the solutions of the following difference equations with the initial conditions as indicated:

   (i) $x_{k+1} - x_k = 2$, $x_0 = 1$;

   (ii) $x_{k+1} + 2x_k - 1 = 0$, $x_0 = 0$;

   (iii) $4x_{k+1} - x_k = 2$, $x_0 = 3$.

2. Determine the general solutions of the following difference equations:

   (i) $x_{k+2} = x_k + x_{k+1}$

   (ii) $x_{k+2} + 2x_{k+1} - 3x_k = 0$

   (iii) $3x_{k+2} + 2x_{k+1} - x_k = 0$.

   In (ii) determine the solution which satisfies $x_0 = 1$, $x_1 = 2$.

3. Determine the general solutions of the following difference equations:

    (i) $4x_k + 4x_{k+1} + x_{k+2} = 0$;

    (ii) $x_{k+2} + 2x_{k+1} + 2x_k = 0$;

    (iii) $x_{k+2} + 3x_{k+1} + 10x_k = 0$.

4. Find the solution of the difference equation

$$x_{k+2} - 4x_{k+1} + 4x_k = 0$$

for which $x_0 = -5$, $x_1 = -1$.

5. Find the solution of the difference equation

$$x_{k+2} + x_{k+1} - 6x_k = 0$$

for which $x_0 = 1$, $x_1 = 2$.

6. Obtain particular solutions of the following difference equations and hence determine the general solution:

    (i) $x_{k+2} - x_{k+1} - 6x_k = k$

    (ii) $x_{k+2} + x_{k+1} + x_k = 2^k k^2$

    (iii) $x_{k+2} + 6x_{k+1} + 9x_k = (-3)^k$

    (iv) $x_{k+2} - x_k = 2$.

7. Determine the complete solutions of the following equations which satisfy $x_0 = 0$ and $x_1 = 1$:

    (i) $x_{k+2} - 9x_k = 1$

    (ii) $4x_{k+2} + 5x_{k+1} + x_k = 4^k$

    (iii) $x_{k+2} - 4x_{k+1} + 3x_k = -1$.

8. Compute the national income of Jedesland as described in Sec. 7.1 by Eq. (7.4), that is,

$$T_k = A(1 + B)T_{k-1} - ABT_{k-2} + 1$$

up to T_{20} when $T_0 = 2$, $T_1 = 3$ and

    (i) $A = 0.5$, $B = 6.0$

    (ii) $A = 0.5$, $B = 0.1$.

Describe the behaviour of the economy in each case. Do these results agree with the conclusions in Sec. 7.3?

9. Investigate solutions of the population model (7.23), that is,

$$N_{k+1} = (1 + a - bN_k)N_k$$

by computing solutions for $N_0 = 1000$, and

(i) $a = 0.5$, $b = 0.0001$

(ii) $a = 1.5$, $b = 0.0001$

(iii) $a = 3.0$, $b = 0.0001$

(iv) $a = 4.0$, $b = 0.0001$.

If N_k tends to a finite value as k increases, show that it must be $(1 + a)/b$.

10. Use the population model in Problem 9 to predict the USA population at ten-yearly intervals given the data

Time	USA population
1890	62.9×10^6
1900	76.0×10^6
1910	92.0×10^6

Compare your predictions with the actual values given in Table 1 on page 147.

11. Extending the cobweb model of supply and demand in Sec. 7.4.2, assume that

$$D(x_n) = S(\tfrac{1}{2}(x_{n-1} + x_{n-2})),$$

and with the forms for S and D as given by (7.26), (7.27), show that the price x_n satisfies

$$2bx_{n+2} + ax_{n+1} + ax_n = 2(a + b)\alpha.$$

Defining $y_n = x_n - \alpha$, show that

$$2y_{n+2} + ky_{n+1} + ky_n = 0, \quad k = a/b.$$

If $0 < k < 2$, show that the price is stable. What happens if $k > 2$?

12. The growth of an insect population in the nth period is k times the growth in the $(n-1)$th period. If x_n denotes the population after n periods, show

that

$$x_n - (1 + k) x_{n-1} + k x_{n-2} = 0 .$$

If $k = 3$, $x_0 = 2$ and $x_1 = 3$, find the population for the first six periods and determine x_n.

13. The response of a person to a drug injected at $t = 0$ depends on the time elapsed and the original dosage. If r_n denotes the reaction after n periods of time, then

$$r_{n+1} = \tfrac{1}{2} r_n + (\tfrac{1}{3})^n .$$

If $r_0 = 1$, find r_n. Evaluate r_5 and r_{10}.

14. The population of a town is such that in each year there would be a 50% increase in numbers with no immigration. If in each year, there is also a loss of 50 members, show that the population x_n satisfies the equation

$$2x_{n+1} - 3x_n = 100 .$$

Determine x_n when the initial population size is 100.

15. Chicken pox is spreading amongst the children of a village. It is estimated that if P_n denotes the probability of at least one new case in the nth week after outbreak, then

$$P_n = P_{n-1} - \tfrac{1}{4} P_{n-2} .$$

If $P_0 = 0$, $P_1 = 1$, find P_n.

16. A whale population is such that if there were no predators, the number of a new generation would be twice the sum of the previous two generations. If 300 of each generation are harvested, show that

$$x_n = 2(x_{n-1} + x_{n-2}) - 300 .$$

If $x_0 = 100$ and $x_1 = 1200$, find x_n.

17. A general model for competing species is given by

$$x_{n+1} = ax_n - by_n$$

$$y_{n+1} = -cx_n + dy_n$$

Show that x_n and y_n both satisfy the difference equation

$$Z_{n+2} - (a + d) Z_{n+1} + (ad - bc) Z_n = 0 .$$

For the special cases

        (i) $a = 3, b = 1, c = 1, d = 3$;

        (ii) $a = 2, b = 1, c = 2, d = 1$,

Solve the equations for x_n and y_n when $x_0 = 200$, $y_0 = 100$. In each case, do either of the species become extinct?

18. Generalise the problem in Problem 17 to the model

$$x_{n+1} = ax_n - by_n$$

$$y_{n+1} = -cx_n + dy_n$$

where a, b, c, and d are positive constants. If initially $x = x_0$, $y = y_0$, under what conditions do either of the species become extinct?

CHAPTER 8

Vectors and Matrices: Linear Models with Several Variables

8.1 THE YUMMY JAM COMPANY

The Yummy Jam Company produces three different varieties of marmalade, namely 'Jelly', 'Medium Yummy', and 'Old British'. At the end of each week the total orders for the three types of marmalade are summed, the required orders are placed for the raw materials, and the required labour is planned.

The main raw materials required are oranges, lemons, and sugar. The quantities in lbs of each required to make 100 jars of each type are summarized below, together with the units (in man hours) of labour required:

	Oranges	Lemons	Sugar	Labour
Jelly	45	5	60	12
Medium Yummy	52	7	50	14
Old British	60	10	40	17

It is important for the management to know not only the required amounts of raw material for the following week but also the cost of these quantities. The evaluation of all these results includes many multiplications and additions, and it is very easy to make errors. A junior manager has suggested that perhaps vectors and matrices will help to simplify the process.

8.2 VECTORS AND MATRICES – PRELIMINARY THEORY

A **matrix** is any rectangular array of numbers arranged in ordered rows and columns. If the rectangular array of numbers has m rows and n columns, it is called an '$m \times n$ matrix', and in general it is denoted by

$$A = \begin{bmatrix} a_{11} & a_{12} & \cdots\cdots & a_{1n} \\ a_{21} & a_{22} & \cdots\cdots & a_{2n} \\ & \cdots\cdots\cdots & \\ a_{m1} & a_{m2} & \cdots\cdots & a_{mn} \end{bmatrix} \tag{8.1}$$

For brevity, we often write, $A = [a_{ij}]$; $i = 1, 2, \ldots m$; $j = 1, 2, \ldots n$. Examples of matrices are

$$\begin{bmatrix} 2 & 1 & 4 \\ -1 & 2 & 3 \end{bmatrix}, \begin{bmatrix} 2 & 1 \\ 6 & -4 \end{bmatrix}, \begin{bmatrix} 3 & 2 & 1 & 4 \end{bmatrix}, \begin{bmatrix} 5 \\ 1 \\ 2 \end{bmatrix}, \begin{bmatrix} -1 & 2 & 5 \\ 2 & -4 & 1 \\ -3 & 1 & 2 \end{bmatrix}$$

The second and fifth matrices are both examples of a **square matrix**, the numbers of rows and columns being equal. The third and fourth illustrate **row vectors** and **column vectors**. Row vectors are matrices with only one row. Column vectors are matrices with only one column.

Having defined what we mean by a matrix, we now begin to develop an algebra for them.

Equality

Two matrices, A and B, are said to be equal if

(i) A and B have the same number of rows (m) and columns (n), that is, they are the same size;

(ii) All the elements of A are equal to the corresponding elements of B, that is, if $A = [a_{ij}]$, $B = [b_{ij}]$, then $a_{ij} = b_{ij}, 1 \leqslant i \leqslant m, 1 \leqslant j \leqslant n$.

Note that, for example, the matrices

$$A = \begin{bmatrix} 1 & 2 \\ 3 & 4 \end{bmatrix}, B = \begin{bmatrix} 1 & 2 & 0 \\ 3 & 4 & 0 \end{bmatrix}$$

are not equal since thay are of different size.

Addition

Matrix addition is defined only for matrices of equal size. If $A = [a_{ij}]$, $B = [b_{ij}]$

are both $m \times n$ matrices, their sum, $C = [c_{ij}]$ is defined by

$$c_{ij} = a_{ij} + b_{ij} \qquad (i = 1,2,\ldots m; \ j = 1,2,\ldots n) \qquad (8.2)$$

For example if

$$A = \begin{bmatrix} 2 & 1 & 4 \\ 3 & -1 & 2 \\ 4 & 5 & 1 \end{bmatrix}, \ B = \begin{bmatrix} 3 & -1 & -4 \\ 2 & 3 & 1 \\ -4 & -5 & 1 \end{bmatrix}, \ A+B = \begin{bmatrix} 5 & 0 & 0 \\ 5 & 2 & 3 \\ 0 & 0 & 2 \end{bmatrix}$$

Multiplication by a Scalar

Given any $m \times n$ matrix $A = [a_{ij}]$ and scalar λ, the product of λ with A is defined by

$$\lambda A = [\lambda a_{ij}],$$

That is, *each* component of the matrix is multiplied in turn by λ. For example, using A above,

$$2A = \begin{bmatrix} 4 & 2 & 8 \\ 6 & -2 & 4 \\ 8 & 10 & 2 \end{bmatrix} (= A + A).$$

We can now define subtraction; for if A and B are both $m \times n$,

$$A - B = A + (-1)B. \qquad (8.3)$$

Again using the example above

$$A - B = \begin{bmatrix} 2 & 1 & 4 \\ 3 & -1 & 2 \\ 4 & 5 & 1 \end{bmatrix} + \begin{bmatrix} -3 & 1 & 4 \\ -2 & -3 & -1 \\ 4 & 5 & -1 \end{bmatrix} = \begin{bmatrix} -1 & 2 & 8 \\ 1 & -4 & 1 \\ 8 & 10 & 0 \end{bmatrix}.$$

Matrix Multiplication

The operation of multiplication on the matrices A and B is defined only when the

'number of columns of A = number of rows of B'.

Thus if $A = [a_{ij}]$ is an $m \times p$ matrix and $B = [b_{jk}]$ is a $p \times n$ matrix, then AB is defined by $C = AB$ where $C = [c_{ik}]$ is an $m \times n$ matrix given by

$$c_{ik} = \sum_{j=1}^{p} a_{ij}b_{jk} \qquad (i = 1,2,...m; \ k = 1,2,...n). \qquad (8.4)$$

This means, for example, that c_{11} is the sum of the products of the elements in the first row of A with the corresponding elements in the first column of B. For example, if

$$A = \begin{bmatrix} a_{11} & a_{12} & a_{13} \\ a_{21} & a_{22} & a_{23} \end{bmatrix}, \qquad B = \begin{bmatrix} b_{11} \\ b_{21} \\ b_{31} \end{bmatrix}$$

then AB is defined (since A is 2×3, B is 3×1) and $C = AB$ is a 2×1 matrix given by

$$C = \begin{bmatrix} a_{11}b_{11} + a_{12}b_{21} + a_{13}b_{31} \\ a_{21}b_{11} + a_{22}b_{21} + a_{23}b_{31} \end{bmatrix}.$$

But BA is not defined, since the number of columns of B is not equal to the number of rows of A. Some numerical examples are now given

(i)
$$A = \begin{bmatrix} 2 & 1 \\ -1 & 3 \end{bmatrix}, \quad B = \begin{bmatrix} 1 & 3 & -1 \\ 2 & 4 & -2 \end{bmatrix}$$

$$AB = \begin{bmatrix} 2 & 1 \\ -1 & 3 \end{bmatrix}\begin{bmatrix} 1 & 3 & -1 \\ 2 & 4 & -2 \end{bmatrix}$$

$$= \begin{bmatrix} 2\times1 + 1\times2 & 2\times3 + 1\times4 & 2\times(-1) + 1\times(-2) \\ (-1)\times1 + 3\times2 & (-1)\times3 + 3\times4 & (-1)\times(-1) + 3\times(-2) \end{bmatrix} = \begin{bmatrix} 4 & 10 & -4 \\ 5 & 9 & -5 \end{bmatrix}.$$

BA is not defined.

(ii) $A = \begin{bmatrix} 3 & 1 & -2 \\ 2 & -1 & 5 \end{bmatrix}, \quad B = \begin{bmatrix} 3 \\ 1 \\ 4 \end{bmatrix}$

$$AB = \begin{bmatrix} 3 & 1 & -2 \\ 2 & -1 & 5 \end{bmatrix} \begin{bmatrix} 3 \\ 1 \\ 4 \end{bmatrix} = \begin{bmatrix} 3\times 3 + & 1\times 1 + (-2)\times 4 \\ 2\times 3 + (-1)\times 1 + & 5\times 4 \end{bmatrix} = \begin{bmatrix} 2 \\ 25 \end{bmatrix}$$

BA is not defined.

(iii)
$$A = \begin{bmatrix} 2 & -3 & 4 \\ 1 & 3 & -2 \end{bmatrix}, \; B = \begin{bmatrix} 1 & -2 \\ 2 & 4 \\ -1 & 5 \end{bmatrix}$$

$$AB = \begin{bmatrix} 2 & -3 & 4 \\ 1 & 3 & -2 \end{bmatrix} \begin{bmatrix} 1 & -2 \\ 2 & 4 \\ -1 & 5 \end{bmatrix}$$

$$= \begin{bmatrix} 2\times 1 + (-3)\times 2 + 4\times(-1) & 2\times(-2) + (-3)\times 4 + 4\times 5 \\ 1\times 1 + 3\times 2 + (-2)\times(-1) & 1\times(-2) + 3\times 4 + (-2)\times 5 \end{bmatrix}$$

$$= \begin{bmatrix} -8 & 4 \\ 9 & 0 \end{bmatrix}.$$

BA is defined and given by

$$BA = \begin{bmatrix} 1 & -2 \\ 2 & 4 \\ -1 & 5 \end{bmatrix} \begin{bmatrix} 2 & -3 & 4 \\ 1 & 3 & -2 \end{bmatrix}$$

$$= \begin{bmatrix} 1\times 2 + (-2)1 & 1\times(-3) + (-2)\times 3 & 1\times 4 + (-2)\times(-2) \\ 2\times 2 + 4\times 1 & 2\times(-3) + 4\times 3 & 2\times 4 + 4\times(-2) \\ (-1)\times 2 + 5\times 1 & (-1)\times(-3) + 5\times 3 & (-1)\times 4 + 5\times(-2) \end{bmatrix}$$

$$= \begin{bmatrix} 0 & -9 & 8 \\ 8 & 6 & 0 \\ 3 & 18 & -14 \end{bmatrix}.$$

As this example shows, $AB \neq BA$.

We finish this section by defining two special matrices

(a) **Zero matrix** of order $m \times n$: matrix all of whose elements are zero. For example, $\begin{bmatrix} 0 & 0 & 0 \\ 0 & 0 & 0 \end{bmatrix}$ is the 2×3 zero matrix, and is usually denoted by 0;

(b) **Unit matrix** of order n : square matrix of order $n \times n$ in which all elements are zero, $a_{ij} = 0$, except when $i = j$, and then $a_{ii} = 1$. It is denoted by I, and for example the 2×2 unit matrix is $\begin{bmatrix} 1 & 0 \\ 0 & 1 \end{bmatrix}.$

8.3   MATRIX REPRESENTATION FOR THE YUMMY JAM COMPANY

We now return to the Yummy Jam's problems. We can clearly represent the raw material inputs and the labour inputs required for the manufacture of the three types of marmalade:

	Oranges	Lemons	Sugar	Labour	
	45	5	60	12	Jelly
$R =$	52	7	50	14	Medium Yummy
	60	10	40	17	Old British

(8.5)

Let the weekly demand be represented by the row vector

$$D = [d_1 \quad d_2 \quad d_3] \tag{8.6}$$

where d_1, d_2, and d_3 are the weekly orders for 100 jar cases of Jelly, Medium Yummy, and Old British respectively. Since D is a 1×3 matrix and R is a 3×4 matrix, the product DR is defined and is a 1×4 matrix. What does it represent? Let us consider one particular week's orders, when the demands are

$$d_1 = 50 \quad d_2 = 30 \quad d_3 = 20.$$

Then

$$DR = [50 \quad 30 \quad 20] \begin{bmatrix} 45 & 5 & 60 & 12 \\ 52 & 7 & 50 & 14 \\ 60 & 10 & 40 & 17 \end{bmatrix}$$

$$= [50 \times 45 + 30 \times 52 + 20 \times 60 \quad 50 \times 5 + 30 \times 7 + 20 \times 10$$

$$50 \times 60 + 30 \times 50 + 20 \times 40 \quad 50 \times 12 + 30 \times 14 + 20 \times 17]$$

$$= [5010 \quad 660 \quad 5300 \quad 1360]$$

The components of this vector are just the total amounts required for oranges, lemons, sugar, and labour; and so the company should buy 5010 lb of oranges, 660 lb of lemons, and 5300 lb of sugar and arrange for 1360 units of labour.

To determine the costs of the required materials we must introduce a price vector

$$P = \begin{bmatrix} 0.08 \\ 0.12 \\ 0.10 \\ 0.55 \end{bmatrix}$$

where 8p is the price of one lb of oranges, 12p for 1 lb of lemons, 10p for 1 lb of sugar, and 55p for one unit of labour. The product RP then gives the direct costs for 100 jars of each type of marmalade; that is,

$$RP = \begin{bmatrix} 45 & 5 & 60 & 12 \\ 52 & 7 & 50 & 14 \\ 60 & 10 & 40 & 17 \end{bmatrix} \begin{bmatrix} 0.88 \\ 0.12 \\ 0.10 \\ 0.55 \end{bmatrix} = \begin{bmatrix} 16.80 \\ 17.70 \\ 19.35 \end{bmatrix}$$

Thus the direct costs of producing 100 jars of 'Jelly' marmalade are £16.80; £17.70 for 'Medium Yummy'; and £19.35 for 'Old British'.

If the individual costs of the inputs are required, then the components of DR must be multiplied by the corresponding prices in P, since the components of DR are the total number of inputs required. Lastly, we can find the total costs of all inputs required to meet the demand by evaluating DRP. That is,

$$DRP = [5010 \quad 660 \quad 5300 \quad 1360] \begin{bmatrix} 0.08 \\ 0.12 \\ 0.10 \\ 0.55 \end{bmatrix}$$

$$= [400.80 + 79.20 + 530.00 + 748.00]$$

$$= [1758].$$

So the total cost of materials and labour for the given week is £1758.

8.4 INPUT-OUTPUT MODELS[†]

Matrix algebra is of particular importance in input-output models for economics and industry. Most industries make products that are either then used in the manufacture of other finished products or have a final use in their own right. Thus the demand for a product can be divided into **interindustry demand** and **autonomous demand**. For example, the total steel output is mainly used for various forms of construction, particularly in the car industry and the railway manufacturing industry. The main inputs to the steel industry come from the iron ore industry, and in the form of services from the railways. We attempt to form a model which depicts these relationships.

Suppose, for example, that in producing £1000 worth of steel, £300 of ore are required, £200 worth of railway services are required, and £100 of steel itself required. In this way we can analyse each industry, and display the results in a matrix form

	Steel	Car	Railways	Ore
Steel	0.1	0.4	0.1	0.1
Car	0	0.1	0.4	0.2
Railways	0.2	0.1	0	0.2
Ore	0.3	0	0	0

For example, for every £1000 worth of output from the car industry, the inputs are £400 from steel, £100 from the car industry itself, and £100 from the railways.

[†]The model is based on an example from Stern (1965).

The $(i,j)^{\text{th}}$ element, that is the element in the ith row and j^{th} column, represents the proportion of the input of the industry in the row i in each £1000 worth of the output of the industry in column j. The expected autonomous demand is 10, 100, 20, and 5 for steel, cars, railways, and ore, but the economists in the steel industry would like to know what the effect would be of, say, an increase of 20% in the final demand of the car industry.

Suppose that, in general, x_s, x_c, x_r, x_o are the total output for each industry. But $\frac{1}{10}$ the output of steel is used by the steel industry itself, and steel also provides $\frac{4}{10}$ of the car industry, and so on. Thus

$$\text{net output of steel} = x_s - (0.1\,x_s + 0.1\,x_r + 0.4\,x_c + 0.1\,x_o).$$

Similarly

$$\text{net car output} = x_c - (0.1\,x_c + 0.4\,x_r + 0.2\,x_o)$$
$$\text{net railway output} = x_r - (0.2\,x_s + 0.1\,x_c + 0.2\,x_o)$$
$$\text{net ore output} = x_o - (0.3\,x_s).$$

The system can be put in matrix form

$$\boxed{(I - A)X = D}$$

$$(8.8)$$

where

$$X = \begin{bmatrix} x_s \\ x_c \\ x_r \\ x_o \end{bmatrix}, \quad D = \begin{bmatrix} d_s \\ d_c \\ d_r \\ d_o \end{bmatrix} \quad \text{is the final demand vector}$$

and

$$A = \begin{bmatrix} 0.1 & 0.4 & 0.1 & 0.1 \\ 0 & 0.1 & 0.4 & 0.2 \\ 0.2 & 0.1 & 0 & 0.2 \\ 0.3 & 0 & 0 & 0 \end{bmatrix} \quad I = \begin{bmatrix} 1 & 0 & 0 & 0 \\ 0 & 1 & 0 & 0 \\ 0 & 0 & 1 & 0 \\ 0 & 0 & 0 & 1 \end{bmatrix}.$$

Writing

$$B = I - A = \begin{bmatrix} 0.9 & -0.4 & -0.1 & -0.1 \\ 0 & 0.9 & -0.4 & -0.2 \\ -0.2 & -0.1 & 1 & -0.2 \\ -0.3 & 0 & 0 & 1 \end{bmatrix}$$

the system of equations can now be written as

$$BX = D.$$ (8.9)

For a specified demand, D, the required output of each industry can be determined by solving this matrix equation for the column vector X. In the next section we shall develop the theory required to solve this problem.

8.5 SYSTEMS OF LINEAR EQUATIONS

Consider a system m linear equations in n unknowns

$$
\begin{array}{l}
a_{11}x_1 + a_{12}x_2 + \ldots\ldots + a_{1n}x_n = b_1 \\[2mm]
a_{21}x_1 + a_{22}x_2 + \ldots\ldots + a_{2n}x_n = b_2 \\[2mm]
a_{m1}x_1 + a_{m2}x_2 + \ldots\ldots + a_{mn}x_n = b_n
\end{array}
$$

which we can write compactly in matrix form

$$AX = B$$ (8.10)

where $A = [a_{ij}]$ is a given $m \times n$ matrix, $B = [b_i]$ is a given column vector, and $X = [x_i]$ is an unknown column vector. The elementary approach to solving for $x_1, x_2, \ldots\ldots x_n$ is to eliminate the unknowns and eventually solve one by one. Sometimes there will be a unique solution, sometimes no solution at all, and at other times an infinity of solutions. We will deal only with the case of equal numbers and equations, that is, $m = n$. [For $m > n$ or $m < n$ the concept of **rank** is required]. In this case A is a square matrix with equal numbers of rows and columns. We first define what is meant by the **inverse** of a square matrix.

Definition
If A and C are $m \times n$ matrices such that

$$AC = CA = I$$

where I is the unit matrix of order n, then C is called the **inverse** of A and written as A^{-1}; that is,

$$AA^{-1} = A^{-1}A = I.$$ (8.11)

Example

If
$$A = \begin{bmatrix} 1 & 2 \\ 1 & 3 \end{bmatrix}, \quad C = \begin{bmatrix} 3 & -2 \\ -1 & 1 \end{bmatrix}, \quad \text{then}$$

$$AC = \begin{bmatrix} 1 & 2 \\ 1 & 3 \end{bmatrix} \begin{bmatrix} 3 & -2 \\ -1 & 1 \end{bmatrix} = \begin{bmatrix} 1 & 0 \\ ^\wedge & 1 \end{bmatrix} = I$$

$$CA = \begin{bmatrix} 3 & -2 \\ -1 & 1 \end{bmatrix} \begin{bmatrix} 1 & 2 \\ 1 & 3 \end{bmatrix} = \begin{bmatrix} 1 & 0 \\ 0 & 1 \end{bmatrix} = I$$

so $C = A^{-1}$.

Returning to our problem of solving (8.10) for X, suppose that A^{-1} exists, then we can multiply (8.10) by A^{-1} to give

$$A^{-1}AX = A^{-1}B$$

$$IX = A^{-1}B$$

that is,

$$\boxed{X = A^{-1}B}.$$

Example

Solve the equations

$$x_1 + 2x_2 = 1$$

$$x_1 + 3x_2 = 3.$$

Solution

We can rewrite the equation in the form $AX = B$ with

$$A = \begin{bmatrix} 1 & 2 \\ 1 & 3 \end{bmatrix}, \quad X = \begin{bmatrix} x_1 \\ x_2 \end{bmatrix}, \quad B = \begin{bmatrix} 1 \\ 3 \end{bmatrix}.$$

Now
$$A^{-1} = \begin{bmatrix} 3 & -2 \\ -1 & 1 \end{bmatrix}$$

so that

$$X = A^{-1}B = \begin{bmatrix} 3 & -2 \\ -1 & 1 \end{bmatrix} \begin{bmatrix} 1 \\ 3 \end{bmatrix} = \begin{bmatrix} -3 \\ 2 \end{bmatrix}$$

that is, $x_1 = -3, \quad x_2 = 2$.

Of course this method works very well if we can find A^{-1}. But as yet we have no method of determining the inverse; in fact we do not even know if it exists!

We will first give one method for evaluating the inverse of a square matrix if it exists. This method starts with writing down the $n \times 2n$ matrix.

$$[A : I] = \begin{bmatrix} a_{11} \, a_{12} \dots a_{1n} & | & 1 & 0 \dots 0 \\ a_{21} a_{22} \dots a_{2n} & | & 0 & 1 \dots 0 \\ \dots\dots\dots & | & \dots\dots\dots \\ a_{n1} a_{n2} \dots a_{nn} & | & 0 & 0 \dots 1 \end{bmatrix}$$

We now perform 'elementary row operations' until this matrix is of the form $[I : B]$, in which case $B = A^{-1}$. By **elementary row operations** we mean
   (i) adding (or subtracting) any multiples of one *row* to any other *row*,
   (ii) multiplying (or dividing) any *row* by a number.
We illustrate the method with this matrix:

$$A = \begin{bmatrix} 2 & 1 & 3 \\ -1 & 2 & 1 \\ 5 & -1 & -3 \end{bmatrix}.$$

Thus we form

$$[A : I] = \begin{bmatrix} 2 & 1 & 3 & | & 1 & 0 & 0 \\ -1 & 2 & 1 & | & 0 & 1 & 0 \\ 5 & -1 & -3 & | & 0 & 0 & 1 \end{bmatrix}.$$

Using R_i to denote row i, we perform the following row operations:

$$R_3 \to R_3 - \tfrac{5}{2} R_1$$
$$R_2 \to R_2 + \tfrac{1}{2} R_1$$

$$\left[\begin{array}{ccc|ccc} 2 & 1 & 3 & 1 & 0 & 0 \\ 0 & \tfrac{5}{2} & \tfrac{5}{2} & \tfrac{1}{2} & 1 & 0 \\ 0 & -\tfrac{7}{2} & -\tfrac{21}{2} & -\tfrac{5}{2} & 0 & 1 \end{array}\right]$$

$$R_3 \to R_3 + \tfrac{7}{5} R_2$$

$$\left[\begin{array}{ccc|ccc} 2 & 1 & 3 & 1 & 0 & 0 \\ 0 & \tfrac{5}{2} & \tfrac{5}{2} & \tfrac{1}{2} & 1 & 0 \\ 0 & 0 & -7 & -\tfrac{9}{5} & \tfrac{7}{5} & 1 \end{array}\right]$$

$$R_3 \to -\tfrac{1}{7} R_3$$

$$\left[\begin{array}{ccc|ccc} 2 & 1 & 3 & 1 & 0 & 0 \\ 0 & \tfrac{5}{2} & \tfrac{5}{2} & \tfrac{1}{2} & 1 & 0 \\ 0 & 0 & 1 & \tfrac{9}{35} & -\tfrac{1}{5} & -\tfrac{1}{7} \end{array}\right]$$

$$R_2 \to R_2 - \tfrac{5}{2} R_3$$
$$R_1 \to R_1 - 3 R_3$$

$$\left[\begin{array}{ccc|ccc} 2 & 1 & 0 & \tfrac{8}{35} & \tfrac{3}{5} & \tfrac{3}{7} \\ 0 & \tfrac{5}{2} & 0 & -\tfrac{1}{7} & \tfrac{3}{2} & \tfrac{5}{14} \\ 0 & 0 & 1 & \tfrac{9}{35} & -\tfrac{1}{5} & -\tfrac{1}{7} \end{array}\right]$$

$$R_2 \to \tfrac{2}{5} R_2$$

$$\left[\begin{array}{ccc|ccc} 2 & 1 & 0 & \tfrac{8}{35} & \tfrac{3}{5} & \tfrac{3}{7} \\ 0 & 1 & 0 & -\tfrac{2}{35} & \tfrac{3}{5} & \tfrac{1}{7} \\ 0 & 0 & 1 & \tfrac{9}{35} & -\tfrac{1}{5} & -\tfrac{1}{7} \end{array}\right]$$

$$R_1 \to R_1 - R_2$$

$$\left[\begin{array}{ccc|ccc} 2 & 0 & 0 & \tfrac{2}{7} & 0 & \tfrac{2}{7} \\ 0 & 1 & 0 & -\tfrac{2}{35} & \tfrac{3}{5} & \tfrac{1}{7} \\ 0 & 0 & 1 & \tfrac{9}{35} & -\tfrac{1}{5} & -\tfrac{1}{7} \end{array}\right]$$

$$R_1 \to \tfrac{1}{2} R_1$$

$$\left[\begin{array}{ccc|ccc} 1 & 0 & 0 & \tfrac{1}{7} & 0 & \tfrac{1}{7} \\ 0 & 1 & 0 & -\tfrac{2}{35} & \tfrac{3}{5} & \tfrac{1}{7} \\ 0 & 0 & 1 & \tfrac{9}{35} & -\tfrac{1}{5} & -\tfrac{1}{7} \end{array}\right]$$

and we see that the inverse of A is given by:

$$A^{-1} = \begin{bmatrix} \frac{1}{7} & 0 & \frac{1}{7} \\ -\frac{2}{35} & \frac{3}{5} & \frac{1}{7} \\ \frac{9}{35} & -\frac{1}{5} & -\frac{1}{7} \end{bmatrix} .$$

We now have a technique for finding the inverse of a square matrix. We next need to know if it exists before we start applying the method. To answer this question we use the concept of a **determinant** of a square matrix.

A determinant is a *number* which is evaluated by a given set of rules from the elements of a square matrix. The determinant of a square matrix of order 2

$$A = \begin{bmatrix} a_{11} & a_{12} \\ a_{21} & a_{22} \end{bmatrix}$$

is defined by

$$D = \begin{vmatrix} a_{11} & a_{12} \\ a_{21} & a_{22} \end{vmatrix} = a_{11}a_{22} - a_{12}a_{21}. \tag{8.12}$$

We sometimes use $|A|$ to denote the determinant of a square matrix A. Note that vertical lines about the matrix elements denote the determinant of the matrix.

If $A = [a_{ij}]$ is a 3×3 square matrix its determinant is given by

$$D = \begin{vmatrix} a_{11} & a_{12} & a_{13} \\ a_{21} & a_{22} & a_{23} \\ a_{31} & a_{32} & a_{33} \end{vmatrix}$$

$$= a_{11} \begin{vmatrix} a_{22} & a_{23} \\ a_{32} & a_{33} \end{vmatrix} - a_{12} \begin{vmatrix} a_{21} & a_{23} \\ a_{31} & a_{33} \end{vmatrix} + a_{13} \begin{vmatrix} a_{21} & a_{22} \\ a_{31} & a_{32} \end{vmatrix}$$

$$- a_{11}(a_{22}a_{33} - a_{23}a_{32}) - a_{12}(a_{21}a_{33} - a_{23}a_{31})$$
$$+ a_{13}(a_{21}a_{32} \quad a_{22}a_{31})$$

$$= a_{11}a_{22}a_{33} - a_{11}a_{23}a_{32} - a_{12}a_{21}a_{33}$$
$$+ a_{12}a_{23}a_{31} + a_{13}a_{21}a_{32} - a_{13}a_{22}a_{31}. \tag{8.13}$$

For example,

$$
\begin{vmatrix}
2 & 1 & 3 \\
-1 & 2 & 1 \\
5 & -1 & -3
\end{vmatrix}
$$

$$= 2[2\times(-3)-1\times(-1)]-1[(-1)\times(-3)-1\times5]+3[(-1)\times(-1)-2\times5]$$

$$= 2(-5)-(-2)+3(-9)$$

$$= -10+2-27$$

$$= -35.$$

Determinants of higher order are introduced in a similar way. For example, if

$$
A = \begin{bmatrix}
2 & 1 & 0 & 1 \\
3 & 0 & 0 & 0 \\
-1 & 2 & 1 & 4 \\
3 & 0 & 2 & 1
\end{bmatrix}
$$

then

$$
|A| = 2\begin{vmatrix} 0 & 0 & 0 \\ 2 & 1 & 4 \\ 0 & 2 & 1 \end{vmatrix} -1\begin{vmatrix} 3 & 0 & 0 \\ -1 & 1 & 4 \\ 3 & 2 & 1 \end{vmatrix} +0\begin{vmatrix} 3 & 0 & 0 \\ -1 & 2 & 4 \\ 3 & 0 & 1 \end{vmatrix}
$$

$$
-1\begin{vmatrix} 3 & 0 & 0 \\ -1 & 2 & 1 \\ 3 & 0 & 2 \end{vmatrix}
$$

$$
= 0 -1 \{3\begin{vmatrix} 1 & 4 \\ 2 & 1 \end{vmatrix} -0 + 0\} +0 -1 \{3\begin{vmatrix} 2 & 1 \\ 0 & 2 \end{vmatrix} -0 +0\}
$$

$$
= -3(1\times1-4\times2)-3(2\times2-1\times0)=21-12=9.
$$

That is, you multiply each element of the top row by the determinant formed by eliminating the row and column through that element. The terms are then added by taking 'plus' the first term, 'minus' the second term, and so on.

The important result is the following theorem.

Theorem
If A is a square matrix, then A^{-1} exists if and only if $|A| \neq 0$. The proof of this theorem, although not difficult, does require further concepts and analysis. We refer the reader to Read (1972) for a full explanation.

Example
If
$$A = \begin{bmatrix} 2 & 1 & 5 \\ 4 & 2 & 10 \\ 3 & 3 & 1 \end{bmatrix},$$
does A^{-1} exist?

Solution
$$|A| = \begin{vmatrix} 2 & 1 & 5 \\ 4 & 2 & 10 \\ 3 & 3 & 1 \end{vmatrix} = 2(2 \times 1 - 3 \times 10) - 1(4 \times 1 - 3 \times 10) + 5(4 \times 3 - 2 \times 3)$$
$$= 2(-28) - 1(-26) + 5(6) = 0.$$

So A^{-1} does not exist.

Definition
We say that the square matrix A is singular if $|A| = 0$, and non-singular if $A \neq 0$. Hence the inverse of a square matrix exists if A is non-singular.

It is also possible to use determinants to calculate the inverse of an $n \times n$ matrix via the formula

$$A^{-1} = \frac{1}{|A|} \text{ adj } A$$

where adj A is another $n \times n$ matrix whose elements are defined from the elements of A. This method is more cumbersome to use and computationally less efficient than the $[A \vdots I]$ method given earlier.

It is also fair to say that many practitioners do not calculate $|A|$ to check that A^{-1} exists before using the $[A \vdots I]$ method. In many cases the work involved in computing $|A|$ is almost as great as in applying the $[A \vdots I]$ method. If A^{-1} fails to exist, this will soon become apparent by the appearance of a row of zeros in the left-hand $n \times n$ submatrix.

We finish this section by solving homogeneous equations of the form

$$\boxed{AX = 0.}$$

(8.14)

Again we are taking $n = m$. If A is non-singular, that is $|A| \neq 0$, then A^{-1} exists, and so

$$A^{-1}AX = 0 \Rightarrow IX = 0 \Rightarrow X = 0.$$

In this case the only solution is the trivial one $X = 0$. If $|A| = 0$, then there will be non-trivial solutions.

Example

Solve the set of equations

$$x_1 + 2x_2 + 3x_3 = 0$$

$$x_1 + x_3 \qquad = 0$$

$$x_1 + x_2 + 2x_3 = 0.$$

Solution

Here

$$A = \begin{bmatrix} 1 & 2 & 3 \\ 1 & 0 & 1 \\ 1 & 1 & 2 \end{bmatrix}$$

and $|A| = 1(0 \times 2 - 1 \times 1) - 2(1 \times 2 - 1 \times 1) + 3(1 \times 1 - 0 \times 1)$

$$= -1 - 1 + 3 = 0.$$

So A^{-1} does not exist, and we expect non-trivial solutions. Using the second equation in the first and third gives

$$-2x_1 + 2x_2 = 0$$

$$-x_1 + x_2 = 0.$$

That is, the equations are identical, and so we have $x_1 = x_2$. Thus if x_1 takes the value, say λ, then $x_2 = \lambda$ and $x_3 = -\lambda$. Hence the general solution is

$$x_1 = \lambda, \quad x_2 = \lambda, \quad x_3 = -\lambda,$$

where λ can take any real value. Note that we have an infinity of solutions.

8.6 INPUT-OUTPUT SOLUTION

We are now in a position to return to the input-output model, where we have to solve

$$BX = D \qquad (8.15)$$

for X. Provided that $|B| \neq 0$, we can formally write the solution as

$$X = B^{-1}D. \qquad (8.16)$$

So we must find the inverse of a 4×4 matrix. We can use the method introduced in Sec. 8.5, but for a 4×4 matrix it involves a considerable amount of algebra. So for simplicity we quote the answer, namely

$$B^{-1} = \begin{bmatrix} 1.31 & 0.62 & 0.38 & 0.33 \\ 0.25 & 1.28 & 0.54 & 0.39 \\ 0.36 & 0.29 & 1.15 & 0.32 \\ 0.39 & 0.19 & 0.11 & 1.10 \end{bmatrix}.$$

If the demand vector is

$$D = \begin{bmatrix} d_s \\ d_c \\ d_r \\ d_o \end{bmatrix},$$

then, for example, the output of steel is given by the first component of $B^{-1}D$, which is

$$x_s = (1.31)d_s + (0.62)d_c + (0.38)d_r + (0.33)d_o$$

Suppose that we have a final demand vector

$$D_1 = \begin{bmatrix} 10 \\ 100 \\ 20 \\ 5 \end{bmatrix}$$

then

$$x_s = 84.35 .$$

It is easy to see the effect of, say, a 10% increase in the final demand for cars. For then

$$D_2 := \begin{bmatrix} 10 \\ 110 \\ 20 \\ 5 \end{bmatrix} = D_1 + \begin{bmatrix} 0 \\ 10 \\ 0 \\ 0 \end{bmatrix}$$

giving

$$x_s = 84.35 + (0.62)10 .$$

That is, the increase is 6.2, and so the percentage increase in steel output for a 10% increase in car demand is $(6.2/84.35) \times 100 = 7.4\%$.

8.7 CASE STUDIES

8.7.1 Co-existence of Bacteria

Three species of bacteria are present in a test tube and fed on three different resources. Denote by C_{ij} the average amount of the ith resource consumed per day by the jth bacteria.

So $C_j = \begin{bmatrix} C_{1j} \\ C_{2j} \\ C_{3j} \end{bmatrix}$ is the consumption vector for the ith species.

For example, suppose that

$$C_1 = \begin{bmatrix} 1 \\ 2 \\ 2 \end{bmatrix}, \quad C_2 = \begin{bmatrix} 3 \\ 2 \\ 1 \end{bmatrix}, \quad C_3 = \begin{bmatrix} 8 \\ 4 \\ 1 \end{bmatrix} ;$$

and that there are 2750 units of the first resource given each day, 1500 units of the second resource, and 500 units of the third resource. Assuming that all the resources are consumed each day, what populations of the three bacteria can coexist in the test tube?

Let x_i ($i = 1, 2, 3$) denote that population of the ith species. For the first resource, equating consumption per day we must have

$$x_1 + 3x_2 + 8x_3 = 2750 .$$

Similarly for the second and third resource, we must have

$$2x_1 + 2x_2 + 4x_3 = 1500$$

$$2x_1 + x_2 + x_3 = 500 .$$

and in matrix form

$$CX = R,$$

$$\text{where } C = [C_{ij}], \quad X = \begin{bmatrix} x_1 \\ x_2 \\ x_3 \end{bmatrix} \quad R = \begin{bmatrix} 10000 \\ 20000 \\ 30000 \end{bmatrix} .$$

Now for the inverse of C to exist, we must have $|C| \neq 0$.
But

$$|C| = \begin{vmatrix} 1 & 3 & 8 \\ 2 & 2 & 4 \\ 2 & 1 & 1 \end{vmatrix} = 1\,(2-4) - 3\,(2-8) + 8\,(2-4) = 0 .$$

So C does not have an inverse, and there is *not* a unique solution for X.

We can, though, find the solution. Taking the third equation from the second gives

$$x_2 = 1000 - 3x_3$$

and from the first,

$$x_1 = x_3 - 250 .$$

Thus provided $250 < x_3 < 100/3$, we have positive solutions for x_1, x_2 and x_3.

8.7.2 Production Explosion

A manufacturer sells five products, denoted by A, B, C, D, and E. Products B and E are manufactured directly from the raw material, whereas A requires $4B$ parts and $1C$ part for its manufacture, C requires $2B$ parts and $3E$ parts, and D requires $6A$ parts, $2C$ parts, and $1E$ part. The required demand for

$$16A, \ 3C, \ 5D \text{ and } 6E,$$

so the manufacturer needs to know the raw material requirements, the total numbers of each product to be manufactured, and the total cost of production. We can 'explode' the production process graphically as shown below. In the first explosion, each part is exploded into its subparts; for example, A is exploded to $4B$ and $1C$. We continue in this way as illustrated in the table below.

Explosion level

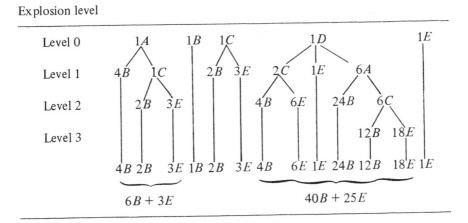

	Level 0	Level 1	Level 2	Level 3

The usual terminology is to call

B,E - parts

C - first level assembly, since it requires only parts

A - second level assembly, since it requires a first level assembly

D - third level assembly, since it requires a second level assembly.

The explosion process is the reverse of the assembly process. The last line indicates the B and E requirements for the manufacture of each product. Hence, for the specified demand, the B and E requirements are

$$16(6B + 3E) + 3(2B + 3E) + 5(40B + 25E) + 6E$$

$$= 302B + 188E.$$

So we have a straightforward graphical method of solution, but we can also use matrix methods to develop an elegant method of solution. We first write the input requirements in the table below:

	A	B	C	D	E
A			6		
B	4		2		
C	1			2	
D					
E			3	1	

The columns represent the requirements to assemble each product. From this array we can define the assembly matrix N:

$$N = \begin{bmatrix} 0 & 0 & 0 & 6 & 0 \\ 4 & 0 & 2 & 0 & 0 \\ 1 & 0 & 0 & 2 & 0 \\ 0 & 0 & 0 & 0 & 0 \\ 0 & 0 & 3 & 1 & 0 \end{bmatrix}$$

where $N = [n_{ij}]$ and $n_{ij} =$ number of i assemblies required to produce one j assembly $(i, j = A, B, C, D, E,)$. The assembly matrix N represents the first explosion process (level 1) since it is just the requirements to assemble one of each assembly.

We now turn to level 2 and consider the matrix NN:

$$NN = \begin{bmatrix} 0 & 0 & 0 & 6 & 0 \\ 4 & 0 & 2 & 0 & 0 \\ 1 & 0 & 0 & 2 & 0 \\ 0 & 0 & 0 & 0 & 0 \\ 0 & 0 & 3 & 1 & 0 \end{bmatrix} \begin{bmatrix} 0 & 0 & 0 & 6 & 0 \\ 4 & 0 & 2 & 0 & 0 \\ 1 & 0 & 0 & 2 & 0 \\ 0 & 0 & 0 & 0 & 0 \\ 0 & 0 & 3 & 1 & 0 \end{bmatrix} = \begin{bmatrix} 0 & 0 & 0 & 0 & 0 \\ 2 & 0 & 0 & 28 & 0 \\ 0 & 0 & 0 & 6 & 0 \\ 0 & 0 & 0 & 0 & 0 \\ 3 & 0 & 0 & 6 & 0 \end{bmatrix}$$

and we see that this matrix does indeed represent the level 2 requirements. For example, in column 1, $2B$ and $3C$ are required for A. Similarly level 3 is represented by N^3:

$$\begin{aligned} N^3 = \\ N(N^2) = \end{aligned} \begin{bmatrix} 0 & 0 & 0 & 6 & 0 \\ 4 & 0 & 2 & 0 & 0 \\ 1 & 0 & 0 & 2 & 0 \\ 0 & 0 & 0 & 0 & 0 \\ 0 & 0 & 3 & 1 & 0 \end{bmatrix} \begin{bmatrix} 0 & 0 & 0 & 0 & 0 \\ 2 & 0 & 0 & 28 & 0 \\ 0 & 0 & 0 & 6 & 0 \\ 0 & 0 & 0 & 0 & 0 \\ 3 & 0 & 0 & 6 & 0 \end{bmatrix} = \begin{bmatrix} 0 & 0 & 0 & 0 & 0 \\ 0 & 0 & 0 & 12 & 0 \\ 0 & 0 & 0 & 0 & 0 \\ 0 & 0 & 0 & 0 & 0 \\ 0 & 0 & 0 & 18 & 0 \end{bmatrix}$$

for at level 3 we just require $12B$ and $18E$ for the construction of $1D$ at level 0.

Since at level 4, there are no assemblies, we would expect N^4 to be the zero matrix, all of whose elements are zero. It is as well to check this:

$$N^4 = N(N^3) = \begin{bmatrix} 0 & 0 & 0 & 6 & 0 \\ 4 & 0 & 2 & 0 & 0 \\ 1 & 0 & 0 & 2 & 0 \\ 0 & 0 & 0 & 0 & 0 \\ 0 & 0 & 3 & 1 & 0 \end{bmatrix} \begin{bmatrix} 0 & 0 & 0 & 0 & 0 \\ 0 & 0 & 0 & 12 & 0 \\ 0 & 0 & 0 & 0 & 0 \\ 0 & 0 & 0 & 0 & 0 \\ 0 & 0 & 0 & 18 & 0 \end{bmatrix} = \begin{bmatrix} 0 & 0 & 0 & 0 & 0 \\ 0 & 0 & 0 & 0 & 0 \\ 0 & 0 & 0 & 0 & 0 \\ 0 & 0 & 0 & 0 & 0 \\ 0 & 0 & 0 & 0 & 0 \end{bmatrix} = 0$$

The total requirement matrix, T, is the sum of the requirements at each level of explosion; at level 0 the assembly matrix is I; the unit matrix

$$I = \begin{bmatrix} 1 & 0 & 0 & 0 & 0 \\ 0 & 1 & 0 & 0 & 0 \\ 0 & 0 & 1 & 0 & 0 \\ 0 & 0 & 0 & 1 & 0 \\ 0 & 0 & 0 & 0 & 1 \end{bmatrix}$$

for an ith assembly, or part, must be assembled to 'produce' one i^{th} assembly or part;

so that

$$T = I + N + N^2 + N^3$$

$$= \begin{bmatrix} 1 & 0 & 0 & 6 & 0 \\ 6 & 1 & 2 & 40 & 0 \\ 1 & 0 & 1 & 8 & 0 \\ 0 & 0 & 0 & 1 & 0 \\ 3 & 0 & 3 & 25 & 1 \end{bmatrix}$$

An element t_{ij} of the matrix gives the *total* number of ith assemblies or parts needed to produce one j^{th} assembly or part; for example, the elements of the fourth column excluding the fourth, are just the requirements needed at all levels to produce $1D$.

We can readily compute the production requirements by defining the demand vector

$$S = \begin{bmatrix} 16 \\ 0 \\ 3 \\ 5 \\ 6 \end{bmatrix}$$

The total production requirement is given by the product

$$X = TS = \begin{bmatrix} 1 & 0 & 0 & 6 & 0 \\ 6 & 1 & 2 & 40 & 0 \\ 1 & 0 & 1 & 8 & 0 \\ 0 & 0 & 0 & 1 & 0 \\ 3 & 0 & 3 & 25 & 1 \end{bmatrix} \begin{bmatrix} 16 \\ 0 \\ 3 \\ 5 \\ 6 \end{bmatrix} = \begin{bmatrix} 46 \\ 302 \\ 59 \\ 5 \\ 188 \end{bmatrix}$$

which shows that $302B$ and $188E$ are required, and to meet the demand $46A$, $59C$, and $5D$ must be produced.

We can also readily determine the total costs, for if

C_A = cost of assembling $1A$ from Bs and already assembled C,
C_B = cost of producing $1B$ from raw material, etc.,

we can define the assembly cost vector

$$C = [C_A \ C_B \ C_C \ C_D \ C_E],$$

and the total cost will be given by

$$CX = C(TS)$$

together with the raw material cost.

Clearly this matrix method generalises to more complicated processes. In general the total production requirement will be given by TS, where

$$T = I + N + \ldots\ldots + N^k$$

and $N^{k+1} = 0$, and N is the assembly matrix. A different method of computing is to note that

$$T(I-N) = (I + N + \ldots\ldots + N^k)(I-N)$$
$$= I - N^{k+1}$$
$$= I, \text{ since } N^{k+1} = 0;$$

so that $T = (I-N)^{-1}$.

8.7.3 Discrete Population Model with an Age Distribution

For accurate predictions of the future population of a species with a varying age distribution, we need to know the birth and death rates for different age groups. Taking for example one year as the unit of time, we define

$N_i(t) =$ number of individuals i years old $(0 \leqslant i \leqslant M)$ where M is the greatest age at which there is an appreciable population.

Also define

$b_i =$ birth rate of the population i years old
$d_i =$ death rate of the population i years old.

The difference equations describing the population change over one year are now

$$N_0(t+1) = b_0 N_0(t) + b_1 N_1(t) + \ldots\ldots + b_m N_m(t)$$

$$N_1(t+1) = (1-d_0)N_0(t)$$

$$\ldots\ldots\ldots\ldots\ldots\ldots\ldots$$

$$N_m(t+1) = (1-d_{m-1})N_{m-1}(t).$$

Knowing all the birth and death rates and initial population distribution we have sufficient information to predict the future population, assuming birth and death rates remain constant over the period in question. This method is used by planners in assessing the need for construction of schools, hospitals, and general welfare facilities.

Matrix methods have been used to simplify the calculations. We first define the population vector

$$N(t) = \begin{bmatrix} N_0(t) \\ N_1(t) \\ \vdots \\ N_m(t) \end{bmatrix}$$

so that the equations can be written as

$$\boxed{N(t + 1) = AN(t)}$$

where A is the $(m+1) \times (m+1)$ matrix

$$A = \begin{bmatrix} b_0 & b_1 & b_2 \ldots \ldots b_{m-1} & b_m \\ (1-d_0) & 0 & 0 \ldots \ldots 0 & 0 \\ 0 & (1-d_1) & 0 \ldots \ldots 0 & 0 \\ 0 & 0 & (1-d_2) \ldots 0 & 0 \\ 0 & 0 & 0 \ldots (1-d_{m-1}) & 0 \end{bmatrix}.$$

Repeated applications of the difference equations give

$$N(t + 2) = AN(t+1) = A[AN(t)] = A^2 N(t)$$

and in general

$$N(t + k) = A^k N(t)$$

and so the predicted population m time intervals later can be readily calculated.

The yearly age distribution is of course arbitrary. For a human population, it might be more appropriate to divide the population into just three groups:

N_1 0 - 14
N_2 15 - 40
N_3 more than 40.

We assume that we know the average birth and death rates for each group (that is, b_1, b_2, b_3 and d_1, d_2, d_3). The population in group 1 after one year consists of the number born plus the numbers who have survived in group 1 but not advanced to group 2. Assuming an even distribution in the first age group this number is estimated by $\frac{14}{15}(1-d_1)\,N_1$. Thus

$$N_1(t+1) = b_1 N_1(t) + b_2 N_2(t) + b_3 N_3(t) + \frac{14}{15}(1-d_1)N_1$$

and similarly

$$N_2(t+1) = \frac{1}{15}(1-d_1)N_1(t) + \frac{24}{25}(1-d_2)N_2(t)$$

$$N_3(t+1) = \frac{1}{25}(1-d_2)N_2(t) + (1-d_3)N_3(t).$$

As before we can define the population matrix

$$N(t) = \begin{bmatrix} N_1(t) \\ N_2(t) \\ N_3(t) \end{bmatrix} \text{ so that } N(t+1) = \begin{bmatrix} b_1 + \frac{14}{15}(1-d_1) & b_2 & b_3 \\ \frac{1}{15}(1-d_1) & \frac{24}{25}(1-d_2) & 0 \\ 0 & \frac{1}{25}(1-d_2) & (1-d_3) \end{bmatrix} N(t)$$

that is,

$$\boxed{N(t+1) = AN(t)}$$

and after repeated applications,

$$N(t+m) = A^m N(t).$$

As a specific example, take

$$b_1 = 0, \quad b_2 = 0.01, \quad b_3 = 0$$

$$d_1 = 0.002, \quad d_2 = 0.001, \quad d_3 = 0.005,$$

then

$$A = \begin{bmatrix} 0.931 & 0.010 & 0.000 \\ 0.067 & 0.954 & 0.000 \\ 0.000 & 0.040 & 0.995 \end{bmatrix}$$

If at, say, $t = 0$,

$$N = \begin{bmatrix} 1000 \\ 2000 \\ 1000 \end{bmatrix}$$

then

$$N(1) = A \begin{bmatrix} 1000 \\ 2000 \\ 1000 \end{bmatrix} = \begin{bmatrix} 951 \\ 1985 \\ 1075 \end{bmatrix}$$

and similarly

$$N(2) = A \begin{bmatrix} 951 \\ 1985 \\ 1075 \end{bmatrix} = \begin{bmatrix} 858 \\ 1968 \\ 1149 \end{bmatrix} .$$

We can continue in this to predict the future age distribution. For the parameters used it is clear that both the first and second groups are showing overall decreases, particularly the first group, whereas the third group is showing a significant increase.

8.8 PROBLEMS

1. if

$$A = \begin{bmatrix} 1 & 2 \\ 6 & 4 \end{bmatrix} \quad B = \begin{bmatrix} 3 & 1 \\ 2 & 1 \end{bmatrix} \quad C = \begin{bmatrix} 1 \\ -1 \end{bmatrix}$$

determine

      (i) AB
     (ii) BA
   (iii) AC
   (iv) BC

and verify that $(A+B)C = AC + BC$.

2. Repeat Problem 1 when

$$A = \begin{bmatrix} 1 & 2 & 3 \\ 0 & 1 & 1 \\ 0 & 0 & -1 \end{bmatrix} \quad B = \begin{bmatrix} 1 & -1 & -1 \\ 0 & 1 & -1 \\ 0 & 0 & 1 \end{bmatrix} \quad C = \begin{bmatrix} 3 \\ 2 \\ 1 \end{bmatrix}.$$

3. If $A = \begin{bmatrix} 1 & 1 \\ -1 & 1 \end{bmatrix}$, calculate A^2, A^3, and A^4.

4. Verify that $AB = 0$ where

$$A = \begin{bmatrix} 1 & 2 & 0 \\ 1 & 1 & 0 \\ -1 & 4 & 0 \end{bmatrix}, \quad B = \begin{bmatrix} 0 & 0 & 0 \\ 0 & 0 & 0 \\ 1 & 4 & 9 \end{bmatrix}.$$

5. Verify that $AB = AC$ even though $B \neq C$ where

$$A = \begin{bmatrix} 1 & 2 & 0 \\ 1 & 1 & 0 \\ 1 & 4 & 0 \end{bmatrix} \quad B = \begin{bmatrix} 2 & 2 & 3 \\ 2 & 1 & -1 \\ 2 & 1 & 2 \end{bmatrix} \quad C = \begin{bmatrix} 2 & 2 & 3 \\ 2 & 1 & -1 \\ 1 & 3 & 1 \end{bmatrix}.$$

6. Referring to the Yummy Jam Company problem described in Sec. 8.1, if the weekly demand is given by

$$D = [d_1 \quad d_2 \quad d_3]$$

determine a general expression for the inputs required to meet this demand and also the total weekly cost.

Evaluate these expressions when

(i) $d_1 = 40 \quad d_2 = 40 \quad d_3 = 20$
(ii) $d_1 = 60 \quad d_2 = 30 \quad d_3 = 10.$

7. Verify that if

(i) $A = \begin{bmatrix} 4 & 1 \\ 6 & 2 \end{bmatrix}$, then $A^{-1} = \begin{bmatrix} 1 & -\frac{1}{2} \\ -3 & 2 \end{bmatrix}$

(ii)

$$A = \begin{bmatrix} 2 & 0 & 4 \\ 2 & 1 & 0 \\ 3 & 1 & 3 \end{bmatrix}, \quad \text{then } A^{-1} = \begin{bmatrix} 3/2 & 2 & -2 \\ -3 & -3 & 4 \\ -1/2 & -1 & 1 \end{bmatrix}.$$

8. Determine the inverse of the following matrices:

(i) $\begin{bmatrix} 1 & 3 \\ 3 & 5 \end{bmatrix}$ (ii) $\begin{bmatrix} 1 & 1 & 5 \\ 0 & 9 & -7 \\ 1 & 6 & 1 \end{bmatrix}$ (iii) $\begin{bmatrix} 1 & 1 & 1 \\ 3 & -1 & 11 \\ 2 & 1 & 4 \end{bmatrix}.$

9. Show that the matrix $A = \begin{bmatrix} a & b \\ c & d \end{bmatrix}$ has

inverse $A^{-1} = \begin{bmatrix} d/A & -b/A \\ -c/A & a/A \end{bmatrix}.$

10. Calculate the inverse of the following matrices (if they exist);

(i) $\begin{bmatrix} 4 & 6 & -3 \\ 0 & 0 & 7 \\ 0 & 0 & 5 \end{bmatrix}$ (ii) $\begin{bmatrix} 1 & 0 & 0 \\ 0 & 5 & 6 \\ 0 & 0 & 2 \end{bmatrix}.$

11. By calculating inverses solve the following systems of equations:

(i) $4x_1 + 2x_2 = 1$
$x_1 + 6x_2 = 2,$

(ii) $2x_1 - x_2 = 2$
$\frac{1}{2}x_1 + 2x_2 - x_3 = 0$
$-x_2 + 2x_3 = 4,$

(iii) $x_1 + x_2 + x_3 = 6$
$x_1 + x_2 - x_3 = 0$
$x_1 + 2x_2 - x_3 = -1.$

12. Evaluate the determinants of the following matrices

(i) $\begin{bmatrix} 1 & 4 \\ 4 & 2 \end{bmatrix}$ (ii) $\begin{bmatrix} 0 & 4 & 7 \\ -1 & 3 & 1 \\ 2 & -2 & 5 \end{bmatrix}$ (iii) $\begin{bmatrix} 1 & 1 & 1 \\ 2 & 3 & 4 \\ 4 & 9 & 16 \end{bmatrix}$.

13. Show that the system of equations

$$x_1 - x_2 + x_3 = 0$$
$$2x_1 + 2x_2 + x_3 = 0$$
$$5x_1 + 7x_2 + 2x_3 = 0$$

has non-trivial solutions, and determine them.

14. In the production of three commodities, x_1, x_2 and x_3, none of each commodity is used in the production of itself, but 1/3 unit of each is used for the production of each other. Using the input–output model of sec. 8.4 determine the output required to meet a demand of 80, 160 and 240 units of x_1, x_2 and x_3 respectively.

15. Referring to Sec. 8.7.1, suppose that

$$C_1 = [1 \quad 1 \quad 1]; \quad C_2 = [1 \quad 2 \quad 3]; \quad C_3 = [1 \quad 2 \quad 5]$$

and that 10 000, 20 000 and 50 000 units of the three foods are supplied each day to the test tube. If all resources are consumed, what populations of the three species can coexist in the environment?

16. A manufacturer produces 7 products, A_1, A_2 .... A_7; these products are made up as follows

> A_1 requires 3 A_2, 2 A_6 and 1 A_3
> A_2 requires only raw material
> A_3 requires 1 A_7 and 2 A_6
> A_4 requires 3 A_6, 1 A_2 and 3 A_3
> A_5 requires 1 A_3 and 1 A_6
> A_6 requires 1 A_2 and 3 A_7
> A_7 requires only raw material.

Compute the requirement matrix and use it to compute the requirements to meet a sales forecast which calls for:

$$15A_1, 1A_2, 0A_3, 6A_4, 1A_5, 7A_6, 0A_7.$$

Verify your results by a graphical explosion, and also verify that the assembly matrix N and the requirements matrix T satisfy the relation

$$T = (I - N)^{-1}.$$

17. The costs of manufacturing washing machines at two plants are given by:

	Plant I	Plant II
Direct labour	2	4
Materials	1	2
Indirect labour	3	1

and the costs of manufacturing driers are:

	Plant I	Plant II
Direct labour	3	5
Materials	2	2
Indirect labour	4	2

The production rates for the two types at the plants are:

	Plant I	Plant II
Number of washing machines	1000	500
Number of driers	6000	7000

Define appropriate matrices and use matrix operations to find:
(a) the cost of each of the three categories for the total production of washing machines.
(b) The cost of each of the three categories for the total production of driers.
(c) The cost of each of the three categories for the total production of all appliances.
(d) The total costs of production of all applicances for the manufacturing firm.

18. Four boys are customers in a fish-and-chip restaurant. A orders fish, chips, and peas; B orders two fish with chips; C orders fish and peas; D orders chips and peas. The prices are £0.30 for fish, £0.15 for chips, and £0.10 for peas.

(a) Express each boy's order as a row vector.
(b) Add together these four vectors to obtain a fifth row vector representing the total quantities ordered.
(c) Express the prices as a column vector.
(d) Multiply each of the row vectors by the price vector, to obtain the amount owed by each boy and the total amount owed.
(e) Check that the fifth result in (d) is equal to the sum of the other four results.

19. A closed environment contains three coexisting species. The population vector

$$n(t) = \begin{bmatrix} n_1(t) \\ n_2(t) \\ n_3(t) \end{bmatrix}$$

Of the system at time t is determined from the transition equation

$$n(t+1) = A(t)n(t), \quad A(t) = \begin{bmatrix} 1 + t/10 & -t/10 & t/20 \\ t/10 & 1 & -t/20 \\ 0 & 0 & 1-t/5 \end{bmatrix}$$

If the initial population vector is

$$n(0) = \begin{bmatrix} 100 \\ 200 \\ 100 \end{bmatrix}$$

find $n(1)$, $n(2)$ and $n(3)$. Do any of the population become extinct during the first three time periods? When does the third population become extinct?

CHAPTER 9

Optimal Policy Decisions: Models based on Optimization Techniques

9.1 THE PRECISION TOOL COMPANY

The Precision Tool Company is a manufacturer of precision screws. It has two main lines, wood screws and metal screws, which it sells for £20 and £25 respectively per box. The material costs for each box are £10 and £8 respectively, and overhead costs are £5000 per week. All the screws have to pass through a slotting and a threading machine. A box of wood screws requires 3 minutes in the slotting machine and 2 minutes on the threading machine, whereas a box of metal screws requires 2 minutes on the slotting machine and 8 minutes on the threading machine. In a week, each machine is available for 60 hours. The company wishes to maximize its weekly earnings.

As in all problems of this type, the decision variables must first be identified. Since the company can produce two types of screws, it is clear that our decision variables are

x = number of boxes of wood screws produced weekly
y = number of boxes of metal screws produced weekly.

Thus the revenue (in pounds) received by the company in a week is

$$20x + 25y$$

and the total overheads are

$$10x + 8y + 5000.$$

Hence the objective is to maximize

$$z = 20x + 25y - (10x + 8y + 5000)$$

that is, $z = 10x + 17y - 5000.$ (9.1)

There are of course a number of constraints on x and y. Since the slotting and threading machines are available for only 3600 minutes per week, we have the inequality constraints

$$3x + 2y \leqslant 3600 \tag{9.2}$$

$$2x + 8y \leqslant 3600. \tag{9.3}$$

Also production is a one-way process, so

$$x \geqslant 0, \quad y \geqslant 0. \tag{9.4}$$

There may be a further constraint on the total demand for the product, an upper limit on the number of boxes of screws of each type that can actually be sold on the market; but we shall assume that all production can be readily sold. We warn the reader that this model will not be valid for a saturated market, when an additional demand constraint must be put in. Thus the company's problem has now been reduced to the maximization of a function of two variables, (9.1), subject to the inequality constraints (9.2), (9.3) and (9.4).

9.2 OPTIMIZATION TECHNIQUES

We have already met a number of techniques for dealing with extremum (maximum or minimum) values of a function. For a function of one variable, say $f(x)$, a necessary condition for a local maximum or minimum at $x = a$ is

$$\boxed{f'(a) = 0} \tag{9.5}$$

If, in addition, $f''(a) < 0$, f has a local *maximum* at $x = a$, and if $f''(a) > 0$, f has a local *minimum* at $x = a$. These results can be generalized to functions of more than one variable. For example, a necessary condition for (a, b) to be a local extremum of $f(x, y)$ is

$$\boxed{\frac{\partial f}{\partial x}(a, b) = 0 = \frac{\partial f}{\partial y}(a, b)^{*}} \tag{9.6}$$

*See Appendix III for partial differentiation.

If, also, at $x = a$, $y = b$

(i) $\dfrac{\partial^2 f}{\partial x^2} \dfrac{\partial^2 f}{\partial y^2} - \left(\dfrac{\partial^2 f}{\partial x \partial y}\right)^2 > 0$, $\dfrac{\partial^2 f}{\partial x^2} < 0$, then f has a local maximum.

(ii) $\dfrac{\partial^2 f}{\partial x^2} \dfrac{\partial^2 f}{\partial y^2} - \left(\dfrac{\partial^2 f}{\partial x \partial y}\right)^2 > 0$, $\dfrac{\partial^2 f}{\partial x^2} > 0$, then f has a local minimum.

In this chapter, though, we will be mainly concerned with extremum values of functions, subject to a number of constraints.

As a simple example, consider the problem of finding among all rectangles with constant perimeter, the one which has the maximum area (this is known as an 'isoperimetric problem'). Let the length of the sides of the rectangle be x and y so that the area, $A = xy$. If L is the constant perimeter length, then we must have $L = 2(x + y)$. Thus the mathematical problem is to maximize the function

$$A = xy$$

subject to the constraint

$$L = 2(x + y).$$

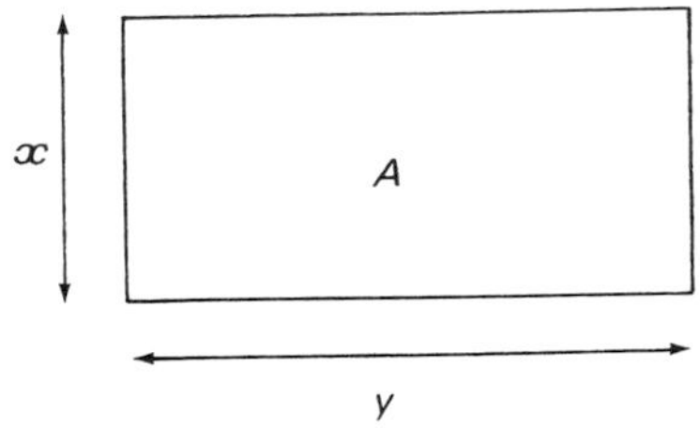

Fig. 9.1   The isoperimetric problem for rectangles.

Clearly the problem can be solved by eliminating one of the variables, say y, so that we need to maximize

$$A = x(\tfrac{1}{2}L - x).$$

Using (9.5), we consider

$$\frac{\mathrm{d}A}{\mathrm{d}x} = 0 = \tfrac{1}{2}L - 2x$$

so that for extremum values, $x = L/4 = y$. Also $d^2A/dx^2 = -2$, so the solution $x = y = L/4$ gives the maximum value to A. Hence the required rectangle is a square.

Not all 'maximization subject to constraint' problems are as simple as this. It is not always possible to use the constraint equation to eliminate one of the variables. We do, though, have an alternative technique, developed by imbedding our problem in a more general class of problems. We first state our problem. Consider the maximization of a function

$$f = f(x,y) \tag{9.7}$$

subject to a constraint of the form

$$g(x,y) = 0. \tag{9.8}$$

There is no loss of generality in choosing this form as, for example, the constraint above, $L = 2(x + y)$, can be put in this way by simply writing

$$L - 2(x + y) = 0.$$

We now consider the problem of maximizing the augmented function

$$h(x,y) = f(x,y) - \lambda g(x,y) \tag{9.9}$$

where λ is a real number known as the **Lagrange multiplier**. Hence we solve

$$\frac{\partial h}{\partial x} = 0, \quad \frac{\partial h}{\partial y} = 0.$$

The solutions will clearly depend on λ: let $x = x^*(\lambda)$, $y = y^*(\lambda)$ denote the solution. Consequently for any value of λ, we have obtained the point (x,y) at which $h(x,y)$ has a maximum value. But if we choose λ so that the constraint is satisfied, that is,

$$g(x^*(\lambda), y^*(\lambda)) = 0 \tag{9.10}$$

then $h = f$, and we have the maximum value of f, as well as h. The above is not a rigorous proof of why the Lagrange multiplier method works, but it does give some indication of the philosophy behind it.

Let us illustrate its working in the simple example introduced above. Writing the constraint in the form

$$L - 2(x + y) = 0,$$

we first form the augmented function

$$h(x,y) = xy - \lambda[L - 2(x + y)].$$

Setting $\dfrac{\partial h}{\partial x} = \dfrac{\partial h}{\partial y} = 0$ gives

$$y - \lambda(-2) = 0$$

$$x - \lambda(-2) = 0.$$

Hence $x = y = -2\lambda$, and substituting into the constraint gives $x = y = L/4$ as expected. Whether the extremum is a maximum or a minimum is usually obvious by inspection, although there is a rigorous method involving the second differential of h to be found in textbooks of mathematical analysis.

   This method of Lagrange multipliers can be readily extended to functions of more than two variables and to more than one constraint. Unfortunately, constraints are not always 'equality' constraints (as defined in (9.3)), and are often inequality constraints of the form

$$g(x,y) \leqslant 0. \tag{9.11}$$

For example, the constraints (9.2), (9.3) and (9.4) in the Precision Tool Company example are all inequality constraints. The problem now is to maximize $f = f(x,y)$ subject to the inequality constraint (9.11).
   We first introduce a new variable z defined by

$$z^2 = -g(x,y) \tag{9.12}$$

which effectively means that g must be non-positive and so the constraint is satisfied. The problem is now to maximize $f(x,y)$ subject to

$$g(x,y) + z^2 = 0. \tag{9.13}$$

Lagrange multiplier methods can now be used. We form the augmented function

$$h(x,y) = f(x,y) - \lambda[g(x,y) + z^2]$$

and for an extremum value

$$\frac{\partial h}{\partial x} = 0, \text{ that is, } \frac{\partial f}{\partial x} - \lambda\frac{\partial g}{\partial x} = 0 \tag{9.14}$$

$$\frac{\partial h}{\partial y} = 0, \text{ that is, } \frac{\partial f}{\partial y} - \lambda \frac{\partial g}{\partial y} = 0 \qquad (9.15)$$

$$\frac{\partial h}{\partial z} = 0, \text{ that is, } 2z\lambda = 0. \qquad (9.16)$$

From (9.16), clearly either $\lambda = 0$ or $z = 0$. If $z = 0$, then from (9.13) $g = 0$. Thus we can write

$$\lambda g(x,y) = 0. \qquad (9.17)$$

It can also be shown that for a local maximum value, the Lagrange multiplier

$$\lambda \geq 0. \qquad (9.18)$$

These conditions are necessary but not always sufficient. Provided that f and g are both concave, these 'Kuhn-Tucker' conditions are also sufficient.

Example
Maximize $f(x,y) = 2x + xy - x^2 - 2y^2$ subject to $x + y \leq \alpha$.

Solution
Necessary conditions for a maximum, with $g = x + y - \alpha$, are

$$\frac{\partial f}{\partial x} - \lambda \frac{\partial g}{\partial x} = 0, \text{ that is, } 2 + y - 2x - \lambda = 0$$

$$\frac{\partial f}{\partial y} - \lambda \frac{\partial g}{\partial y} = 0, \text{ that is, } x - 4y - \lambda = 0$$

$$\lambda g = 0, \qquad\qquad \text{that is, } \lambda(x + y - \alpha) = 0.$$

Thus either $\lambda = 0$ or $x + y = \alpha$. If $\lambda = 0$, then

$$2x - y = 2$$

$$x - 4y = 0$$

which has solution $x = 8/7$, $y = 2/7$. The constraint $x + y \leq \alpha$ must also be satisfied. This is so if $\alpha \geq 10/7$. Consequently f has a maximum value at $x = 8/7$, $y = 2/7$ provided that $\alpha \geq 10/7$. In fact the maximum value is 56/49.

Now if $\alpha < 10/7$, then we must have $x + y = \alpha$, and so

$$3x + \lambda = 2 + \alpha$$

$$5x - \lambda = 4\alpha$$

giving

$$x = \frac{1}{4} + \frac{5\alpha}{8}, \qquad y = -\frac{1}{4} + \frac{3\alpha}{8},$$

and the maximum value of f is now

$$f = \frac{1}{4} + \frac{5\alpha}{4} - \frac{7\alpha^2}{16}.$$

In many problems we have the special case where the function f which we wish to maximize (or minimize) is a *linear* function, as in the next example.

Example
Maximize $f = 6x + 10y$, subject to the constraints

$$x + y \leqslant 3, \qquad x + 4y \leqslant 4.$$

Solution
We require a slight generalization of the above theory in order to deal with the inequalities. We form the augmented function

$$h(x,y) = 6x + 10y - \lambda(x + y - 3) - \mu(x + 4y - 4)$$

where λ and μ are Lagrange multipliers, and

$$\lambda(x + y - 3) = 0$$

$$\mu(x + 4y - 4) = 0$$

with $\lambda \geqslant 0, \quad \mu \geqslant 0.$

For maximum h, we have

$$\frac{\partial h}{\partial x} = 0, \text{ that is, } 6 - \lambda - \mu = 0$$

$$\frac{\partial h}{\partial y} = 0, \text{ that is, } 10 - \lambda - 4\mu = 0$$

and so $\lambda = 14/3$ and $\mu = 4/3$. Since $\lambda \neq 0$, $\mu \neq 0$, the inequality constraints are satisfied by the equality case; that is,

$$x + y = 3$$

$$x + 4y = 4$$

giving $x = 8/3$, $y = 1/3$. Thus the maximum of f occurs at this point and has value $f = 58/3$.

This simple example has an easy graphical interpretation. The regions defined by $x + y \leqslant 3$ and $x + 4y \leqslant 4$ can be illustrated as in Fig. 9.2. The area in

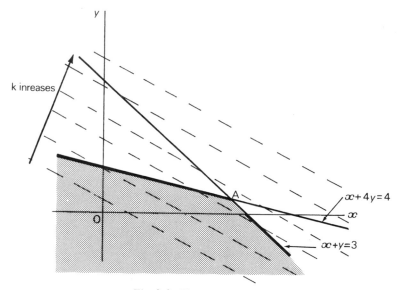

Fig. 9.2   The accessible region.

common to these two regions defines what is called the accessible region, that is the region of points (x,y) which satisfy both the inequalities. We require the maximum of $f(x,y) = 6x + 10y$ for (x,y) in this **accessible region**. But f can also be illustrated graphically. For instance, if f takes a constant value k, we have

$$6x + 10y = k,$$

which defines a family of parallel straight lines, some of which are illustrated in the figure. The value of k and hence the value of f increase in the direction indicated by the arrow. Consequently the maximum value of f in the accessible region occurs on the straight line which passes through A. In other words the maximum of f occurs at the intersection of the two lines

$$x + 4y = 4, \quad x + y = 3,$$

which gives the same solution as above.

For the more general problem of finding the maximum value of

$$f(x,y) = ax + by$$

subject to a number of constraints of the form

$$g_i(x,y) = c_i x + d_i y - e_i \leqslant 0 \qquad\qquad (i = 1, 2, \ldots n)$$

we first consider the accessible region defined by the inequalities. If this defines a convex region, as illustrated in Fig. 9.3, then the equation

$$ax + by = k$$

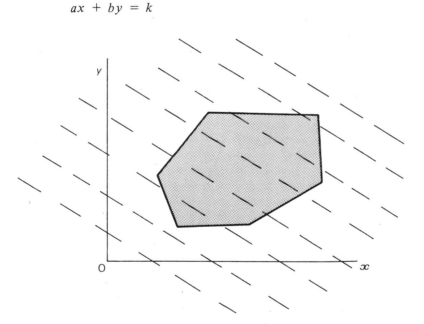

Fig. 9.3 Convex accessible region.

is again a one-parameter family of straight lines. Clearly the maximum value of f in the accessible region must occur either

  (i) at an intersection point of the constraint equation; or

 (ii) along one of the constraint equations

$$g_i(x,y) = 0.$$

In either case the maximum value of f occurs on the constraint boundary, and one method of finding this value is simply to compute the value of f at each of the intersections, which may be found by solving the set of simultaneous equations $g_i(x,y) = 0$ $(i = 1, 2, \ldots n)$.

Example

Find the maximum value of $f(x,y) = x + 2y$ subject to the constraints

$$x + 3y \leqslant 3, \quad 4x + y \leqslant 8, \quad x \geqslant 0, \quad y \geqslant 0.$$

Solution

When we sketch the constraint lines $g_i(x,y) = 0$ we obtain a convex accessible region as shown in Fig. 9.4.

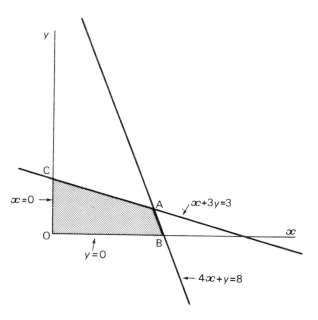

Fig. 9.4   The accessible region.

Clearly the maximum value of f occurs at A, but just to check we will compute the values of f at all the intersection points:

O. $(0,0)$, $f(0,0) = 0$,

B: $(2,0)$, $f(2,0) = 2$,

C: $(0,1)$, $f(0,1) = 2$,

A: $(21/11, 4/11)$, $f(21/11, 4/11) = 29/11$.

Hence the maximum value of $f(x,y)$ subject to the given constraints is 29/11.

The method described in these last two examples can be generalized to cope with extremum values of linear functions of n variables subject to linear inequality constraints. [The 'simplex' method is a very useful technique for computing the solution of such problems.]

We have briefly reviewed some of the optimization techniques available. In the following section we will see their use in a number of case studies.

9.3 SOLUTION OF THE PRECISION TOOL COMPANY'S PROBLEM

With the theory developed in Sec. 9.2 we are now in a position to solve the problem in Sec. 9.1, namely, to maximize

$$z = 10x + 17y - 5000, \tag{9.19}$$

subject to the constraints

$$3x + 2y \leqslant 3600,$$

$$2x + 8y \leqslant 3600,$$

$$x \geqslant 0,$$

$$y \geqslant 0.$$

These four inequality constraints define a convex accessible region as indicated in Fig. 9.5.

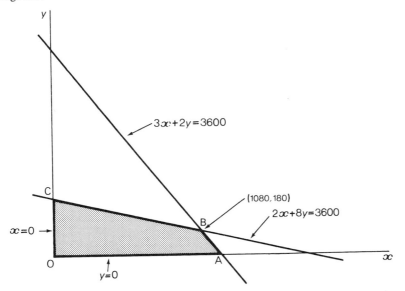

Fig. 9.5 Convex accessible region for the Precision Tool Company's problem.

We know that the maximum will occur at a corner (vertex), so we evaluate (9.19) at each point in turn.

$$O: \quad (0,0), \; z = -5000$$

$$A: \quad (1200,0), \; z = 7000$$

$$B: \quad (1080,180), \; z = 8860$$

$$C: \quad (0,400), \; z = 1300.$$

Clearly the maximum occurs at B, and so the company's best policy is to produce 1080 boxes of used screws and 180 boxes of metal screws weekly. The resulting profit is £8860 per week.

9.4 CASE STUDIES

9.4.1 Stock Control with Shortages

We have already met a simple model for stock control, in which we assumed that a retailer holds goods to meet a constant demand rate r per unit time. We assumed that the new supplies could be obtained instantly at a set-up cost c_1, and that holding costs were c_2 per unit stock per unit time. If x is the order quantity, the time taken for this to be used up is x/r, and then a new batch is ordered. This is illustrated in Fig. 9.6.

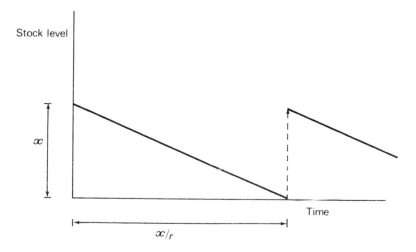

Fig. 9.6 Stock level.

The stock level, $s(t)$, is given by

$$s = x - rt \qquad (9.20)$$

and the costs per cycle are

$$c_1 + c_2 \int_0^{x/r} s \, dt$$

$$= c_1 + c_2 x^2/2r^2 \, ;$$

using (9.20). Hence costs per unit time are given by

$$\boxed{F(x) = \frac{r}{x}(c_1 + c_2 x^2/2r^2).} \qquad (9.21)$$

For minimum total costs, we find the economic order quantity, [E.O.Q.], $x = (2rc_1/c_2)^{1/2}$.

We now improve the model by introducing an estimated cost c_3 per unit stock per unit delay on delivery of the product. It may be worth paying the costs incurred by delayed deliveries in order to reduce the storage costs if these are high. This is illustrated in Fig. 9.7.

Let x be the initial stock level after the shortages have been met. Let r denote the demand rate per unit time, so that shortages begin after time x/r. If τ denotes

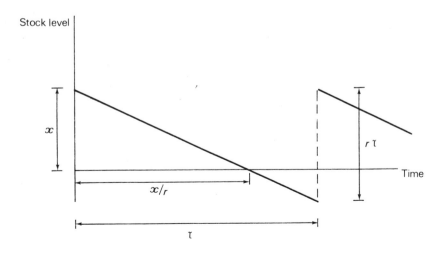

Fig. 9.7 Stock control with shortages.

the time between reordering, then the batch size is $r\tau$, and the quantity $(r\tau - x)$ is immediately required to meet the shortages.

The total costs per cycle are made up of the set-up costs, stock-holding costs, and shortage costs, that is,

$$c_1 + c_2 \int_0^{x/r} s \, dt + c_3 \int_{x/r}^{\tau} (-s) \, dt$$

where $s = x - rt$ is the stock level. This gives

$$c_1 + c_2 \int_0^{x/r} (x - rt) \, dt + c_3 \int_{x/r}^{\tau} (rt - x) \, dt$$

$$= c_1 + c_2(xt - \tfrac{1}{2}rt^2)\big|_0^{x/r} + c_3(\tfrac{1}{2}rt^2 - xt)\big|_{x/r}^{\tau}$$

$$= c_1 + \frac{c_2 x^2}{2r} + \frac{c_3}{2r}(r^2\tau^2 - 2rx\tau + x^2)$$

$$= c_1 + \frac{c_2 x^2}{2r} + c_3 \frac{(r\tau - x)^2}{2r}$$

and the total costs per unit time are now

$$F(x, \tau) = \frac{c_1}{\tau} + \frac{c_2 x^2}{2r\tau} + \frac{c_3(r\tau - x)^2}{2r\tau}. \tag{9.22}$$

F is a function of two variables x and τ, and for a minimum, from (9.6), we require

$$\frac{\partial F}{\partial x} = \frac{\partial F}{\partial \tau} = 0$$

and

$$\frac{\partial^2 F}{\partial x^2} \frac{\partial^2 F}{\partial \tau^2} - 2 \frac{\partial^2 F}{\partial x \partial \tau} > 0, \qquad \frac{\partial^2 F}{\partial x^2} > 0.$$

Applying these conditions gives

$$0 = \frac{c_2 x}{r\tau} - \frac{c_3(r\tau - x)}{r\tau}, \quad \text{that is, } (c_2 + c_3)x = c_3 r\tau$$

$$0 = -\frac{c_1}{\tau^2} - \frac{c_2 x^2}{2r\tau^2} + \frac{c_3}{2r\tau^2}(r^2\tau^2 - x^2)$$

that is, $2rc_1 + (c_2 + c_3)x^2 = c_3 r^2 \tau^2$.

These two equations can be solved to obtain

$$x = [2rc_1 c_3/c_2(c_2 + c_3)]^{\frac{1}{2}}$$
$$\tau = [2c_1(c_2 + c_3)/rc_2 c_3]^{\frac{1}{2}}$$

$$(9.23)$$

It is interesting to note that the E.O.Q. formula in the first model can be determined simply by letting $c_3 \to \infty$ in (9.23). Then

$$x \to (2rc_1/c_2)^{\frac{1}{2}}$$

as expected.

As an illustration, consider a dealer who supplies ten machines per day. The cost of holding one machine in stock is £1 per day, and the penalty for late delivery is £4 per machine per day. The set-up costs of each order are £1000.

In terms of the constants defined above, we have

$$c_1 = 1000, \quad c_2 = 1, \quad c_3 = 4, \quad r = 10,$$

taking a unit of time as 1 day, and £1 as the unit cost. The formula (9.23) gives $\tau = 16$, to the nearest whole day, so that the total order size is 160. Also by (9.23), $x = 130$, and so the maximum shortage is 30 machines.

9.4.2 Optimal Warehouse Area

In this study we consider how large a territory should be served by a warehouse to result in a minimum total cost. The costs are made up of
  (i) holding the goods in the warehouse,
  (ii) delivery from warehouse to customer.
In this particular model we assume that sales of these goods are fixed, so that maximizing profits is equivalent to minimizing costs. The 'measure of effectiveness' to be used will be cost per unit value of goods distributed.

If C denotes the total cost per unit value of goods distributed in the warehouse region, then we model c by

$$C = a + b/V + c\sqrt{A}$$

$$(9.24)$$

where V is the value of the volume of goods handled per unit of time, A is the area in square miles served by the warehouse, a is cost not affected either by warehouse volume or area served, b and c are constants. Hence if V increases, the total cost per unit value of goods decreases, whereas if the catchment area increases, so do the costs due to the longer journey now made.

If we assume that customers are evenly spread throughout the country we have

$$V = kA$$

where k is a constant. Thus

$$C = a + \frac{b}{kA} + c\sqrt{A}.$$

A quick look at the graph of C as a function of A shows that any extremum with A positive must be a minimum. Thus for minimum costs

$$\frac{dC}{dA} = 0,$$

that is, $$-\frac{b}{kA^2} + \frac{C}{2\sqrt{A}} = 0$$

which gives

$$A = \left[\frac{2b}{Ck}\right]^{2/3} \tag{9.25}$$

9.4.3 Production Planning

A labour-intensive firm produces the same item in each of three successive months. It has received orders for 5 units of this item at the end of the first month, 10 at the end of the second, and 15 at the end of the third. Because of the special structure of overtime agreements with the union, the cost of producing x items in any given month is x^2 (measured in £1000). From this point of view it would appear advantageous for the firm to spread out production as evenly as possible, carrying over any unsold units in inventory. On the other hand, there is a holding cost of £4000 per month for each unit kept in inventory. Assuming no initial inventory, what policy should the firm pursue to minimize total costs?

We must first identify the relevant variables. In this problem these are the numbers of units produced in the first, second, and third months, say x_1, x_2, and x_3.

Let C be the total cost (in £1000). Then

$$C = \text{production costs} + \text{holding costs}$$

$$= x_1^2 + x_2^2 + x_3^2 + 4(x_1 - 5) + 4(x_1 + x_2 - 15). \qquad (9.26)$$

The constraints defining the feasible region are

$$x_1 \geqslant 5$$

$$x_1 + x_2 \geqslant 15$$

$$x_1 + x_2 + x_3 = 30$$

$$x_2 \geqslant 0$$

$$x_3 \geqslant 0$$

Since the function C, (9.26), is non-linear we apply the usual conditions to the augmented function, assuming that the inequality constraints are in fact satisfied,

$$F(x_1, x_2, x_3) = x_1^2 + x_2^2 + x_3^2 + 4(x_1 - 5) + 4(x_1 + x_2 - 15)$$

$$- \lambda(x_1 + x_2 + x_3 - 30)$$

that is, $\dfrac{\partial F}{\partial x_1} = 0$ gives $2x_1 + 4 + 4 - \lambda = 0$ or $2x_1 = -8 + \lambda$

$\dfrac{\partial F}{\partial x_2} = 0$ gives $2x_2 + 4 - \lambda = 0$ or $2x_2 = -4 + \lambda$

$\dfrac{\partial F}{\partial x_3} = 0$ gives $2x_3 - \lambda = 0$.

Substituting these values of x_1, x_2, x_3 into the equality constraints gives $\tfrac{1}{2}(-8 + \lambda) + \tfrac{1}{2}(-4 + \lambda) + \tfrac{1}{2}(\lambda) = 30$. This gives $\lambda = 24$ and so

$$\boxed{x_1 = 8, \quad x_2 = 10, \quad x_3 = 12} . \qquad (9.27)$$

This means that three units are stored in the second and third months. The solution does in fact satisfy all the inequalities, and so the optimum occurs at an *interior* point of the feasible region. Of course in many cases the inequalities will not be satisfied, showing that there is *no* interior solution, and the solution will remain at a boundary point of the feasible region.

For example, consider the same problem but with requirements 4, 10, and 4 units at the end of each month.
The constraints are now

$$x_1 \geqslant 4$$

$$x_1 + x_2 \geqslant 14$$

$$x_1 + x_2 + x_3 = 18$$

$$x_2 \geqslant 0$$

$$x_3 \geqslant 0.$$

The augmented function is:

$$F(x_1, x_2, x_3) = x_1^2 + x_2^2 + x_3^2 + 4(x_1 - 4) + 4(x_1 + x_2 - 14)$$
$$- \lambda(x_1 + x_2 + x_3 - 18).$$

Applying the usual formulae we obtain (as in the first case)

$$2x_1 = -8 + \lambda, \quad 2x_2 = -4 + \lambda, \quad 2x_3 = \lambda,$$

and, on substituting into the constraint, we obtain

$$\tfrac{1}{2}(-8 + \lambda) + \tfrac{1}{2}(-4 + \lambda) + \tfrac{1}{2}(\lambda) = 18.$$

This gives $\lambda = 16$, and so

$$x_1 = 4, \quad x_2 = 6, \quad x_3 = 8. \tag{9.28}$$

This is *not* a feasible solution, for although the total number of units produced is correct for three months, there will not be sufficient to meet the demand at the end of the second month. The solution to the problem then must be on the boundary of the feasible region, and to determine it we can use the Kuhn-Tucker conditions equation (9.14), (9.15) and (9.17) from Sec. 9.2, or use a more direct method as outlined below.

First eliminate the variable x_3, using the equality constraint $x_1 + x_2 + x_3 = 18$.

This gives the total cost as

$$C = x_1^2 + x_2^2 + (18 - x_1 - x_2)^2 + 4(x_1 - 4) + 4(x_1 + x_2 - 14)$$

$$= 2x_1^2 + 2x_1 x_2 + 2x_2^2 - 28x_1 - 32x_2 + 252 \qquad (9.29)$$

which we wish to minimize subject to the conditions

$$x_1 \geqslant 4, \quad x_2 \geqslant 0, \quad x_1 + x_2 \geqslant 14.$$

The feasible region is illustrated in Fig. (9.8).

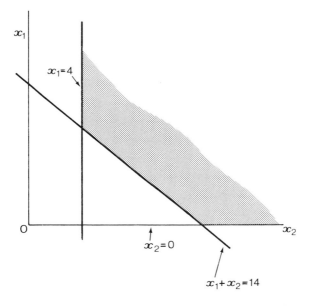

Fig. 9.8 Feasible region for $x_1 \geqslant 4, x_2 \geqslant 0, x_1 + x_2 \geqslant 14$.

We already know that there is no interior solution, so we can consider the three boundary cases:

(i) $x_1 = 4, \quad x_2 = 10$; then

$$C = 2x_2^2 - 24x_2 + 172$$

and for a turning point $dC/dx_2 = 0$ which gives $x_2 = 6$. This is outside the feasible region, and so the minimum will in fact occur on the boundary at $x_2 = 10$ and has value $C = 132$. (See Fig. 9.9)

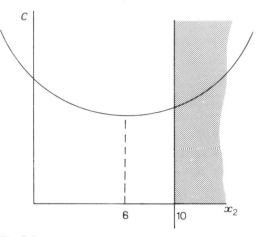

Fig. 9.9   Minimum value on boundary of feasible region.

(ii) $x_1 + x_2 = 14$;   then eliminating, say, x_1 gives

$$C = 2x_2^2 - 32x_2 + 252.$$

For minimum C we require $dC/dx_2 = 0$, giving $x_2 = 8$ and hence $x_1 = 6$. This is on the boundary of the feasible region, and the minimum value is given by $C = 124$.

(iii) $x_2 = 0$, $x_1 \geqslant 14$;   then

$$C = 2x_1^2 - 28x_1 + 252$$

and for a minimum $dC/dx_1 = 0$, that is, $x_1 = 7$. (See Fig. 9.10)

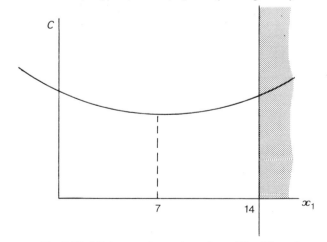

Fig. 9.10   Minimum value on boundary of feasible region.

This is again not in the feasible region, and the minimum will occur at $x_1 = 14$ and its value is 252.

Having considered the three cases, it is clear that the solution to the problem is

$$x_1 = 6, \quad x_2 = 8, \quad x_3 = 4 \tag{9.30}$$

and two units are held in stock in the second month.

9.4.4 Routeing Problem[*]

In the figure below, a network of roads is shown between two towns A and H. The length of the roads is given on the lines; for example 7 miles from A to B. The problem is to find the path from A to H which minimizes the distance between A and H.

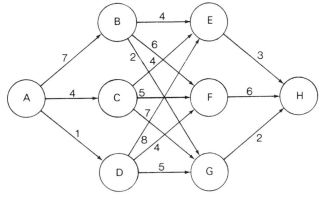

Fig. 9.11.

We will use a technique called **dynamic programming** (D.P.) to solve this relatively simple problem. As D.P. was not introduced in Sec. 9.2, we will first define the problem in the usual D.P. terminology:

STATE	Town
STAGE	Transition from town to adjacent town
ACTION	Taking a particular route from a town
RETURN	Distance from town to adjacent town
VALUE OF STATE	Distance from town to terminal town under given plan.

[*]This approach to D.P. is based on Hastings (1973).

We now solve the problem, not using the D.P. notation, but using the D.P. philosopy. Consider the last stage ending at H. There is no choice here from each state E, F, G. Consider the previous stage. From B we have three possible paths BEH, BFH, BGH, with values 4+3, 6+6, 2+2 respectively. Clearly BGH with value 4 is the best choice here. For C, we consider CEH, CFH, CGH with values 4+3, 5+6, 7+2, and so CEH is the best choice. For D, consider DEH, DFH, DGH with values 8+3, 4+6, 5+2, giving DGH as the best choice. Finally we look at A. We have three choices, to B, C or D and then on the best choice from there. Thus for AB, we move on ABGH with value $4+7 = 11$, and for AD, we move on ADGH with value $1+7 = 8$. Thus our optimum path is:

   A   D   G   H

with value 8.

We note two important points. Firstly we have assumed that each part of an optimal path is optimal. That is, if the overall optimal path from A to H pases through D, it will necessarily move on the optimal path from D to the terminal town H. Secondly, the number of additions made at each stage is 0, 3+3+3, 3; a total of twelve. If the value of each possible path (and there are 9) is evaluated, we would have 18 additions, that is, we have a 30% saving in additions. In fact the saving in additions becomes quite remarkable as the number of stages increases.

To be able to formulate in a precise way, suitable for computation, other D.P. problems we introduce a stage and state variable notation. The stage variable, n, indicates the number of stages which remain until a terminal state is reached. The states are numbered in groups corresponding to each stage. We denote the ith state at stage n by (n,i). The routeing problem is labelled as follows:

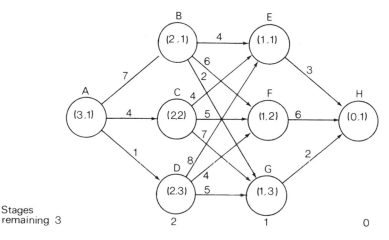

Fig. 9.12.

In the state (n, i) there will be a number of possible actions. Let K_{ni} denote the set of actions available at the state (n, i) and we number the actions $k = 1, 2 \ldots \ldots k_{ni}$, that is,

$$K_{ni} = \{1, 2, \ldots \ldots k_{ni}\}.$$

For example

$$K_{21} = \{1, 2, 3\}$$

where 1 denotes move to $(1,1)$, 2 denotes move $(1, 2)$, 2nd 3 denotes move to $(1, 3)$.

In general, the successor state $(n-1, j)$ from state (n, i) is determined from the current stage, state, and action variable, but in the routeing problem this transition function takes the simple form

$$j = k. \tag{9.31}$$

Thus at state $(2, 1)$, action $k = 1$, moves system to $(1, 1)$; $k = 2$ moves system to $(1, 2)$ etc.

We also define the return associated with state (n, i) and action k or $r(n, i, k)$, where r is called the **return function**. Thus, in the example,

$$r(2,1,1) = 4, \quad r(2,1,2) = 6, \quad r(2,1,3) = 2.$$

We now solve the routeing problem again, using the notation introduced above and a tabular presentation.

Stage n	State i	Action k	Value v
1	1	1	3
	2	1	6
	3	1	2
2	1	1	$4 + 3 = 7$
		1	$6 + 6 = 12$
		3	$2 + 2 = 4$
	2	1	$4 + 3 = 7$
		2	$5 + 6 = 11$
		3	$7 + 2 = 9$

	3	1	$8 + 3 = 11$
		2	$4 + 6 = 10$
		3	$5 + 2 = \underline{7}$
3	1	1	$7 + 3 = 10$
		2	$4 + 7 = 11$
		3	$1 + 7 = \underline{8}$

The value of state (n,i) under an optimal plan is denoted by $v(n,i)$, where v is the optimal value function; so that, for example,

$$v(2,1) = 4, \quad v(2,2) = 7, \quad v(2,3) = 7.$$

Now $v(0,1) = 0$. In states $(1,1)$, $(1,2)$, $(1,3)$, there is only one possible action $k = 1$, that is,

$$v(1,1) = 3$$

$$v(1,2) = 6$$

$$v(1,3) = 2$$

At stage 2, we consider each state in turn. For $(2,1)$ there are three possible actions, $k = 1,2,3$, which gives values

$$r(2,1,1) + v(1,1) = 4 + 3 = 7$$

$$r(2,1,2) + v(1,2) = 6 + 6 = 12$$

$$r(2,1,3) + v(1,3) = 2 + 2 = 4$$

Thus the value under the optimal system is 4 for $v(2,1)$. These results are indicated in the table, the optimal plans for each stage and state being indicated by underlining. We can summarize the method of obtaining the optimal actions and value for state $(2,1)$ by

$$v(2,1) = \min_{r = 1,2,3} [r(2,1,k) + v(1,k)]$$

We continue in this way and complete the table. The optimal policy is found by retracing the optimal path through the table.

9.4.5 Resource Allocation

A dairy manufacturer can make three products: cheese, butter, and yoghurt from his incoming resource, milk. The profit which he can obtain by using 1, 2, 3, or 4 units of milk are given in the table:

Units of milk	1	2	3	4
Cheese	8	18	22	24
Butter	3	6	9	12
Yoghurt	6	7	8	10

The manufacturer wishes to find the resource allocation to the three products so as to maximize his profits when using a total of *four* units of milk.

This problem is quite simple, and it would not take long to find the solution by a trial and error method. We will use the problem, though, to illustrate the techniques of D.P. again. We must first define the relevant terms.

STAGE, n Number of products available (label product cheese as 1 etc.)

STATE, i Number of units of milk available

ACTION, k Number of units of milk allocated to product n

RETURN, r Profit obtained on allocating k units of milk to product n

VALUE, v Total profit on allocation of i units.

The same procedure as in Sec. 9.4.4 is followed. We first consider just product 1, cheese, the first stage, and the allocation of up to four units of milk to this product. At the second stage, products 1 and 2 are utilized, and so on. The optimal policies are underlined, and having reached stage 3 at state 4 the overall optimum policy is

         1 resource unit to product 1, Yoghurt
         0   ,,   ,, ,,   ,,   2, Butter
         3   ,,   ,, ,,   ,,   3, Cheese

giving a maximum profit of 28 units.

Stage	State	Action	Value
1	0	0	0
	1	1	8
	2	2	18
	3	3	22
	4	4	24
2	0	0	0
	1	$\underline{0}$	$0 + 8 = \underline{8}$
		1	$3 + 0 = 3$
	2	$\underline{0}$	$0 + 18 = \underline{18}$
		1	$3 + 8 = 11$
		2	$6 + 0 = 6$
	3	$\underline{0}$	$0 + 22 = \underline{22}$
		1	$3 + 18 = 21$
		2	$6 + 8 = 14$
		3	$9 + 0 = 9$
	4	0	$0 + 24 = 24$
		$\underline{1}$	$3 + 22 = \underline{25}$
		2	$6 + 18 = 24$
		3	$9 + 8 = 17$
		4	$12 + 0 = 12$
3	4	0	$0 + 25 = 25$
		1	$6 + 22 = \underline{28}$
		2	$7 + 18 = 25$
		3	$8 + 8 = 16$
		4	$10 + 10 = 20$

9.5 PROBLEMS

1. Show that the function

$$x^2 y - 4x^2 - y^2$$

has a maximum value at (0,0).

2. Find the minimum value of the function

$$x^2y + 2x^2 - 2xy + 3y^2 - 4x + 7y.$$

3. Find the dimension of the rectangular box which encloses a volume v with minimum surface area.

4. Find the minimum of $x^2 + y^2 + z^2$ subject to the constraint

$$x + 3y - 2z = 4$$

by   (i) using the constraint to eliminate one of the variables,
        (ii) using a Lagrange multiplier.

5. Find the maximum value of xy^3 subject to the constraint

$$x + y = 1.$$

6. Determine the maximum value of the function

$$f(x,y) = x^2 + 2xy + y^2 + 2x + 2y + 4$$

subject to

$$x + y \leqslant 2.$$

7. Determine the maximum value of the function

$$f(x,y) = x^2 + xy - 2y^2 + x - y + 1$$

subject to

$$x + y \leqslant 1,$$

$$x + 4y \leqslant 3.$$

8. Solve, graphically, the following linear programming problems;

(i) maximize $40x + 50y$ subject to

$$5x + 2y \leqslant 30,$$

$$5x + 7y \leqslant 35,$$

$$2x + 5y \leqslant 20,$$

$$x,y \geqslant 0.$$

(ii) maximize $3x + 2y$ subject to

$$2x + y \leqslant 6,$$

$$x + 2y \leqslant 8,$$

$$x,y \geqslant 0.$$

(iii) minimize $10x - 9y$ subject to

$$2x + 3y \geqslant 1,$$

$$x + y \geqslant 3,$$

$$x,y \geqslant 0.$$

9. Solve graphically the non-linear programming problem:

maximize $3xy - y^2$ subject to

$$2x + 5y \geqslant 20,$$

$$x - 2y = 5,$$

$$x,y \geqslant 0.$$

10. The earnings of a department store are estimated to be given by the function

$$E(x,y) = 4x + 5y + xy - x^2 - y^2 + 5,$$

where E is the earnings, x the investment in inventory, and y the floor space for display. Determine the values for x and y which maximize E. If working capital requires the constraint

$$\frac{x}{2} + y \leqslant 6$$

again determine the maximum value of the earnings E. If the working capital is increased so that

$$\frac{x}{2} + y \leqslant 8$$

does the maximum value of E change?

11. A lake in a pleasure park is stocked each spring with two species of fish, F_1 and F_2. The average weight of species F_1 is 2 kg and of species F_2 is 1 kg. There are two foods, X_1 and X_2, available in the lake. Each day there are 50 units of X_1 and 101 units of X_2, and species F_1 requires 1 unit of X_1 and 4 units of X_2 each day whilst species F_2 requires 3 units of X_1 and 1 unit

of X_2 each day. How should the lake be stocked in order to maximise the weight of fish in the lake.

12. A farmer has £200 of capital to invest in hens. Each class 1 hen costs £4, produces 20 large eggs and 5 standard eggs per month and costs 90 pence per month to keep. Each class 2 hen costs £3, produces 15 large eggs and 6 standard eggs per month and costs 74 pence per month to keep. The farmer sells large eggs for 4 pence each, and standard eggs for 3 pence each, and he has space for only 60 hens. How many of each class of hen should be buy in order to maximize his net income per month?

If any of the £200 which is not spent on buying hens is deposited in a bank, where each pound earns $1\frac{1}{10}$ pence per month interest, how may of each class of hen should he now buy in order to maximize his net income per month (including bank interest)?

13. A manufacturer makes two kinds of chairs, high-back and rockers. A high-back requires three hours on the lathe and two hours on the sander. Each rocker requires two hours on the lathe and four hours on the sander. The profit from high-back chairs is 14 units each, and the profit on each rocker is 12 units. If the lathe operates twelve hours daily and the sander operates sixteen hours daily, how many chairs should be produced to maximize the profit?

14. A chemical product is a mixture of two ingredients A and B. The total quantity produced per day must equal or exceed 1000 gallons but not be more than 1500 gallons. At least 200 gallons of the mixture must be ingredient A. The mixture must contain at least 300 gallons of pure alcohol. Ingredient A has 40% alcohol and ingredient B has 24% alcohol. If ingredient A costs 1 unit per gallon and ingredient B 2 units per gallon, how much of each should be used in the mixture to minimize costs?

15. A Newcastle family wish to have a holiday in one of the following towns:

Clacton, Southend, London, Oxford, Gloucester.

To minimize their costs they wish to select the town which minimizes the distance from Newcastle. The route network with distance in miles is shown in Fig. 9.13.
Find the optimal plan. Using dynamic programming, how many additions are made? How many possible paths are there, and how many additions would be made if the total distance for each path was evaluated separately?

16. The cost of taking an admissible step between nodes from left to right is indicated in Fig. 9.14. Find, using D.P. techniques, the path from A to B which gives minimum cost.

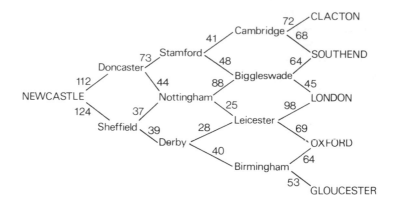

Fig. 9.13.

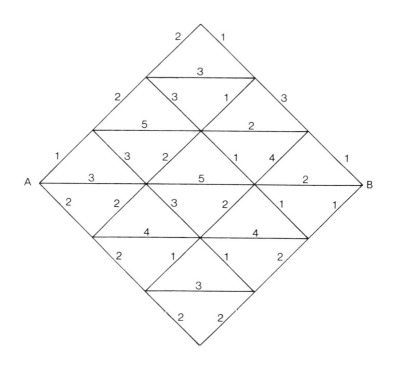

Fig. 9.14.

17. A boatbuilder has orders for boats of a certain type to be delivered at the end of the months shown.

Boatbuilder's orders

Month	No. of boats
Feb.	1
Mar.	2
Apr.	5
May	3
June	2
July	1

Stock is zero at the beginning of February and is to be zero after the July delivery. If the boats are built in a particular month there is an overhead cost of 4 units. Stock holding costs 1 unit per boat per complete month. Demands must be met. In what months should boats be built, and in what quantities, to minimize costs? (Assume that no more than 5 boats can be built in any one month, and no more than 3 stored).

18. A plant overhaul has to be completed in ten days. The overhaul has three stages, stripping, repairing, and rebuilding, and these stages must be completed sucessively. The time taken to complete each stage is related to the cost of the resources which are used at that stage in the way shown in Table 1.

Table 1

Time to complete in days	Cost of stage (£1000s)		
	Stripping	Repairing	Rebuilding
2	18	11	20
4	17	8	15
6	8	7	9
8	6	5	8

Develop a general dynamic programming formulation for allocating the available time to the stages of the overhaul in such a way as to minimize costs, and use your formulation to obtain the optimal allocation with the given data.

19. A company can buy t tons of a raw material for $£c(t)$. It can use the raw material to make products A, B, C in various amounts. The return resulting when k tons of raw material are allocated to the production of A is $r(A, k)$,

and similar relationships apply for B and C. Use dynamic programming to formulate a method for determining how much raw material the company should buy and how much it should allocate to the various products. Using your formulation, solve this problem with the data shown in Tables 2 and 3. Note that the variables k and t can take only the values which appear in the tables, or zero.

Table 2   The cost of raw materials

t tons	2	4	6	8
£$c(t)$	15	28	40	50

Table 3   Returns from raw materials usage

Allocations in tons	Returns (£)		
	$r(A,k)$	$r(B,k)$	$r(C,k)$
1	9	6	8
2	18	12	10
3	23	21	11

CHAPTER 10

The Theory of Games

10.1 THE PRISONER'S DILEMMA

We introduce the idea of game theory with the classical example of the prisoner's dilemma. Two men are apprehended by the police, and both are found to be in possession of a number of forged bank notes. At the police station, they are kept in different rooms for interrogation. The detective in charge of the case is convinced that not only are both men passing forged notes but that they are in fact the counterfeiters. But he has no proof of this which would stand up in court. So he hopes to gain confessions, and to do this he poses the same proposition to each of the men separately. If neither of the men confess to be a counterfeiter, then both will be charged with passing forged notes and will probably get about an 18 month prison sentence. If both confess to be counterfeiters, they will be prosecuted for forgery but given a lenient sentence of about 3 years each. On the other hand if only one of them confesses, he will secure a free pardon, whereas the other will be dealt with as harshly as possible, probably getting a seven year prison sentence.

We can illustrate the possible strategies by using a tabular representation.

| | | PRISONER B | |
		Confess	Refuse
PRISONER A	Confess	(3,3)	(0,7)
	Refuse	(7,0)	(1½,1½)

The numbers represent the number of years' imprisonment for various actions, the first of each pair of numbers being Prisoner A's result, the second Prisoner B's. Each prisoner is anxious to achieve the minimum number of years in prison for himself. If, for instance, A refuses to confess, then provided that his partner does the same he could get away with only 18 months. On the other hand if his partner confesses he risks 7 years in jail! Suppose, instead, that A agrees to confess, then either he might get off with no sentence (if his partner does not confess) or at worst he will get three years (if his partner also confesses). So his safest action is to confess – in this way he minimizes his worst outcome. These arguments are just as valid for Prisoner B, so by playing safe, both prisoners confess, the detective succeeds in getting his confession in spite of the fact that if both had refused to talk the prisoners could halve their terms in prison!

10.2 RECTANGULAR TWO-PERSON GAMES

The example considered in Sec. 1 is a special case of a rectangular two-person game which we will now describe. Let the players be A and B, and suppose that A has m choices open to him, numbered $\{1, 2, \ldots m\}$ and B has n choices numbered $\{1, 2, \ldots n\}$. We denote by a_{ij} the gain to A if he chooses i and B chooses j, and for the same choices, let the gain to B be b_{ij}. We call a_{ij} and b_{ij} the pay-off, and we can represent them by the table

		B's choices			
	1	2	i		n
1	(a_{11}, b_{11})	(a_{12}, b_{12})	$\ldots$ (a_{1j}, b_{1j})	$\ldots$	(a_{1n}, b_{1n})
2	(a_{21}, b_{21})	(a_{22}, b_{22})	$\ldots$ (a_{2j}, b_{2j})	$\ldots$	(a_{2n}, b_{2n})
A's choices i	(a_{i1}, b_{i1})	(a_{i2}, b_{i2})	$\ldots$ (a_{ij}, b_{ij})	$\ldots$	(a_{in}, b_{in})
m	(a_{m1}, b_{m1})	(a_{m2}, b_{m2})	$\ldots$ (a_{mj}, b_{mj})	$\ldots$	(a_{mn}, b_{mn})

We should emphasize at this stage that neither A nor B knows, at the time of making his own choice, what the choice of the other will be, but both A and B are aware of all the information in the table.

As a particular example, consider the game tabulated below.

		B		
		1	2	3
	1	(8,2)	(0,9)	(7,3)
	2	(3,6)	(9,0)	(2,7)
A	3	(1,7)	(6,4)	(8,1)
	4	(4,2)	(4,6)	(5,1)

First consider A's alternatives. At worst, choice 1 will give him 0; choice 2 might give him only 2, choice 3 might give him 1, and choice 4 will give him at least 4.

So that if A is going to maximize his minimum earnings, he chooses row 4. Suppose that B argues in the same way. His minimum earnings for each choice are 2, 0, 1 respectively, so he will choose column 1. So if both players play safe, we will end up with the result (4,2), that is, A gains 4, and B gains 2.

But suppose player A guesses what player B will do? He might now argue that it would be better to play row 1, since if he assumes that B will play column 1, he obtains the result (8,2), that is, he wins 8 and B gains 2. This plan for A is fine provided, of course, that B continues to play safe. But suppose that B argues in the same way, that is he assumes that A will play safe and so play row 4. In this case B will play column 2, and if both argue in this way, the result will be (0,9) – zero gain to A and 9 to B!

Note also that in this game collaboration will be of benefit. While they both play safe, they get the pay-off (4,2) but by collaborating they can do better, for example, (7,3) or (6,4) so that their total gain is 10 rather than 6. Collaboration will not always help; for example, consider the game with pay-off table

	Player B		
	1	2	3
1	(8,2)	(1,9)	(7,3)
2	(4,6)	(9,1)	(3,7)
3	(2,8)	(6,4)	(8,2)
4	(6,4)	(4,6)	(6,4)

(Player A labels rows 1–4)

This game offers no incentive to collaborate, for the total gain to both players is the same amount, 10, regardless of the outcome. The pay-off table can be simplified by taking 5 from all entries in the table to give

	Player B		
	1	2	3
1	(3,−3)	(−4,4)	(2,−2)
2	(−1,1)	(4,−4)	(−2,2)
3	(−3,3)	(1,−1)	(3,−3)
4	(1,−1)	(−1,1)	(1,−1)

(Player A labels rows 1–4)

The two entries in each cell add to zero; what one player gains the other loses.

Such a game is called a **zero-sum** game, and we will confine our analysis to such games.

For a general zero-sum game, $b_{ij} = -a_{ij}$ for all i,j, and we can clearly simplify the pay-off table by omitting all the b_{ij}, and so we have a pay-off matrix of the form

Player B

Player A
$$\begin{bmatrix} a_{11} & a_{12} & \cdots & a_{1n} \\ a_{21} & a_{22} & \cdots & a_{2n} \\ \vdots & & & \\ a_{m1} & a_{m2} & \cdots & a_{mn} \end{bmatrix}$$

We begin by analysing what happens if both players play safe. If A plays row i, he knows that he will receive at least the smallest amount in that row, that is:

$$\min_j a_{ij}.$$

But he wants this guaranteed minimum to be as large as possible, and he achieves this by choosing the row for which $(\min_j a_{ij})$ is largest. In this way he will receive at least the amount μ where

$$\mu = \max_i (\min_j a_{ij}). \tag{10.1}$$

In a similar way, if B chooses column j, he will receive at least

$$\min_i (-a_{ij})$$

(remember that B's gains are $b_{ij} = -a_{ij}$). To make this as large as possible, he chooses the column that maximizes this quantity. In this way B will receive at least the amount v where

$$v = \max_j (\min_i (-a_{ij}))$$
$$= \max_j (-\max_i (a_{ij}))$$

that is,
$$v = -\min_j (\max_i (a_{ij})). \tag{10.2}$$

We can illustrate these definitions by returning to the zero-sum game introduced earlier, that is, the game with pay-off matrix

$$\begin{bmatrix} 3 & -4 & 2 \\ -1 & 4 & -2 \\ -3 & 1 & 3 \\ 1 & -1 & 1 \end{bmatrix}$$

We can evaluate μ and ν as shown below:

	1	2	3	row min.
1	3	-4	2	-4
2	-1	4	-2	-2
3	-3	1	3	-3
4	1	-1	1	-1
col. max.	3	4	3	

$$\mu = \max(-4, -2, -3, -1) = -1$$

$$\nu = -\min(3, 4, 3) = -3$$

So by choosing row 4, A holds his losses to 1, whatever B does; and if B plays column 1 or 3, he holds his losses to 3, whatever A does. In this example we see that $\mu + \nu = -4$. For a zero-sum game we have the following result.

Lemma

For a zero-sum game $\mu + \nu \leqslant 0$.

Proof

With cautious play on both sides, A gains at least μ and B gains at least ν, so that the two of them together gain at least $\mu + \nu$. But it is a zero-sum game, and thus the total gain is always zero. Hence $\mu + \nu$ cannot exceed zero, and we have

$$\mu + \nu \leqslant 0. \tag{10.3}$$

There are of course some games in which $\mu + \nu = 0$, and these are particularly easy to analyse. For example, consider the game with pay-off matrix

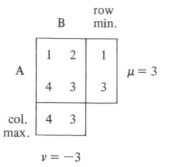

$$v = -3$$

We see that $\mu = 3$, $v = -3$; that is, by choosing row 2, A can guarantee a gain of at least 3, whilst B, by choosing column 2, can guarantee to hold his loss to 3. So if both players act in this way we do indeed get the outcome $(3, -3)$, with A winning 3 and B losing 3. Moreover, neither player has good reason to depart from the safe choice. If A chooses row 1 he has no chance of getting more than 2, and if B chose column 1 he would improve matters only if A actually chose row 1. So for this game the 'best' outcome is clear - both players play safe, and we have what we call a **stable solution.**

In general terms for a zero-sum game, we define a stable solution as an outcome, say row r and column s, such that neither player can improve his result by altering his choice, unless the other player alters his choice too.

Thus for a stable solution, if A sticks to his choice of row r, then B cannot do better than choose column s; so that no entry in row r is less than a_{rs}, that is, $a_{rs} = \min_{j} a_{rj}$.

$$
A \rightarrow
\begin{bmatrix}
 & a_{1s} & \\
 & \vdots & \\
a_{r1} & \cdots & a_{rs} & \cdots & a_{rn} \\
 & \vdots & \\
 & a_{ms} &
\end{bmatrix}
$$

with B indicated by $\overset{B}{\downarrow}$ above the s column.

Secondly, if B sticks to his choice of column s, then A can do no better than choose row r. There, $a_{rs} = \max_{i} a_{is}$. Consequently the element a_{rs} must be the smallest element in its row, and largest in its column. We call such an element a **saddle point** of the matrix. So a stable solution gives rise to a saddle point of the pay-off matrix, and the converse result is true. We started the analysis with a simple example in which $\mu + v = 0$ and we have a stable solution. This is an illustration of the following theorem.

Theorem

A zero-sum game has a stable solution if and only if $\mu + \nu = 0$.

Proof

We have two things to prove. Suppose, firstly, that $\mu + \nu = 0$. By definition of μ, there is a row, say r^{th}, in which the smallest entry is μ. Similarly there is a column, say s^{th}, in which the largest entry is $-\nu$. So that we must have $a_{rs} \geqslant \mu$, and $a_{rs} \leqslant -\nu = \mu$, since $\mu + \nu = 0$. Thus $\mu \leqslant a_{rs} \leqslant \mu$, and clearly $a_{rs} = \mu = -\nu$. Hence a_{rs} is a saddle point, and so a stable solution.

Secondly, suppose that we have a stable solution, say row r, column s. Then from the definition of

$$\mu = \max_{i} \left(\min_{j} a_{ij} \right)$$

$$\geqslant \min_{j} a_{rj}$$

$$= a_{rs} \text{ (since it is a saddle point).}$$

Similarly

$$-\nu = \min_{j} \left(\max_{i} a_{ij} \right)$$

$$\leqslant \max_{i} a_{is}$$

$$= a_{rs},$$

since again a_{rs} is a saddle point. Thus

$$\mu + \nu \geqslant 0$$

and using the Lemma proved above ($\mu + \nu \leqslant 0$), it is clear that $\mu + \nu = 0$.

Example

Analyse the game with pay-off matrix

$$\begin{bmatrix} 4 & -1 & 2 & 3 \\ 4 & 6 & 3 & 7 \\ 1 & 2 & -2 & 4 \end{bmatrix}$$

Solution

$$
\begin{array}{cc}
 & \text{row} \\
 & \text{min.}
\end{array}
$$

$$
\left.\begin{bmatrix} 4 & -1 & 2 & 3 \\ 4 & 6 & 3 & 7 \\ 1 & 2 & -2 & 4 \end{bmatrix} \begin{array}{l} -1 \\ 3 \leftarrow \\ -2 \end{array}\right\} \mu = 3
$$

col.
max.   4   6   3   7
                ↑

$$
\underbrace{\qquad\qquad\qquad}_{v = -3}
$$

We see that $\mu + v = 0$, giving a stable solution. So A will choose row 2, B column 3, and neither will gain by changing his choice.

We now move on to zero-sum games which do not have stable solutions. This means that $\mu + v < 0$. Consider as a simple example the zero-sum game with pay-off matrix

$$
\begin{array}{cc}
 & \text{row} \\
\text{B} & \text{min.}
\end{array}
$$

$$
A \left.\begin{bmatrix} 4 & -3 \\ -4 & 3 \end{bmatrix} \begin{array}{l} -3 \leftarrow \\ -4 \end{array}\right\} \mu = -3
$$

col.
max.   4   3
              ↑

$$
\underbrace{\qquad\qquad}_{v = -3}
$$

In this example, $\mu + v = -6$, so there is no stable solution. The play safe choices result in the outcome $(-3, 3)$ but both players can possibly improve their result by an alternative choice. To achieve this, though, each player has to try to guess the other player's choice, and we have a vicious circle, with each player trying to outguess the other. This just illustrates the fact that there is no stable solution. Suppose, though, that A and B were playing the game not just once but a number of times. Would it be better to have a mixed strategy, such as tossing a coin, to see if A should play row 1 or row 2? The strategy must, of course, be such that for a particular game any row is chosen at random, otherwise B will soon see the strategy.

So suppose that in a large number of games, A chooses row 1 with probability p and row 2 with probability $1-p$. (He can effect this strategy at random when, for example, $p = 1/6$ by having 5 white and 1 black counters in a bag. For each game played he takes a counter out and plays row 1 if it is black, and row 2 if it is white. In this way, if the game is played a sufficient number of times, row 2 will be chosen approximately five times as often as row 1. So the probability of row 1 being played is about 1/6.) The expected pay-off to A will, of course, depend on B's strategy. If B chooses column 1, A will receive on average

$$4p + (-4)(1 - p) = 8p - 4,$$

whereas if B chooses column 2, A's expectation is

$$-3p + 3(1 - p) = 3 - 6p.$$

We can plot A's expectation for varying p as shown in Fig. 10.1.

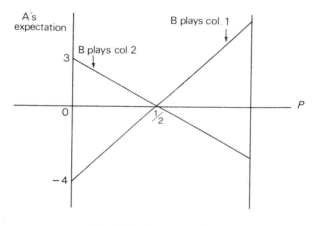

Fig. 10.1   A's expected gain.

If, for example, A uses a value of p less than ½, then B, by always choosing column 1, can make A's expected pay-off negative and so his positive. Similarly if $p > ½$, B can expect gains by always choosing column 2. It is only at $p = ½$ that A can hold his losses to zero, and this is his best mixed strategy; that is, to play rows 1 and 2 at random but with equal probability.

In the same way we can find B's optimum mixed strategy. Suppose that B plays column 1 with probability q and column 2 with probability $(1-q)$. Then when A plays row 1, B's average gain will be

$$4q + (-3)(1 - q) = 7q - 3,$$

whereas if A plays row 2, B's expected gain is

$$-4q + 3(1 - q) = -7q + 3.$$

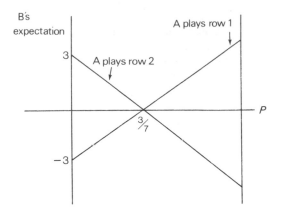

Fig. 10.2   B's expected gain.

Again we can show this situation graphically.

Analysing the situation as before, the best mixed strategy for B is to play column 1 with probability 3/7 and column 2 with probability 4/7. In this way he also holds his expected loss to zero.

So we have determined optimum mixed strategies for both A and B. With these strategies both A and B should hold their losses to zero in the long run. You might well like to try to play this game with a friend and see if you agree with the result!

10.3   CASE STUDIES

10.3.1   Competitive Strategies

Suppose that two firms, A and B, are competing for the same market. They each produce three different brands of their particular product. The management of firm A has decided to increase by £50 000 its advertising expenditure next year in the hope of obtaining a greater proportion of the market. However, firm B also hopes to increase its share, not by increased advertising, but by possibly investing a similar sum of money to increase the quality of its products. Both firms, though, are undecided about which of their three brands should be promoted. So A's alternatives are

    1:   increase advertising of brand 1 by £50 000
    2:   increase advertising of brand 2 by £50 000
    3:   increase advertising of brand 3 by £50 000

and similarly B's alternatives are

1:   increase quality of brand 1 by investing £50 000
2:   increase quality of brand 2 by investing £50 000
3:   increase quality of brand 3 by investing £50 000
4:   no action.

Both firms have a sales forecasting function which predicts the sales for each brand in terms of the decisions taken by each firm. For example, if A employs strategy 1 and B employs strategy 1, the net sales revenue gain for A is predicted as £120 000. The resulting gains (expressed in £1000s) for firm A for the various possible strategies that can be employed by A and B are given in the matrix below.

$$
\begin{array}{c}
 & & \text{Firm B} & & \\
 & 1 & 2 & 3 & 4 \\
\text{Firm A } \begin{matrix} 1 \\ 2 \\ 3 \end{matrix} &
\begin{bmatrix}
120 & -60 & 300 & -220 \\
140 & 20 & 180 & 100 \\
-60 & 0 & -100 & 160
\end{bmatrix}
\end{array}
$$

It is assumed that B's gains are the negative of A's gains for all the varying strategies. So let us apply our game theory analysis to this problem by evaluating μ and ν.

$$
\begin{array}{cccccl}
 & & & & & \text{row} \\
 & & & & & \text{min.} \\
\begin{bmatrix}
120 & -60 & 300 & -220 \\
140 & 20 & 180 & 100 \\
-60 & 0 & -100 & 160
\end{bmatrix} &
\begin{matrix}
-220 \\
20 \leftarrow \\
-100
\end{matrix} &
\left.\vphantom{\begin{matrix}1\\2\\3\end{matrix}}\right\} \mu = 20
\end{array}
$$

col.
max.   140   20   300   160
               $\uparrow$

$$\underbrace{\hspace{4cm}}$$

$$\nu = -20$$

So for this pay-off matrix, there is a stable solution (saddle point) and the play safe strategies are

A: strategy 2 - increase advertising on product 2.
B: strategy 2 - increase investment on product 2.

These are the optimal strategies, provided that both firms are playing conservatively.

10.3.2 How to beat General von Kluge[†]

In August 1944, shortly after the invasion of Normandy, the Allied forces advanced from their beach-head position through a narrow gap at Avranches. The military positions are shown in Fig. 10.3 below:

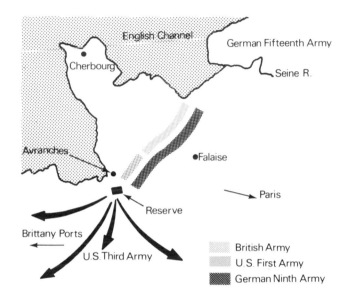

Fig. 10.3 Military positions.

The U.S. First Army and the British Army were threatening the German Ninth Army, whilst the U.S. Third Army had moved south of Avranches. The commander of the U.S. forces was General Bradley, and the German forces commander was General von Kluge. Each had a tactical decision to take.

Von Kluge could either attack towards the west in order to secure his west flank and cut off the U.S. Third Army, or he could withdraw to the east in order to take up a better defensive position near the River Seine.

General Bradley's problem was what to do with his reserves, which were standing just south of the gap. He could order his reserve back to defend the gap; he could send it eastwards to harass and possibly cut off the German's Ninth Army withdrawal; or he could leave it in position for a further day before

[†] This case study is based on 'Military Decisions and Game Theory' by O. G. Haywood, *Journal of the Operations Research Society of America*, Nov. 1954.

committing it. So Bradley had three options, and in terms of game theory there are six possible outcomes. These are illustrated in Fig. 10.4, with the expected results for each decision.

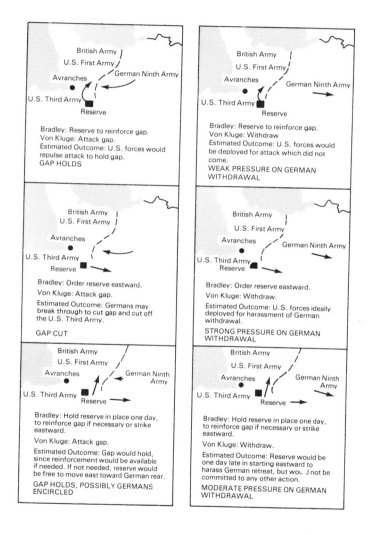

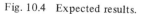

Fig. 10.4   Expected results.

We now construct a pay-off matrix for the game, using Bradley's ordinal figures, from one to six, for the most preferable outcome

General von Kluge

Attack   Withdraw

	Reserve ordered back to gap	Attack	Withdraw
	Reserve ordered back to gap	2	3
General Bradley	Sent eastward	1	5
	Left in position for one day	6	4

The first thing to note is that General Bradley's row 1 choice (ordered back to the gap) is always inferior to his row 3 choice no matter what General von Kluge decides. So we can abandon it and look at the 2×2 game with pay-off matrix

$$\begin{bmatrix} 1 & 5 \\ 6 & 4 \end{bmatrix} \begin{matrix} \text{row} \\ \text{min.} \\ 1 \\ 4 \leftarrow \end{matrix} \Big\} \mu = 4$$

$$\begin{matrix} \text{col.} \\ \text{max.} \end{matrix} \quad 6 \quad 5 \\ \uparrow \\ \underbrace{\qquad} \\ \nu = -5$$

Now $\mu + \nu = -1$, so we do not have a saddle point. There is no stable solution, and we must consider mixed strategies. If the game is being played a number of times, and if Bradley plays row 1 with probability p, then his expected gain if von Kluge always plays column 1 is

$$p1 + (1 - p)6 = 6 - 5p;$$

whereas if von Kluge always plays column 2, his expected gain is

$$p5 + (1 - p)4\ 2 = 4 + p.$$

These are illustrated in Fig. 10.5.

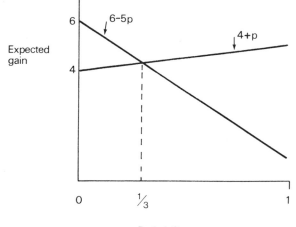

Probability p

Fig. 10.5 Optimum strategy for General Bradley.

If the game were played a number of times, Bradley's optimum strategy would be to play row 1 with probability 1/3 and row 2 with probability 2/3. He would then expect to gain at least 13/3. In a similar way, von Kluge's optimum strategy is to play column 1 with probability 1/6, and column 2 with probability 5/6.

So according to game theory both commanders should have played these strategies, using a random device to determine their actual decisions. Bradley, for instance, should put one red and two blue counters in a bag and choose one at random. If red, he sends his reserve eastward, and if blue, he leaves them in position for a day. Of course this would be fine if the same battle was being played a large number of times – but this is a single very important battle, and it would hardly be likely that the commander would trust the fate of his forces to counters in a bag!

A better way to argue would be to maximize their worst positions. Bradley, for example, would choose row 2 and von Kluge column 2. In this way Bradley gets at least 4, and von Kluge will not lose more than 5. So if they both play safe, we have the outcome

'Reserve stays in position for one day, Germans withdraw'.

This is, in fact, exactly what the two commanders decided to do. But the story doesn't end there. After von Kluge had made his decision to withdraw, Hitler countermanded it and ordered him to attack. In this way Hitler handed over to Bradley his best possible outcome. The gap held on the first day without reinforcements, so the reserve was then used to encircle the Germans. After extricating the shattered remains of his army, von Kluge committed suicide.

10.3.3 Jamaican Fishermen[†]

William Davenport spent some time studying a fishing village of about 200 people, on the south shore of Jamaica. All the male villagers were fishermen making their living exclusively by fishing in the local waters and selling their catches. There were 26 fishing crews which fished the area in dugout canoes by setting fish pots, which are drawn and reset on three regular fishing days each week.

The fishing grounds are divided into inside and outside banks; the inside banks lie from 5 to 15 miles offshore, and the outside banks lie beyond. The distinction between inside and outside banks is made not only on their distance from the shore but on the basis of the strength of the sea currents which flow across them. The outside banks are subject to very strong currents which flow frequently and unpredictably, whereas the inside banks are almost fully protected from these currents. The fishermen have three alternatives

    (1)   set their pots inside

    (2)   set some inside and some outside

    (3)   set their pots outside.

Each action has both advantages and disadvantages. Fishing outside is more expensive since bigger and stronger canoes are required. Pots are often swept away altogether. On the other hand, better quality fish are obtained when the current is not running. Also the price of fish varies according to quality and quantity available, which of course depend on where they are fishing and whether a current is running.

We can try to quantify these arguments by conceiving the situation as one in which the village as a whole is playing against nature. The village has three alternatives, whilst nature has two, to send a current or not to send one. Thus there are six possible outcomes, and Davenport evaluated the respective monetary pay-offs (which were the average net income per canoe during a fishing month). These are shown below.

NATURE

	current	no current	row min.
inside	17.3	11.5	11.5
in and out	5.2	17.0	5.2
outside	−4.4	20.6	−4.4

VILLAGE $\left\{ \begin{array}{l} \end{array} \right.$ $\left. \begin{array}{l} \end{array} \right\} \mu = 11.5$

col. max.   17.3   20.6

$$v = -17.3$$

[†]This case study is based on *Jamaican Fishing: A Game Theory Analysis* by W. Davenport, Yale Univ. Publications in Anthropology, 59, (1960).

Given this pay-off matrix, how should the village play? We see that there is no stable solution, and so the village should have a mixed strategy. Unfortunately, our theory so far does not cover mixed strategies for 3 X 2 games, but it can be proved that such a game contains a particular 2 X 2 game, the solution of which is the solution of the larger game. For this case, the 2 X 2 game is determined by omitting the last row, so that there should be no 'outside' fishing at all. So we are left with finding the village's optimum mixed strategy for the game with pay-off matrix

$$
\begin{array}{cc}
\text{Current} & \text{No current}
\end{array}
$$

$$
\begin{array}{c}
\text{inside} \\
\\
\text{in and out}
\end{array}
\begin{bmatrix}
17.3 & 11.5 \\
\\
5.2 & 17.0
\end{bmatrix}
$$

If the village plays row 1 with probability p and row 2 with probability $(1-p)$, the expected pay-off to the village if there is a current is

$$p(17.3) + (1 - p)(5.2)$$

and if there is no current, it is

$$p(11.5) + (1 - p)(17.0).$$

To find the optimum strategy we must equate these expressions, that is,

$$p(17.3) + (1 - p)(5.2) = p(11.5) + (1 - p)(17.0)$$

giving $p = 0.67$, so that the optimum strategy for the village is to fish 'inside' with probability 0.67 and 'in and out' with probability 0.33 and not 'outside' at all. But the village has 26 canoes, so that the number used for 'inside' fishing should be $0.67 \times 26 = 17.4$ and for 'in and out' fishing 8.6.

Having worked out what strategy the village should undertake, Davenport went on to see what did in fact happen. During his period of observations, 18 canoes fished 'inside', 8 fished 'in and out', and none 'outside'. The observed facts were almost in exact conformity with the optimum strategy evaluated by using game theory!

It should of course be noted that this optimum solution assumes that nature itself is out to minimize the village's gains! It can be evaluated that the optimum strategy for nature to do just that is to send a current with probability 0.31, that is, 31% of the time. Observations show that a current flows about 25% of the time. If we make the assumption that nature plays column 1 with probability 0.25 and column 2 with probability 0.75, then the village's optimum strategy is *not* the one calculated earlier. It would in fact be better to put all canoes on 'outside' fishing, something that was not done at all before! So if nature is indifferent to the fisherman's problems and always plays 'current', 'no current' in the ratio 1:3, the village is not using an optimum strategy at all. It appears as if their strategy has been worked out over the years on the assumption that nature was malevolent!

10.4 PROBLEMS

1. For which of the following games is collaboration of benefit to both players?

(i)

	B	
A	1	2
1	(4,6)	(1,10)
2	(3,5)	(2,2)

(ii)

	B	
A	1	2
1	(4,7)	(1,10)
2	(8,3)	(5,6)

(iii)

	B		
A	1	2	3
1	(6,2)	(4,4)	(7,1)
2	(5,3)	(1,7)	(2,6)
3	(2,6)	(0,8)	(3,5)
4	(4,4)	(2,6)	(5,3)

2. Calculate μ, ν, and $\mu + \nu$ for the following zero-sum games:

(i) $\begin{bmatrix} 1 & 2 \\ 4 & 3 \end{bmatrix}$

(ii) $\begin{bmatrix} 4 & -2 & -5 \\ -2 & 8 & -3 \\ -5 & -3 & 14 \end{bmatrix}$

(iii) $\begin{bmatrix} -2 & -3 & 2 \\ 5 & 4 & 3 \\ 0 & 6 & 1 \end{bmatrix}$.

3. In the children's game of 'stone-scissors-paper' the two players simultaneously thrust forth

    (a) clenched fist (stone),
    (b) two fingers (scissors),
    (c) flat palm (paper).

If both players present the same object, the play is drawn; otherwise the winner is determined by,

    'stone blunts scissors; scissors cut paper; paper wraps stone'.

Construct the pay-off matrix for this game, assuming that the loser pays the winner one unit.

    How would you rate the merits of the three possible moves?

4. Find μ and v for the zero-sum game with pay-off matrix

$$\begin{bmatrix} -3 & -2 & -1 & 0 \\ 4 & 3 & 2 & 1 \\ 3 & 2 & 1 & 0 \\ -4 & -3 & -2 & -1 \end{bmatrix}.$$

Verify that $\mu + v = 0$; find the saddle point of the matrix and the solution to the game.

5. Determine the optimal strategies for the following zero-sum games

(i) $\begin{bmatrix} 5 & 8 \\ 3 & -1 \end{bmatrix}$

(ii) $\begin{bmatrix} -2 & 0 \\ 2 & 4 \\ 6 & 8 \end{bmatrix}$

(iii) $\begin{bmatrix} 1 & 2 & 3 \\ 0 & 3 & 5 \\ -1 & 2 & -2 \end{bmatrix}.$

6. Find all saddle points for the zero-sum games with pay-off matrix

$$\begin{bmatrix} 5 & 5 & 3 & 4 & 3 \\ 4 & 3 & 2 & 4 & 1 \\ 4 & 6 & 2 & 7 & 2 \\ 7 & 5 & 3 & 4 & 3 \end{bmatrix}$$

and determine the solution to this game.

7. Is it possible for a pay-off matrix to have two saddle points with different pay-offs?

8. What are the expected returns to A and B for the zero-sum game with pay-off matrix

$$\begin{bmatrix} 1 & 3 \\ 2 & -1 \end{bmatrix}$$

if

 (i) A plays row 1 with probability ½ and B plays column 1 always:
 (ii) A plays row 1 always and B plays column 1 with probability ¾?
Determine the optimal mixed strategies for A and B and their respective gains.

9. How would you advise the players of a zero-sum game with the following pay-off matrix?

$$\begin{bmatrix} -2 & 5 \\ 3 & -1 \end{bmatrix}$$

For each player, find the best mixed strategy and his expected gain if he uses it.

10. Determine optimal strategies for both players for the zero-sum game with pay-off matrix

$$\begin{bmatrix} -2 & -2 \\ 2 & -1 \\ -1 & 2 \end{bmatrix}.$$

11. In a game between a parent and child, the parent places either two smarties in Box 1 and none in Box 2 and Box 3 *or* one smartie in both Box 1 and Box 2 and none in Box 3. Find the 3 × 2 matrix for this game. what are the optimal strategies for the child and for the parent (assuming he wishes to conserve his smartie stock).

12. Two publishing companies publish competing specialist magazines for fresh water fishing enthusiasts. The total sales revenue is assumed to remain constant, but each publisher can either increase its advertising, action A, or increase its quality, action Q. The pay-off matrix is estimated as

	A	Q
A	4	1
Q	2	5.

Determine the optimal strategy for each publisher.

13. In a certain tomato-growing region of England, the average weather during the growing season is either 'cool' or 'hot'. Two types of tomatoes 'Moneymaker' and 'Gardener's Delight' can be cultivated on a farm of 100 acres. If the season turns out to be cool, the expected profits from Moneymaker are £300 per acre and from Gardener's Delight £100 per acre. On the other hand if the growing season is hot, the expected profits are £100 per acre from Moneymaker and £200 per acre from Gardener's Delight. Describe this game in matrix form assuing competition between the tomato grower and the weather. With no information about the probabilities of hot or cool weather, what is the grower's optimal strategy. If the probabilities of hot or cool weather are equal, how many acres should be devoted to the two types of tomato?

14. Firm A and firm B are competing in the printing of headed notepaper, and A has a somewhat higher quality product, even though the prices are the same. The two actions of price decrease and quality increase are available

to both firms, and it has been determined that if both companies decrease price, A will take way two units of business from B, whereas if A's price decrease is countered by B's quality increase, then firm A will lose three units of business to B. On the other hand, if A chooses to increase quality even further and B counters with a price decrease, the market is more sensitive to price than to an increase in the already high-quality product and, thus, A will lose three units of business to B. Lastly, if B attempts to counter a quality increase of A with its own quality increase, the present higher quality of A's product will be brought home to more customers, and A will obtain four units of business from B. Find the optimal strategies for each company and the value of the game. Discuss the result.

15. Many medical procedures involve substantial risk to the patient and should only be undertaken when the patient is exposed to greater risk if no treatment is given. The problem is further complicated if it is not certain that the patient does have the disease suspected.

    We can model this problem as a game theory problem with pay-off matrix

$$\begin{bmatrix} a & b \\ c & d \end{bmatrix}$$

where a, b, c, and d are the expected lengths of life if the patient has the operation and the disease, the operation and no disease, the disease and no operation, and no disease and no operation respectively. Assuming that the patient wishes to maximize his expected length of life, show that the operation can be recommended if the probability that the patient has the disease is greater than

$$\frac{d - b}{a + d - b - c}.$$

(The actual probability is found by performing various tests.)

    A patient has a suspected tumour on the brain. The estimated values of the parameters in years introduced above are $a = 6$, $b = 10$, $c = 1$, $d = 15$. Determine the required value of the probability that the patient has the tumour in order to recommend the operation.

CHAPTER 11

An Explanation of Discontinuous Phenomena: Models based on Catastrophe Theory

11.1 THE CASE OF THE TATOPOPS LAUNCH

Years of product research have led the Continental Cereal Corporation to the development of a new potato-based breakfast food, Tatopops, combining the properties of the potato crisp with those of the conventional puffed breakfast cereal. Before launcing this revolutionary product, the board has asked the marketing director for an analysis of likely consumer reactions and the mechanism by which public beliefs about Tatopops might be translated into an intention to purchase. The market research department has spent a great deal of time on identifying and measuring factors affecting the customers' intentions to purchase, and has split these into two categories:

    (i) Social normative factors, S, which measure the customer's perception of what he supposes other people expect him to do;

and (ii) Attitude factors, A, which measure the views that the customer holds directly about the attributes of the product.

Thus the intention to purchase, I, may be given by the equation

$$\boxed{I = F(S,A)}$$

where F is a function describing the relative importance of socially normative and attitude factors to a particular subset of potential customers. While much is known of the effect that S and A have separately on the intention to purchase, I, little attention has been paid to their interaction. In particular, there are several observed phenomena which have not been satisfactorily explained. We discuss these now.

When social normative factors against a new product are small, it is generally observed that the intention to purchase increases steadily with increasing awareness of its attributes, that is, with an increasingly favourable attitude towards the product.
This case is shown in Fig. 11.1.

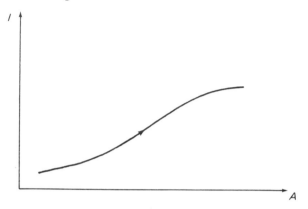

Fig. 11.1 Early stages of the life cycle of new product – low social normative factors against.

This occurs when the new product is similar to other products already in the field and there is no particular public feeling against it. But where public opinion is hostile towards a new product, that is social normative factors are high against the product and prior intention to purchase in low, a positive increase in attitude factor will have little or no effect on the intention to purchase until a certain threshold point is reached, where a further small increase in attitude will lead to a large increase in intention to purchase, perhaps even a jump in intention as shown in Fig. 11.2. This typically happens where the product is of radical design, where consumers hold back for fear of being 'thought odd', but once a few 'pioneers' have been seen to adopt it, these inhibitions are overcome and its superior attributes are appreciated. For instance, the sales of a foreign car of unconventional design but good performance may not begin to rise significantly until a certain proportion of cars seen on the road are of this type. The size of this proportion determines the length of time until the threshold point is reached.

Conversely, where there is high prior intention to purchase and high social normative pressure against the product, a decrease in attitude towards the product will not result in a corresponding decrease in intention to purchase until a threshold point is reached where a small decrease in attitude results in a large decrease in intention (see Fig. 11.3), the **delay phenomenon**.

For an example of high social normative factors against an established product with high prior intention to purchase, consider the effect of smoking and health reports on cigarette sales. In general the point a_2 will be to the left of the point a_1.

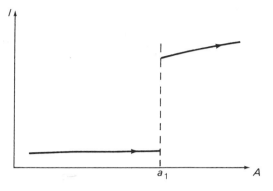

Fig. 11.2 The threshold effect – high social normative factors against; increasing attitude.

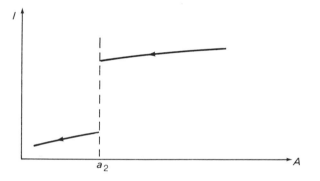

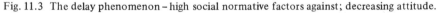

Fig. 11.3 The delay phenomenon – high social normative factors against; decreasing attitude.

The problem facing the marketing director of Continental Cereal is how to reconcile these three types of behaviour in the one model, particularly the cases where a continuous change in one of the controlling variables (A) leads to discontinuous change in the intention to purchase (I). The behaviour is not only non-linear, but the various smoothness conditions on functions are absent.

If a suitable model can be found, there remains the problem of whether to use advertising to increase attitude towards or to reduce social normative factors against Tatopops, or perhaps a combination of both. The first can be achieved by playing up the taste of the product, or the fact that it does you good: for example, 'provides x% of your daily requirement of vitamin y'. Social normative factors can be influenced by having it sponsored by successful sportsmen or by showing it in a happy family setting with Mum serving Tatopops to appreciative children.

After several months, a young pure mathematics graduate, recently recruited, put forward a model based on catastrophe theory, which is described in the next section.

11.2 THE CUSP CATASTROPHE

There is little doubt that of all the fields of human knowledge, the physical services have been most successfully modelled by mathematics. Sir Isaac Newton first used differential equations to describe 'smooth' natural phenomena such as the acceleration of a falling body. This in turn led to the further development of calculus and modern analysis in modelling continuous systems. We have also seen how matrix algebra can be used to model linear systems with a finite number of degrees of freedom. Thus any phenomenon which is continuous, or linear, or both, may be modelled by well-tried methods. But when we meet discontinuous functions, divergent series, or non-linear systems the situation becomes much more difficult.

This is one reason why the quantification of the social and life sciences has proceded so slowly. As has been clear from the examples in this book, economics is the most highly quantified of the social sciences. In the others, and in biology, discontinuity and divergence abound, leading to the label of the 'inexact sciences', because of the limitations of existing mathematical models in describing phenomena in these fields. A similar impasse had been reached in the development of the theory of dynamical systems along quantitive liness although a quantitive theory had been proposed by Poincaré. In recent years a French mathematician, René Thom, developed a qualitative method based on the theory of singularities of mappings, known as catastrophe theory because of the sudden jumps from one state to another. This work has been popularised by E. C. Zeeman and others in wide-ranging applications in the non-physical sciences. The method hinges on a classification theorem stated by Thom and proved by J. N. Mather. Consider a situation where the state of the system is controlled by up to four variables (this will include all real situations with three space variables and one time variable).

In practical terms this theorem states that if continuous changes in control variables cause discontinuous changes in state, then it is possible to choose coordinates in such a way that the kinds of discontinuity which occur are one of a standard list of seven **elementary catastrophes**. These same seven catastrophes govern all physical phenomena.

The seven elementary catastrophies			
Cuspoids	Fold Cusp Swallowtail Butterfly	*Umbilics*	Hyperbolic Elliptic Parabolic

When there is only one control variable, only one type of singularity, the **fold**, can occur. This is shown in Fig. 11.4.

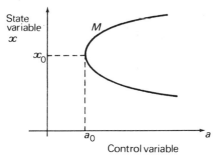

Fig. 11.4 The fold singularity.

At the point a_0 it is possible to move onto either the upper branch of the curve M describing possible states of the system. This might occur in the branching of solutions of an equation or in a double-valued function, where either sign may be taken in the square root, for example

$$x = (a-a_0)^{\frac{1}{2}} + x .$$

When there are two control variables (as in our case, when the state of the system, given by the level of intention to purchase I, is controlled by the two factors S and A) only the fold or the **cusp catastrophe** can occur. The possible states of the system are described by the partly folded surface M given by the equation

$$x^3 = a + bx$$

in the state space with coordinates (a, b, x) (see Fig. 11.5).

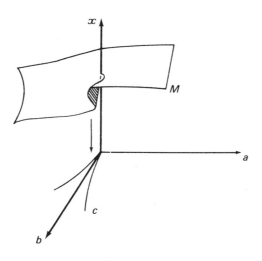

Fig. 11.5 The cusp catastrophe.

If we project the surface M down onto the control plane with coordinates (a, b) (imagine the edges of the shadow cast by a light shining down on a translucent surface M from above) the fold in M shows up in the control plane as a **cusp** C with equation

$$27a^2 - 4b^3 = 0.$$

This equation is obtained by eliminating x from the equation of the surface M and the equation of the fold which is given by

$$3x^2 = b.$$

11.3   THE CUSP CATASTROPHE MODEL FOR THE TATOPOPS LAUNCH

In this case the intention to purchase I is controlled by the two factors S and A. The classification theorem assures us that we can find a change of scale along the three axes that allows us to represent this situation by the cusp catastrophe (we can reject the other possibility, the fold, because it could not account for the changes in the behaviour of I against A for different S). By studying the observed data it is possible to orient the cusp with respect to the S and A axes as shown in Fig. 11.6.

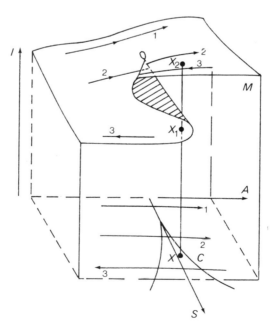

Fig. 11.6.

We see that for many values of S and A there is exactly one point on the intention surface M corresponding to a given point in the (S,A) plane, but for those points lying inside the cusp C (for instance, the point X in Fig. 11.6) there corresponds a point X_1 on the lower leaf of the surface M and a point X_2 on the upper leaf of M.

The paths marked $1, 2, 3$ on the intention surface M correspond to the phenomena described in Figs 11.1 and 11.3 respectively. These paths are also shown projected down onto the control plane in Fig. 11.6. We see that the path 1 in the control plane does not enter the region bounded by the cusp, hence for each point on the path there is a unique point on the intention surface. This gives the case of a continuous increase in intention I arising from a continuous increase in attitude A.

On path 2 we start in a state of low intention to purchase. As attitude to the product increases we enter the cusp region where two states of intention are open, but we remain on the lower leaf until the last possible moment (that is, when the right-hand branch of the cusp is crossed) when we jump on to the top leaf. This gives the threshold effect described in Sec. 10.1. For path 3 the reverse applies: we start with high intention to purchase and remain on the upper leaf until the left-hand branch of the cusp in the control plane is crossed, when we drop down to the lower leaf of the intention surface. Notice that in both cases 2 and 3 the jump in intention does not take place until the second branch of the cusp is crossed. Hence similar paths in the control plane produce different paths on M, depending on the direction in which the branches of the cusp C are crossed. This explains the delay phenomenon encountered in Sec. 10.1.

Once the present position on the intention surface has been found by examining market research data, the correct promotional policy of increasing or decreasing S relative to A may be worked out to obtain a jump up to the upper leaf or to avoid a fall on to the lower leaf. There are situations where decreasing advertising can lead to an increase in intention to purchase. This **surprise reversal effect** is shown in Fig. 11.7. Consider the case of a new product (point P) with low intention to purchase and high social pressures against. Advertising has increased the attitude A towards the product, but not sufficiently to overcome the social pressure. Advertising is abandoned (point Q) and attitude decreases slowly. However, in the absence of advertising, the social pressures also decline and the cusp C is crossed at point R giving a marked increase in intention to purchase.

In this case the cusp in the control plane was bisected by one of the control variable axes S. We say that S is the **splitting factor**. In other cases we may find the cusp between the axes in the control plane, as in Fig. 11.8(ii). In this case we say that the two control dimensions are conflicting factors. We give an example of conflicting factors in Sec. 11.4.1.

Notice that a limitation of catastrophe theory is that it does not produce any figures predicting possible outcomes. What it does provide is a deep understanding of the processes at play in the model and of their interaction. Such a model is *qualitative* rather than quantitive.

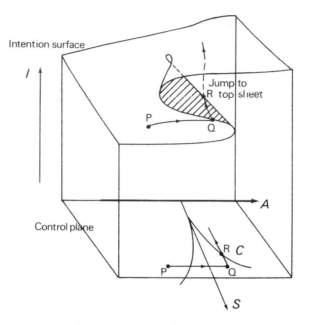

Fig. 11.7 The Surprise Reversal Effect.

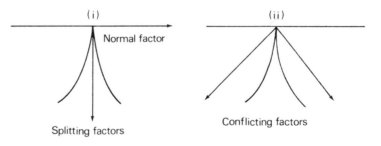

Fig. 11.8.

11.4 CASE STUDIES

11.4.1 'Never pat a cowering dog'

It is often held that fear and rage are conflicting drives influencing aggression. The level of aggression in dogs ranges over a continuous spectrum from attack, threat, barking, and growling to whimpering, cowering, cringing, and flight. Rage on its own causes attack, and fear on its own causes flight; and when both are present, behaviour at either end of the spectrum can occur depending on whether rage or fear occurs first. A small dog may well attack a larger dog which enters its home (rage before fear) whereas, in the street, on neutral territory, it would give it a wide berth (fear before rage). The levels of the rage and fear factors may be measured from observations of facial expressions. These suggest that the cusp catastrophe model is oriented as in Fig. 11.9.

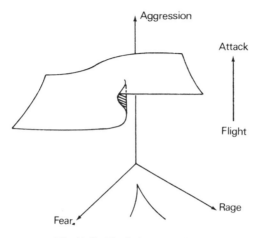

Fig. 11.9   The behaviour of dogs.

It is well-known that relaxation of the threat can lead to a sudden change from threat to attack, and that one should never attempt to pat a strange dog that shows signs of fear. This is another example of the surprise reversal effect. The path in the control plane is shown in Fig. 11.10. If the path is between the branches of the cusp when the threat is relaxed (at point P) the resulting decrease in fear takes the path across the second branch of the cusp with a resulting jump from the lower (flight) leaf of the aggression surface to the upper (attack) leaf. On the other hand, threatening an enraged dog can put it to flight.

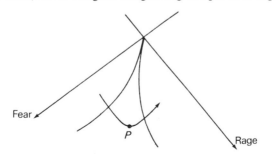

Fig. 11.10   The surprise reversal effect in dogs.

A number of other situations have been examined, using the same model, and we list a few below. The reader may like to consider whether the model in each case is a realistic interpretation of the situation.

Example	Splitting factor	Normal factor
Level of national defence	Cost of achievement	Sense of threat
Censorship	Aesthetic value	Erotic content
Committee decisions	Reaction of opposing group	Action in favour
Nervous impulse	Potassium conductance	Electrical potential
Heartbeat	Muscular tension	Chemical control

11.4.2 Catastrophes in higher dimensions

The five new catastrophes that appear when the number of control variables is increased to 3 or 4 are much more difficult to describe, and we merely mention their existence in this simple account. Models have been constructed for such diverse natural phenomena as the breaking of waves (3 variables) and gastrulation of frogs (4 variables). In the field of personnel management a model for wage bargaining has been put forward with four control variables: (i) concern over worker's wages; (ii) concern over profits; (iii) union over management side; and (iv) time. In the social sciences there have been catastrophe theory explanations for systematic choice, prison riots, and urban growth. The reader who wishes to pursue this subject further should consult the collection of papers by Zeeman (1978).

11.4.3 Mathematical Publication

The mirror of catastrophe theory has even been turned on the published work of mathematicians, with speculative content as the splitting factor and mathematical ability as the normal factor. We reproduce the Figure below without further comment.

11.5 PROBLEMS

1. Aggression in fish

    Certain species of tropical fish exhibit aggressive behaviour in defending their nesting territory against intruders. The behaviour of the fish, ranging from fight to flight, is thought to depend on two factors: distance from the nest and size of opponent. Observation of the fish encounters gives the cusp in the control plane shown in Fig. 11.12.

    In this case are distance and size normal and splitting factors or conflicting factors? Sketch the level of aggression surface corresponding to Fig. 11.12.

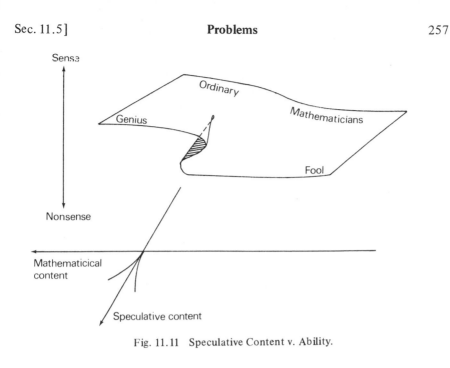

Fig. 11.11 Speculative Content v. Ability.

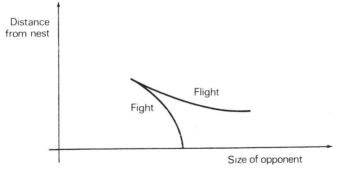

Fig. 11.12 Encounters of tropical fish.

Draw the paths on the aggression surface and in the control plane which describe the behaviour of the fish when:

(i) it meets a large intruder near the nest; and

(ii) it meets a large opponent far from the nest.

In some species it has been observed that whichever partner is nearer the nest will put up a stronger defence, regardless of sex. How can this be explained in terms of the cusp catastrophe model?

2. 'Bulls and Bears'

When the stock market is rising (as measured by the *Financial Times* Index, say) it is usually called a 'bull' market, while it is a 'bear' market if the index is falling. Thus the state of the market may be roughly described by the rate of change of the index. In a normal market the main reason for rise in the index is excess demand for stock by investors. But the market may also rise when few transactions are taking place, and this is thought to be due to speculative factors induced by a feeling of confidence when bank rate falls, the trade figures are good, or a strike is called off. Conversely, a set of bad trade figures or gloomy prognostications from leading bankers may rapidly lead to a 'bear' market. The closed world of the stock market is very sensitive to events when it is in this abnormal state of high speculative content but low excess demand.

By taking rate of change of index as the state variable, excess demand as a normal factor, and speculative content as a splitting factor, construct a cusp catastrophe model of the stock market which will explain stock market 'crashes', or catastrophic falls in the index.

Given that there are two main groups of investors, the 'chartists', who base their policy on charts of previous performance, and the 'fundamentalists', who base their policy on their view of the economic situation and growth potential of the firms, show, using the model, how this may precipitate a crash but also lead to a recovery in the post-crash situation.

[Based on an example in Zeeman (1978).]

APPENDIX I

Number Systems

Consider the set of natural numbers $\mathbf{N} = \{0, 1, 2, 3, \ldots\}$. It is easy to see that the sum and product of two natural numbers is again a natural number (we say that $\mathbf{N}$ is **closed** under addition and multiplication), but if we subtract two elements of $\mathbf{N}$ we need not obtain an element of $\mathbf{N}$ (try taking 3 from 2). Algebraically, this means that we cannot form additive inverse within the set $\mathbf{N}$; given any $n \in \mathbf{N}$ there is no element $m \in \mathbf{N}$ such that $n + m = 0$.

We overcome this difficulty by moving to the set of integers

$$\mathbf{Z} = \{\ldots, -2, -1, 0, 1, 2 \ldots\}$$

which contains $\mathbf{N}$ as a subset. $\mathbf{Z}$ is closed under addition, multiplication, and subtraction, but not under division. Given $n \in \mathbf{Z}$ there is no $p \in \mathbf{Z}$ such that $np = 1$. For this reason we prefer to work with the set of rational numbers

$$\mathbf{Q} = \{p/q : p, q \in \mathbf{Z}\}.$$

Notice that $\mathbf{Z}$ is the subset of $\mathbf{Q}$ obtained when $q = 1$. It is easily seen that $\mathbf{Q}$ is closed under all four operations of addition, subtraction, multiplication and division.

Many algebraic equations with coefficients in $\mathbf{Q}$ have solutions in $\mathbf{Q}$: for instance

$$4x^2 - 1 = 0$$

has solutions $x = \frac{1}{2}$ and $x = -\frac{1}{2}$. There are, though, other equations of this type which have no solutions in $\mathbf{Q}$. The equation

$$x^2 - 2 = 0$$

can be shown to have no solution in $\mathbf{Q}$; that is, there is no rational number whose square is 2. We know, of course, that the solutions of this equation are the irrational numbers $\pm\sqrt{2}$. We therefore consider the real number system **R** which includes both rational and irrational numbers and whose elements may be thought of as points on a line.

We assume then the existence of a set **R** equipped with:

(a) an operation of addition, $+$, such that to each pair of numbers $a, b \in \mathbf{R}$ there corresponds a unique number $a + b$, the **sum** of a and b;

(b) an operation of multiplication such that to each pair $a, b \in \mathbf{R}$ there corresponds a unique number ab, the **product** of a and b; and

(c) a relation of **ordering** $a < b$, read as 'a is less than b', on **R**,

which satisfies the axioms:

additive axioms
$\begin{cases}
\text{(i) } a + b = b + a \\
\text{(ii) } (a + b) + c = a + (b + c) \\
\text{(iii) there is an element } 0 \in \mathbf{R} \text{ such that } a + 0 = a \text{ for all} \\
\quad a \in \mathbf{R} \\
\text{(iv) for all } a \in \mathbf{R} \text{ there is } a -a \in \mathbf{R} \text{ such that } -a + a = 0
\end{cases}$

multiplicative axioms
$\begin{cases}
\text{(v) } ab = ba \\
\text{(vi) } a(bc) = (ab)c \\
\text{(vii) there is an element } 1 \in \mathbf{R}, 1 \neq 0 \text{ such that for all } a \in \mathbf{R}, \\
\quad 1a = a \\
\text{(viii) if } a \in \mathbf{R}, a \neq 0, \text{ there is } a^{-1} \in \mathbf{R} \text{ such that } aa^{-1} = 1
\end{cases}$

distributive law (ix) $a(b + c) = ab + ac$

order axioms
$\begin{cases}
\text{(x) if } a \in \mathbf{R} \text{ either } a > 0 \text{ or } a = 0 \text{ or } a < 0 \\
\text{(xi) if } a, b \in \mathbf{R} \text{ and } 0 < a, 0 < b \text{ then } 0 < a + b, 0 < ab \\
\text{(xii) for } a, b \in \mathbf{R}, a < b \text{ if and only if } a - b < 0
\end{cases}$

completeness axiom
(xiii) if A is a non-empty subset of **R** and A is bounded above (that is, there is $ab \in \mathbf{R}$ such that $a \leqslant b$ for all $a \in A$) then A has a least upper bound. (We say that c is a least upper bound for A if there is no other upper bound b which is less than c).

This last property (xiii) that every non-empty subset which is bounded above has a least upper bound is very important in the subsequent development of mathematical analysis. An equivalent statement is that every non-empty subset of the real numbers bounded below has a greatest lower bound. Either statement allows us to deduce the **Archimedean property of the real numbers**. Given any real number $a > 0$, for any other real number b we can find a natural number n such that $na > b$.

From the same axiom the existence of a real number whose square is 2 can also be proved. The absolute value of a real number a is the non-negative real number $|a|$ given by

$$|a| = \begin{cases} a & \text{if} \quad a \geqslant 0 \\ -a & \text{if} \quad a < 0. \end{cases}$$

If we define $\sqrt{a}$ to be the unique non-negative real number whose square is a, we may show that

$$|a| = \sqrt{a^2}.$$

Going back to our concept of real numbers as points on a line (the **real line**), the distance $d(a,b)$ between two real numbers a and b is given by

$$d(a,b) = |a - b|.$$

We can verify that for any a, b, $c \in \mathbf{R}$, d has the properties
  (i) $d(a,b) \geqslant 0$
  (ii) $d(a,b) = 0$ if and only if $a = b$
  (iii) $d(a,b) = d(b,a)$
  (iv) $d(a,b) \leqslant d(a,c) + d(c,b)$.
It may also be proved from the Archimedean property that there is a rational number q arbitrarily close to any real number a, that is, given any $\epsilon > 0$, we can find q such that $|a - q| < \epsilon$ (see Fig. AI.1).

Fig. AI.1   The rationals and the reals.

For, given $\epsilon > 0$, we can choose n so that $1/n < \epsilon$. Then there is a $k \in \mathbf{N}$ such that $(k-1)/n \leqslant a < k/n$. Choosing $q = (k-1)/n$, which is rational, gives the required result.

One disadvantage of the real numbers is that there are equations whose coefficients are real numbers but which do not have real numbers as solutions. For instance the equation

$$x^2 + 2 = 0$$

has no solution $x \in \mathbf{R}$. We overcome this difficulty by introducing a set of objects, called **complex numbers**, with the operations of addition and multiplication defined so that the sum and product of two complex numbers is again a complex number, and satisfying:
  (a) every real number is a complex number, and if a and b are real numbers

then their sum and product as complex numbers are the same as their sum and product as real numbers;

(b) there is a complex number i such that $i^2 = -1$;

(c) every complex α can be written uniquely as $a + ib$ where a,b are real; and

(d) the ordinary laws of arithmetic, given in axioms (i) -(ix) for the real numbers, are satisfied (N.B: The elements 0 and 1 are the same for both real and complex numbers, by (a)).

We denote the set of complex numbers by **C**. the real numbers a and b in (c) are usually called the **real** and **imaginary** parts of the complex number α. We may also express α in **polar form** $\alpha = re^{i\theta}$ where $r = (a^2 + b^2)^{1/2}$ and $\tan\theta = {}^b\!/a$.

This enables us to think of complex numbers as points in a plane whose axes are the real and imaginary parts as shown in Fig. AI.2.

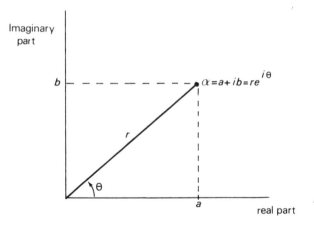

Fig. AI.2   The complex plane.

The complex numbers **C** have the important property that every equation with coefficients in **C** has solutions in **C**. Thus the equation $x^2 + 2 = 0$, which we saw had no solutions in **R**, has solutions $\pm i\sqrt{2}$ in **C**.

Integration

Given a suitable function $f(x)$ we have seen that it is possible to associate with it another function $f'(x)$, the derivative of f. We now pose the converse question: Given a function $f(x)$, can we find a function $F(x)$ whose derivative is $f(x)$, that is, $F'(x) = f(x)$? When such an $F(x)$ exists we call it an **antiderivative** or a **primitive integral** of $f(x)$ and write

$$F(x) = \int f(x) dx.$$

For example, an antiderivative of $3x^2$ is x^3, since $\dfrac{d}{dx}(x^3) = 3x^2$; but so too is $x^3 + k$, where k is any constant, since $\dfrac{d}{dx}(x^3 + k) = \dfrac{d(x^3)}{dx} + \dfrac{d(k)}{dx} = 3x^2 + 0 = 3x^2$.

Thus the primitive integral is not unique, but contains an arbitrary additive constant k. The following standard primitive integrals can be verified by differentiation:

$$\int x^n dx = \frac{x^{n+1}}{n+1} + k \qquad\qquad (n \neq -1)$$

$$\int k f(x) dx = k \int f(x) dx$$

$$\int (f(x)) + (g(x)) dx = \int f(x) dx + \int g(x) dx$$

$$\int (f(x))^n f'(x) dx = (f(x))^{n+1} + k \qquad\qquad n \neq -1$$

$$\int \frac{1}{x} dx = \log |x| + k$$

$$\int e^x dx = e^x + k$$

$$\int e^{f(x)} f'(x) dx = e^{f(x)} + k$$

$$\int \frac{f'(x)}{f(x)} \, dx = \log | f(x) | + k.$$

Now let $f(x)$ be a continuous function defined on an interval I of $\mathbf{R}$. Let $F(x)$ be a primitive integral of $f(x)$. For $a, b \in I$ we define the **definite integral** of $f(x)$ from a to b to be the real number

$$F(b) - F(a).$$

Thus the definite integral of $3x^2$ from 1 to 2 is

$$F(2) - F(1) = 2^3 - 1^3 = 8 - 1 = 7.$$

The definite integral of $f(x)$ from a to b is usually denoted by

$$\int_a^b f(x) \, dx = F(b) - F(a) = [F(x)]_a^b .$$

Thus in the above example

$$\int_1^2 3x^2 \, dx = [x^3]_1^2 = 7.$$

Notice that the definition is independent of the choice of primitive integral of $f(x)$, for if $G(x) = F(x) + k$ is another primitive integral of $f(x)$ then

$$G(b) - G(a) = F(b) + k - (F(a) + k) = F(b) - F(a).$$

We remark that whereas the primitive integral is a function, the definite integral is a real number obtained by taking a difference of function values. As a consequence of the definition and from the properties already given for primitive integrals we can prove that:

$$\int_a^b f(x) \, dx = - \int_b^a f(x) \, dx, \quad \text{and, in particular,} \quad \int_a^a f(x) \, dx = 0.$$

$$\int_a^b f(x) \, dx = \int_a^c f(x) \, dx + \int_c^b f(x) \, dx \quad \text{for} \quad a < c < b.$$

$$\int_a^b k f(x) \, dx = k \int_a^b (f(x) \, dx)$$

$$\int_a^b (f(x) + g(x)) \, dx = \int_a^b f(x) \, dx + \int_a^b g(x) \, dx .$$

The definite integral of $f(x)$ from a to b has the geometrical interpretation of the area lying between the graph $y=f(x)$ and the x-axis enclosed by the lines $x=a$ and $x=b$ (see Fig. AII.1).

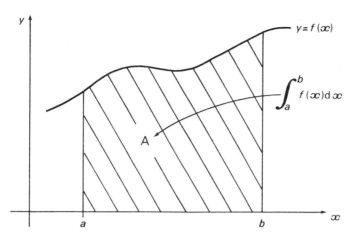

Fig. AII.1 Geometrical interpretation of the definite integral.

The concept of the definite integral as the area under the graph can be given a more precise definition as follows. This interpretation, due to Riemann, depends on approximating the area under the graph by rectangles. If we denote by A the area under the graph between $x=a$ and $x=b$ then we can see, from Fig. AII.2,

$$R_1 > A > r_1,$$

where R_1 is the area of the rectangle based on (a, b) whose height is the maximum

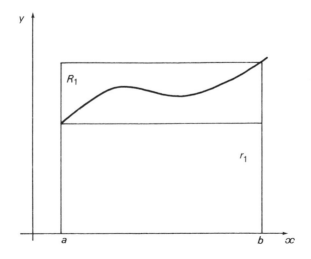

Fig. AII.2 First approximation by rectangles.

value of $f(x)$, and r_1 is the area of the rectangle based on (a, b) whose height is the minimum value of $f(x)$ on (a, b).

Suppose now that (a, b) is divided into n equal subintervals, and that corresponding to each subinterval we construct a sequence of upper rectangles with areas $R_1, R_2, \dots R_n$ and a sequence of lower rectangles with areas $r_1, r_2, \dots r_n$ as in Fig. AII.3. Then it is clear from the figure that

$$R_1 + R_2 + \dots + R_n > A > r_1 + r_2 + \dots + r_n$$

and that as n increases we obtain a better approximation to A. If the series $\sum_{n=1}^{\infty} R_n$ and $\sum_{n=1}^{\infty} r_n$ both converge to the value A we say that $f(x)$ is **integrable** from a to b and

$$\int_a^b f(x)\mathrm{d}x = A.$$

It can be shown that Riemann's definition of the integral is equivalent to the definition of the definite integral given earlier in terms of the primitive integral.

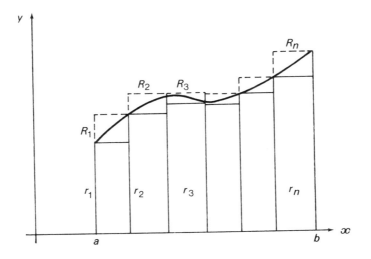

Fig. AII.3   Approximation by n rectangles.

Partial Differentiation

Suppose $f = f(x,y)$ is a real single-valued function of two independent variables x and y. We define the partial derivative of f with respect to x as

$$\frac{\partial f}{\partial x} = \lim_{\delta x \to 0} \left\{ \frac{f(x+\delta x, y) - f(x,y)}{\delta x} \right\}$$

and, similarly, the partial derivative of f with respect to y as

$$\frac{\partial f}{\partial y} = \lim_{\delta y \to 0} \left\{ \frac{f(x, y+\delta y) - f(x,y)}{\delta y} \right\}.$$

These definitions mean that the partial derivative with respect to x effectively means differentiating with respect to x, regarding y as a constant.

Examples

(i) If $f(x,y) = x^2 - 2y^2,$ then $\dfrac{\partial f}{\partial x} = 2x, \dfrac{\partial f}{\partial y} = -4y$

(ii) If $f(x,y) = e^x \cos y,$ then $\dfrac{\partial f}{\partial x} = e^x \cos y, \dfrac{\partial f}{\partial y} = -e^x \sin y$

(iii) If $f(x,y) = x^2 + 2xy + y^2,$ then $\dfrac{\partial f}{\partial x} = 2x + 2y, \dfrac{\partial f}{\partial y} = 2x + 2y.$

We can readily extend these definitions to second order partial derivatives; namely

$$\frac{\partial^2 f}{\partial x^2} = \frac{\partial}{\partial x}\left(\frac{\partial f}{\partial x}\right), \frac{\partial^2 f}{\partial y \partial x} = \frac{\partial}{\partial y}\left(\frac{\partial f}{\partial x}\right), \frac{\partial^2 f}{\partial y^2} = \frac{\partial}{\partial y}\left(\frac{\partial f}{\partial y}\right), \frac{\partial^2 f}{\partial x \partial y} = \frac{\partial}{\partial x}\left(\frac{\partial f}{\partial y}\right).$$

The mixed partial derivatives $\dfrac{\partial^2 f}{\partial y \partial x}$, $\dfrac{\partial^2 f}{\partial x \partial y}$ are, for well behaved functions, equal.

Example

If $f(x,y) = x^2 y + y^2 x$, then

$$\frac{\partial f}{\partial x} = 2xy + y^2, \quad \frac{\partial^2 f}{\partial x^2} = 2y, \quad \frac{\partial^2 f}{\partial y \partial x} = 2x + 2y$$

and

$$\frac{\partial f}{\partial y} = x^2 + 2yx, \quad \frac{\partial^2 f}{\partial y^2} = 2x, \quad \frac{\partial^2 f}{\partial x \partial y} = 2x + 2y \ .$$

[As expected, the mixed derivatives $\dfrac{\partial^2 f}{\partial y \partial x}$ and $\dfrac{\partial^2 f}{\partial x \partial y}$ are equal.]

Bibliography and References

Andrews, J. G. and McLone, R. R., Mathematical Modelling (Butterworth, 1976)

Bailey, N. T. J., The Mathematical Theory of Infectious Diseases (Griffin, 1975)

Battersby, A., Mathematics in Management (Penguin, 1966)

Bender, E. A., An Introduction to Mathematical Modelling (Wiley, 1978)

Bittinger, M. L., Calculus, A Modelling Approach (Addison-Wesley, 1976)

Bradford, M. G. and Kent, W. A., Human Geography (Oxford, 1977)

Braun, M., Differential Equations and their Applications (Springer Verlag, 1975)

Burley, D., Mathematical Model for a Kidney Machine, (*Mathematical Spectrum* 8 69)

Central Statistical Office, Financial Statistics (London H.M.S.O.)

Davenport, W., Jamaican Fishing: A Game Theory Analysis (Yale Univ., 1960)

Derrick, W. R. and Crossman, S., Elementary Differential Equations with Applications (Addison-Wesley, 1977)

Gandolfo, G., Mathematical Methods and Models in Economics (North Holland 1971)

Goult, R., Hoskins, R., Milner, J. and Pratt, M., Applicable Mathematics (Macmillan, 1973)

Grossman, S. and Turner, J., Mathematics for the Biological Sciences (Macmillan, 1974)

Haberman, R., Mathematical Models (Prentice Hall, 1977)

Hastings, N. A. J., Dynamic Programming with Management Applications (Butterworth, 1973)

Haywood, O. G., Military Decision and Game Theory, *J. Operational Res. of America,* Nov. 1954

Holt, M. and Marjoram, D. T. E., Mathematics in a Changing World (Heinemann, 1973)

Hull, J., Mapes, J. and Wheeler, B., Model Building Techniques for Management (Saxon House, 1976)

Kememy, J. and Snell, J., Mathematical Models in the Social Sciences (MIT Press, 1962)

Keynes, J. M., General Theory of Employment, Interest and Money (MacMillan, 1942)

Lancaster, P., Mathematical Models of the Real World (Prentice Hall, 1976)

Lial, M. L. and Miller, C. D., Mathematics with Applications in Management, Natural and Social Sciences (Scott Foresman, 1973)

Lighthill, J., Newer Uses of Mathematics (Penguin, 1978)

McDonald, T., Mathematical Methods for Social and Management Scientists, (Haughton Mifflin, 1974)

Maki, D. P. and Thompson, M., Mathematical Models and Applications (Prentice Hall, 1973)

Mather, J. N., Stability of C^{∞} mappings, *Annals of Mathematics* 87 (1968) 89-104

Murdick, R., Mathematical Models in Marketing (Intext, 1971)

Notari, R. E., Biopharmaceutics and Pharmacokinetics (Dekker, 1975)

Open University, Mathematics Foundation Course, M 101, Block V, (1978)

Open University, Modelling by Mathematics, TM 281, (1977)

Read, R. C., A Mathematical Background for Economics and Social Scientists (Prentice Hall, 1972)

Samuelson, P., Economics (McGraw Hill, 1973)

Sanchez, D., Ordinary Differential Equations with Stability Theory, (Freeman, 1968)

Sturn, M. E., Mathematics for Management (Prentice Hall, 1965)

Teichroew, D., Introduction to Management Science Deterministic Models (Wiley, 1964)

Thom, R., *Stabilité structurelle et morphogénèse*, Benjamin, 1972

Vidale, M. L. and Wolfe, H. B., An Operations-Research Study of Sales Response to Advertising, *Operations Research* June 1957

Wagner, M., Principles of Management Science (Prentice Hall, 1975)

Walford, R., Games in Geography (Longman, 1969)

Wilson, A. G. and Kirkby, M. J., Mathematics for Geographers and Planners (Clarendon, 1975)

Zeeman, E. C., Catastrophe Theory: Selected Papers 1972-1977 (Addison-Wesley, 1978)

Answers to Problems

SOLUTIONS TO CHAPTER 2

1. (i) $\ldots, 14, 17, 20, n$ $a_n = 3n - 1$
   (ii) $\ldots, -9, -15, -21, \ldots$ $a_n = 21 - 6n$
   (iii) $\ldots, 8, 9, 9, \ldots$ $a_n = 1/2n^2 + 7/2n - 10$
   (iv) $\ldots, \frac{7}{8}, \frac{8}{9}, \frac{9}{10}, \ldots$ $a_n = (n+3)/(n+4)$
   (v) $\ldots, 7/5, 7/6, 1, \ldots$ $a_n = 7/n \to 0$ as $n \to \infty$

2. From formula (2.5) $S_n = 21/2 \times (14 + 20 \times 3) = 777$

3. $\{4, 11, 18, 25, 32, 39, 46, 53, 60, 67, 74, \ldots\}$.

4. From (2.5) (i) $S_n = (n/2)(9 + 5n)$; (ii) $S_n = n(3n - 20)$.

5. $a_n = 16n - 203$.

6. $\{2, 12, 72, 432, 2592, 15552, 93312, \ldots\}; S_7 = 111974$

7. $S_n = 48(1 - (1/2)^n) \to 48$ as $n \to \infty$.

8. $a_n = 10 \times 4^{n-1}$.

9. Let a_n be number of bacteria after $4(n-1)$ hours. Then $a_1 = 20, r = 3$ and answer is $a_7 = 20 \times 3^6 = 14580$.

10. £5250.

11. £2400.

12. Depreciation is £1350 per year.

13. 1976.

14. First option £3680, but he should choose second which gives £3800.

15. From (2.7). P.V. = £5000.

16. (2.9) gives (i) a_5 = £140.26; (ii) a_{10} = £196.72; (iii) a_{20} = £386.97.

17. From (2.10). P.V. = £3855.43.

18. From (2.9) rate of interest is 7½% per annum.

19. Option (i).

20. 16 years.

21. From (2.12). P.V. = £1404.72.

22. (i) £1761.89; (ii) £1652.52; (iii) £1591.19. In case 2 monthly payment less tax relief is £96.40.

23. Formula follows from (2.12). The new machine will have paid for itself in the seventeenth year.

24. Using $Y_t = C_t + I_t$, $C_t = cY_{t-1}$ we obtain $c = 0.85$ and may construct the tables

t	Y_{t-1}	C_t	I_t	Y_t	$Y_t - Y_{t-1}$
£1m extra spent in month 0					
−1	100	85	15	100	0
0	100	85	16	101	1
1	101	85.85	15	100.85	−0.15
2	100.85	85.72	15	100.72	−0.13
3	100.72	85.61	15	100.61	−0.11
4	100.61	85.52	15	100.52	−0.09
5	100.52	85.44	15	100.44	−0.08
6	100.44	85.38	15	100.38	−0.06
£2m extra spent in month 0					
−1	100	85	15	100	0
0	100	85	17	102	2
1	102	86.7	15	101.7	−0.3
2	101.7	86.45	15	101.45	−0.25
3	101.45	86.23	15	101.23	−0.22
4	101.23	86.04	15	101.04	−0.19
5	101.04	85.89	15	100.89	−0.15
6	100.89	85.75	15	100.75	−0.14

SOLUTIONS TO CHAPTER 3

1. (i) both; (ii) onto only; (iii) one-to-one only; (iv), (v) both.

4. (i) $(1+x)^2$; (ii) $\sin(x^2)$; (iii) x.

5. (i) $y = x-1$; (ii) $y = 1-x$; (iii) $y = 2x-1$.

6. (i) $x = -b/a$.

7. (i) 3, 4; (ii) 8 (twice); (iii) $-1, -4$.

8. (i) 2; (ii) 1/6; (iii) 2; (iv) fails to exist.

9. (i) infinite discontinuity at $x = 0$.
   (ii) continuous.
   (iii) infinite discontinuities at $x \pm 1$.

10. $f^{-1}(y) = +\sqrt{1/y - 1}$; no inverse if $x \in \mathbf{R}$ since inverse would be double valued and not a function.

11. Gross profit $= (p-D)x - F$.

12. (a) £1519; (b) £126; (c) production 31 tons, price £24.

13. (a) £145080; (b) £24420; (c) production 910 tons, total production costs £106470.

14. Expected sales $= 20000 + 6$ (amount spent $- 150$), £20180.

15. 16 yards of A, 12 yards of B.

16. $t = 70 - 0.003$ h.

18. Equilibrium price $= (b+c)/(a+d)$.

19. $S = 3500p - 3900, D = 189000 - 2500p$, £38, 94000 tons.

20. $S = \begin{cases} 7p + 50 & (p \leqslant 30) \\ 16p - 220 & (p \geqslant 30) \end{cases}$ $D = \begin{cases} 330 - 22p & (p \leqslant 25) \\ 470 - 8p & (p \geqslant 25) \end{cases}$; £28; 24600 tons

21. Equilibrium price $= 81.67p$.

SOLUTIONS TO CHAPTER 4

1. (i) $6x + 2$; (ii) $4x^3$; (iii) $2\cos x - 5\sin x$; (iv) $x\sin x + \frac{1}{2}(1+x^2)\cos x$;
   (v) $\sin 2x$; (vi) $4x/(1-x^2)^2$; (vii) $-2\sin x/(1-\cos x)^2$; (viii) $4\cos(4x)$;
   (ix) $36x^2(1+4x^3)^2$; (x) $3x^2 e^{x^3}$; (xi) $1/(1+x)$; (xii) $2x(\log x^2 + 1)$.

2. (i) $4x(1+x^2)$, $4(1+3x^2)$.
   (ii) $2x + 4$, 2.
   (iii) $2\cos(2x)$, $-4\sin(2x)$.
   (iv) $e^x/1 + e^x)$, $e^x/(1+e^x)^2$.
   (v) $(x^2 - 2x - 1)/(1+x^2)^2$, $2(x-1)(1+2x-x^2)/(1+x^2)^3$.

3. (i) minimum at $x = 0$; (ii) minimum at $x = 2$.
   (ii) minimum at $x = 2$, maximum at $x = -2$.
   (iii) minimum at $x = 3$, maximum at $x = -1$.

4. (i) $\dfrac{dy}{dx} = 3x^2 + 6x + 2$, $\dfrac{d^2y}{dx^2} = 6(x+1)$; maximum at $x = -1.577$,
   minimum at $x = -0.423$

   (ii) $\dfrac{dy}{dx} = -8x/(4+x^2)^2$, $\dfrac{d^2y}{dx^2} = 24(x^2-1)/(4+x^2)^3$; maximum at $x = 0$,

   (iii) $\dfrac{dy}{dx} = (1-2x-x^2)/(1+x^2)^2$, $\dfrac{d^2y}{dx^2} = 2(x-1)(x^2+4x+1)/(1+x^2)^3$;
   maximum at $x = 0.41$, minimum at $x = -2.41$

5. M.P. $= Ax(2-x^3)/(1+x^3)^2$, A.P. $= Ax/(1+x^3)$; $(0, 0.71)$, $(0.71, 1.26)$,
   $(1.26, \infty)$; $E = (2-x^3)/(1+x^3)$.

6. $T = \begin{cases} 1000x \\ -1000 + 1200x - 10x^2 \end{cases}$ $P = \begin{cases} 500x & , x \leqslant 10 \\ -1000 + 700x - 10x^2, & x > 10 \end{cases}$

   For max. revenue, fleet size $= 60$
   For max profit,   fleet size $= 35$.

7. $V = 4x(4-x)(5-x)$ is a maximum when $x = 1.47$ m., with maximum value 52.51 m^3.

8. The square.

10. $p(0) = 100$ and maximum population reached at $t = 20$ days.

11. £410, £38 950, 95.

12. £210, £3100, 90.

13. 750.

14. 43.

15. 37, 0, 38, £12781.33.

16. $\dfrac{dF}{dx} = -rc_1/x^2 + \tfrac{1}{2}c_2 = 0$ when $x = \sqrt{2rc_1/c_2}$.

SOLUTIONS TO CHAPTER 5

1. (i) $x\,t = k$; (ii) $x\,\cos t = k$; (iii) $x = k\,e^{bt/a}$; $x\,t = 1, x\,t = 2$.

2. (i) $x = e^{2t} + Ae^{t}$; (ii) $x = (A - \cos t)/t$; (iii) $x = t + A/t$; $x = t + 1/t$.

4. $x = t^2 + A/t^2$.

6. (i) $x^2/4 + t^2/9 = A$; (ii) $x = A\,e^{-t^2}$; (iii) $x = \tan(t + t^2/2 + A)$;
   (iv) $x^3 = \tfrac{3}{4}(2t + \sin 2t) + A$; $x^3 = \tfrac{3}{4}(2t + \sin 2t)$.

7. $N = \dfrac{\gamma N_0^{\alpha-1}\,e^{(\alpha-1)t}}{[\gamma - \eta N_0^{\alpha-1} + \eta N_0^{\alpha-1}\,e^{(\alpha-1)t}]}$.

8. $\eta = \gamma/N_\infty$, $N_\infty = 197 \times 10^6$.

9. If $\alpha = N_0/N_\infty$, $\alpha_1 = N_0/N_1$, $\alpha_2 = N_0/N_2$, then
   $$\alpha = (\alpha_2 - \alpha_1^2)/(1 - 2\alpha_1 + \alpha_2),\ \gamma = \log[(1-\alpha_1)/(\alpha_1 - \alpha_2)];$$
   i.e. $N_\infty = 259.6 \times 10^6$.

13. $S = M(1 - e^{2ar\,(1-t/\tau)^2/M})$.

14. $w = 1/(\alpha/\beta + A\,e^{-\beta t/2})^2$.

15. $x = x_0\,e^{a(1-\cos bt)/b}$.

16. $Q = \dfrac{a}{b}(1 - e^{-bt}) + Q_0 e^{-bt}$

   $Q \to \dfrac{a}{b}$ as $t \to \infty$.

17. $x = mn\,(1 - e^{-(m-n)kt})/(m - ne^{-(m-n)kt})$

   $x \to n$ as $t \to \infty$.

18. $x = bx_0/[be^{-bat} + x_0(1 - e^{-bat})]$

$x \to b$ as $t \to \infty$.

19. $w = [c(1 - \alpha)t]^{1/(1-\alpha)}$.

As $\alpha \to 1$, the model approaches exponential growth.

20. $\dfrac{x_0^2(k-x)(k+x)}{x^2(k-x_0)(k+x_0)} = e^{-2k^2\alpha t}$.

SOLUTIONS TO CHAPTER 6

1. $x = A e^t + B e^{2t}$.

2. (i) $x = Ae^t + B e^{-2t}; A = 1/(1-e^3), B = e^3/(e^3-1)$.

(ii) $x = Ce^t \cos(4t + \omega)$.
(iii) $x = C \cos(5t + \omega)$.
(iv) $x = C e^{-t} \cos(\sqrt{3}t + \omega)$.
(v) $x = (A + Bt) e^t; A = 2, B = 2(e^{-1}-1)$.

3. $x = At + B/t$.

4. $x = A \cos(t + \omega) + e^t$.

5. $x = \left[\dfrac{1 + e^2}{(1 - e^2)} + t\right] e^t + \left[\dfrac{2e^2}{(e^2 - 1)}\right]e^{-t}$.

6. (i) $x = A e^t + B e^t + 5t + 15/2$.
(ii) $x = A \cos(2t + \omega) + \frac{1}{5} e^{-t}$.
(iii) $x = (A + Bt) e^{-t} + 2t^2 - 8t + 12$.
(iv) $x = A e^t + B e^{-t} - \frac{1}{2} \sin t$.
(v) $x = A \cos t + (B - t/2) \sin t$.

7. (a) As $\alpha \to \omega$, $|x(t)| \to \infty$.

8. $y = \pm \sqrt{c^2 - x^2}$.

9. $Y = (-2.775 e^{0.91t} + 4.775 e^{0.11t} + 1) G$.

10. Forecast price $p(t) = Ae^{\lambda_1 t} + Be^{\lambda_2 t} + \left(\dfrac{a_1 - a_2}{b_1 - a_2}\right)$ is stable if real parts of $\lambda_{1,2} =$

$\dfrac{-\gamma(c_1 - c_2) \pm \sqrt{\gamma^2(c_1 - c_2)^2 - 4(b_1 - b_2)\gamma}}{2} < 0$ which will be true if $c_1 > c_2$

and $b_1 > b_2$.

11. Multiply 2nd equation by b and subtract from c times 1st equation to obtain an expression for $\dot{y}$ in terms of x, $\dot{x}$. Substitute this in the 1st equation differentiated once

$$\alpha_{1,2} = \frac{a+c}{2} \pm \tfrac{1}{2}\sqrt{(a-c)^2 + 4db},\; y(t) = \frac{(a-\alpha_1)}{b}Ae^{\alpha_1 t} + \frac{(a-\alpha_2)}{b}Be^{\alpha_2 t}.$$

with values given $x(t) = -150\,e^{3t} + 250e^t$
$$y(t) = \quad 75\,e^{3t} + 125e^t$$

Thus x species is eliminated when $e^{2t} = \tfrac{5}{3}$ i.e. $t = 0.255$.

12. Preceding as above $\alpha_{1,2} = -\dfrac{a+c}{2} \pm \tfrac{1}{2}\sqrt{(a+c)^2 - 4(ac-db)}$

Both real parts of α_1 and $\alpha_2 < 0$ unless $ac \leqslant bd$.
With values given $x(t) = 150e^{2t} - 50e^{-6t}$
$$y(t) = 150e^{2t} + 50e^{-6t}$$

Hence both populations increase indefinitely.

13. For constant advertising $B(t) = C_1 e^{\lambda_1 t} + C_2 e^{\lambda_2 t} + \dfrac{cA}{ab\,(\alpha\beta-1)}, c_1, c_2$ constants

and where $\lambda_{1,2} = \dfrac{b\beta+a\alpha}{2} \pm \tfrac{1}{2}\sqrt{(b\beta + a\alpha)^2 - 4\,ab(\alpha\beta - 1)}$

Thus $B(t)$ tends to limiting value if the real parts of $\lambda_1, \lambda_2 < 0$ which will be true if $\alpha\beta > 1$.

For $0 < t < 10$ $B(t) = 100(-\tfrac{1}{2}e^t + \tfrac{1}{6}e^{-3t} + \tfrac{1}{3})$
$$M(t) = 100(-\tfrac{1}{2}e^t - \tfrac{1}{6}e^{-3t} + \tfrac{2}{3})$$

SOLUTIONS TO CHAPTER 7

1. (i) $x_k = 1 + 2k$.
    (ii) $x_k = [1 - (-2)^k]/3$.
    (iii) $x_k = 3(1/4)^k + 2[1 - (1/4)^k]/3$.

2. (i) $x_k = A\left(\dfrac{-1+\sqrt5}{2}\right)^k + B\left(\dfrac{-1-\sqrt5}{2}\right)^k$.

    (ii) $x_k = (-3)^k A + B$.
    (iii) $x_k = A\,(1/3)^k + B(-1)^k$.

3. (i) $x_k = (A\,k + B)\,(-2)^k$.
    (ii) $x_k = (A\,k + B)\,(-1)^k$.
    (iii) $x_k = (\sqrt{10})^k\,[A\cos\Theta k + B\sin\Theta k],\; \cos\Theta = -3/2\sqrt{10}$,
    $$\sin\Theta = \sqrt{31}/2\sqrt{10}.$$

6. $x_k = -\dfrac{1}{36}(1 + 6k) + A3^k + B(-2)^k$.

(ii) $x_k = \dfrac{2^k}{343}(49k^2 - 140k + 84) + A \cos \dfrac{2\pi k}{3} + B \sin \dfrac{2\pi k}{3}$.

(iii) $x_k = \dfrac{(-3)^k k^2}{18} + (A k + B)(-3)^k$.

(iv) $x_k = k + A(-1)^k + B$.

7.   (i) $x_k = \dfrac{1}{32}(13 \times 3^k - 9 \times 3^{-k} - 4)$.

(iii) $x_k = \dfrac{1}{4}(3^k - 1 + 2k)$.

12. $x_n = \dfrac{1}{2} \cdot 3^n + \dfrac{3}{2}$.

13. $r_n = \dfrac{5}{6}\left(\dfrac{1}{2}\right)^n - \dfrac{1}{6}\left(\dfrac{1}{3}\right)^n$

$r_5 = 0.0254 \quad r_{10} = 0.0008$

14. $x_n = 200\left(\dfrac{3}{2}\right)^n - 100$.

15. $p_n = 2_n\left(\dfrac{1}{2}\right)^n$

16. $x_n = \dfrac{50}{\sqrt{3}} \cdot \{(9\sqrt{3} + 2)(1 + \sqrt{3})^n + (9\sqrt{3} - 2)(1 - \sqrt{3})^n\}$

17.   (i) $Xn = 50.4^n + 150.2^n$
      $Yn = 150.2^n - 50.4^n$ $\Big\}$ y becomes extinct

(ii) $Xn = 100(2 - n)3^n$
      $Yn = 100(1 + n)3^n$ $\Big\}$ x becomes extinct

SOLUTIONS TO CHAPTER 8

1. (i) $\begin{bmatrix} 7 & 3 \\ 16 & 10 \end{bmatrix}$ (ii) $\begin{bmatrix} 9 & 10 \\ 8 & 8 \end{bmatrix}$ (iii) $\begin{bmatrix} -1 \\ 2 \end{bmatrix}$ (iv) $\begin{bmatrix} 2 \\ 1 \end{bmatrix}$.

2. (i) $\begin{bmatrix} 1 & 1 & 0 \\ 0 & 1 & 0 \\ 0 & 0 & -1 \end{bmatrix}$ (ii) $\begin{bmatrix} 1 & 1 & 3 \\ 0 & 1 & 2 \\ 0 & 0 & -1 \end{bmatrix}$ (iii) $\begin{bmatrix} 10 \\ 3 \\ -1 \end{bmatrix}$ (iv) $\begin{bmatrix} 0 \\ 1 \\ 1 \end{bmatrix}$.

3. $\begin{bmatrix} 0 & 2 \\ -2 & 0 \end{bmatrix}$, $\begin{bmatrix} -2 & 2 \\ -2 & -2 \end{bmatrix}$, $\begin{bmatrix} -4 & 0 \\ 0 & -4 \end{bmatrix}$.

8. (i) $\begin{bmatrix} -5/4 & 3/4 \\ 3/4 & -1/4 \end{bmatrix}$ (ii) $\begin{bmatrix} -51 & -29 & 52 \\ 7 & 4 & -7 \\ 9 & 5 & -9 \end{bmatrix}$ (iii) inverse does not exist.

10. (i) does not exist; (ii) $\begin{bmatrix} 1 & 0 & 0 \\ 0 & 1/5 & -3/5 \\ 0 & 0 & 1/2 \end{bmatrix}$.

11. (i) $x_1 = 1/11, x_2 = 7/22$.
(ii) $x_1 = 10/7, x_2 = 6/7, x_3 = 17/7$.
(iii) $x_1 = 5, x_2 = -1, x_2 = 2$.

12. (i) -14; (ii) 0; (iii) 2.

13. $x_1 = \lambda, x_2 = -\lambda/3, x_3 = -4\lambda/3$; λ arbitrary.

14. Output required is 420, 480, 540 units of x_1, x_2 and x_3 respectively.

15. Solution $x_1 = 15000, x_2 = -20\,000, x_3 = 15000$ is not possible since x_2 negative.

16.

$$N = \begin{bmatrix} 0 & 0 & 0 & 0 & 0 & 0 & 0 \\ 3 & 0 & 0 & 1 & 0 & 1 & 0 \\ 1 & 0 & 0 & 3 & 1 & 0 & 0 \\ 0 & 0 & 0 & 0 & 0 & 0 & 0 \\ 0 & 0 & 0 & 3 & 0 & 0 & 0 \\ 2 & 0 & 2 & 0 & 1 & 0 & 0 \\ 0 & 0 & 1 & 0 & 0 & 3 & 0 \end{bmatrix}, \quad T = \begin{bmatrix} 1 & 0 & 0 & 0 & 0 & 0 & 0 \\ 7 & 1 & 2 & 16 & 3 & 1 & 0 \\ 1 & 0 & 1 & 6 & 1 & 0 & 0 \\ 0 & 0 & 0 & 1 & 0 & 0 & 0 \\ 0 & 0 & 0 & 3 & 1 & 0 & 0 \\ 4 & 0 & 2 & 15 & 1 & 0 & 0 \\ 13 & 0 & 1 & 48 & 6 & 3 & 0 \end{bmatrix},$$

18. $[1 \quad 1 \quad 1]$, $[2 \quad 1 \quad 0]$, $[1 \quad 0 \quad 1]$, $[0 \quad 1 \quad 1]$; £1.95.

19. (a)

$$n(1) = \begin{bmatrix} 95 \\ 205 \\ 80 \end{bmatrix}, \quad n(2) = \begin{bmatrix} 88 \\ 194.5 \\ 64 \end{bmatrix}, \quad n(3) = \begin{bmatrix} 80.6 \\ 200.1 \\ 51.2 \end{bmatrix}; \text{ No}; \quad t = 6.$$

SOLUTIONS TO CHAPTER 9

2. Minimum -5 at $x = 1, y = -1$.

3. Each side $= v^{1/3}$.

4. $44/49$.

5. $27/256$ at $x = 1/4, y = 3/4$.

6. 12.

7. $1/9$.

8.   (i) maximum 274 at $x = 28/5, y = 1$.
   (ii) maximum $32/3$ at $x = 4/3, y = 10/3$.
  (iii) minimum 27 at $x = 0, y = 3$.

10. $x = 13/3, y = 14/3$, earnings $= 83/4$ at $x = 13/3, y = 23/6$; earnings $= 76/3$ at $x = 13/3, y = 14/3$.

11. $F_1 = 23, \quad F_2 = 9$.

12. (i) Class 1 = 20, class 2 = 40; (ii) Class 1 = 0, class 2 = 60.

13. 2 High-back and 3 rockers.

14. A $-$ 200 gallons; B $- 916\frac{2}{3}$ gallons.

15. Newcastle—Doncaster—Nottingham—Leicester—Oxford; 12, 16, 48.

16. minimum cost 8 (three possible paths).

17.

	Feb.	Mar.	April	May	June	July
Boats built	3	0	5	3	3	0
Boats stored	0	2	0	0	0	1

18. Optimum plan: Stripping — 2 days
   Repairing — 2 days
   Rebuilding — 6 days.
   Cost £38,000.

19. 6 tons used and allocated:
   2 for A, 3 for B, 1 for C.

SOLUTIONS TO CHAPTER 10

1. (i) Yes; (ii) No; (iii) No.

2. (i) 3, -3, 0; (ii) $-3, -4, -7$; (iii) 3, -3, 0.

3.

	paper	scissors	stones
paper	0	-1	1
scissors	1	0	-1
stones	-1	1	0

No stable solution.

9. A: plays row 1 with $p = 4/11$, expected gains $13/11$.
    B: plays column 1 with $p = 6/11$, expected gains $-13/11$.

10. A plays row 1 with $p = 0$, row 2 with $p = \frac{1}{2}$, row 3 with $p = \frac{1}{2}$;
    B plays column 1 with $p = \frac{1}{2}$, column 2 with $p = \frac{1}{2}$.

11. Stable solution – child chooses Box 1 – parent puts 1 smartie in Box 1 and
    1 in Box 2.

13. 40 acres for 'Moneymaker' and 60 acres for 'Gardener's Delight';
    100 acres for 'Moneymaker'.

SOLUTIONS TO CHAPTER 11

1.

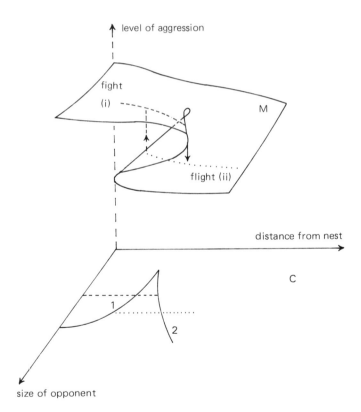

(i) A fish near the nest will pursue a large intruder until its path in the
    control plane crosses the second branch of the cusp when its level of
    aggression will drop sharply from fight to flight.

(ii) A fish far from the nest will flee from a large opponent towards the nest until it crosses branch 1 of the cusp when it will turn to fight. If its partner is near to the nest, that partner will exhibit aggressive behaviour out to branch 2 of the cusp. whereas the original fish will flee until it reaches branch 1.

2.

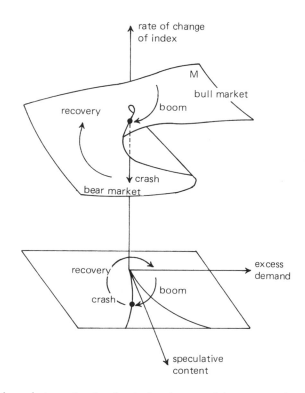

In a normal market, a rise in the index is caused by excess demand for stock, and this is the normal factor. In an abnormal market there is low excess demand and high speculative content. A small event may cause a loss of confidence leading to a crash.

A bull market encourages speculation, but overvaluation of stock causes profit-taking with consequent reduction in excess demand. Thus the arrows on the top sheet point forward and bend to the left, eventually leading to a crash. A bear market discourages speculation, hence the arrows on the lower sheet point backwards, but undervalued stock leads fundamentalists to reinvest, therefore the arrows bend to the right as demand increases, leading eventually to a situation of excess demand and a boom once again. This also offers an explanation of why the market tends to rise steadily but fall suddenly.

4. $\mu = 1, \nu = -1$; A plays row 2, B plays column 2.

5. (i) A plays row 1, B plays column 1.
   (ii) A plays row 3, B plays column 1.
   (iii) A plays row 1, B plays column 1.

6. A plays row 1 or row 4; B plays column 3 or column 5.

7. No.

8. (i) 3/2, −3/2; (ii) 3/2, −3/2.
   A: plays row 1 with probability 3/5 and expected gains 7/5.
   B: plays column 1 with probability 4/5 and expected gains −7/5.

Index